Ohio Univers

READINGS ON
WRITING

Fourth Edition | Editors: Mara Holt, Rachael Ryerson, and Zoë Bossiere

VAN-GRINER

Readings on Writing
Ohio University Composition Program
Fourth Edition

Printed in the United States of America
10 9 8 7 6 5 4 3 2 1
ISBN: 978-1-61740-635-5

Van-Griner Publishing
Cincinnati, Ohio
www.van-griner.com

CEO: Mike Griner
President: Dreis Van Landuyt
Project Manager: Maria Walterbusch
Customer Care Lead: Julie Reichert

Holt 635-5 Su18
207726
Copyright © 2019

Table of Contents

The Inspired Writer vs. The Real Writer

SARAH ALLEN

Several years ago, in a first year writing course, a student nervously approached me after class, asking if we could talk about her latest draft of a formal paper.* She was worried about the content of the draft, about the fact that in writing about her writing process (the assignment for the paper), she found her tone to be at best frustrated, at worst grumbling and whiney. "I don't really like writing. Is that okay?" she asked.

This is the first time that I remember a student confessing aloud (to me) that she did not like writing, and I remember struggling for an appropriate response—not because I couldn't fathom how she had the gall to admit this to me, a writing teacher, but because I couldn't understand why admitting to not liking writing worried her. In the next class, I asked my students if they liked writing. I heard a mixed response. I asked them if they assumed that someone like me, a writing teacher/scholar, always liked writing. The answer was a resounding "yes." I rephrased, "So you believe that every day I skip gleefully to my computer?" Again, though giggling a bit, my students answered "yes." And, at last, one student piped up to say, "Well, you're good at it, right? I mean, that's what makes you good at it."

My student, quoted above, seems to suggest that I am good at writing because I like doing it. But I'd have to disagree on at least two points: First, I wouldn't describe my feelings toward writing as being a "like" kind of thing. It's more of an agonistic kind of thing. Second, I am not "good" at writing, if being good at it means that the words, the paragraphs, the pages come easily.

On the contrary, I believe that I write because I am driven to do so—driven by a will to write. By "will," I mean a kind of purposefulness, propensity, diligence, and determination (which, I should mention, does not lead to perfection or ease … unfortunately). But, I should qualify this: the will to write is not innate for me, nor is it always readily available. In fact, the common assumption that a will to write must be both innate and stem from an ever-replenishing source never ceases to surprise (and annoy) me. I've worked with a lot of enviably brilliant and wonderful writers—teachers, students, scholars, and freelancers. I've yet to meet one who believes that she/he is innately and/or always a brilliant writer, nor have I met one who says she/he always wants to write.

5   And yet, I confess that I find myself to be genuinely surprised when some well-respected scholar in my field admits to struggling with his writing. For example, David Bartholomae (a very successful scholar in the field of Rhetoric and Composition) confesses that he didn't learn to write until after he completed his undergraduate studies, and that he learned it through what must have been at least one particularly traumatic experience: his dissertation was rejected for being "poorly written" (22–23).

If at first glance the rejection of a dissertation means little to you, let me explain: imagine spending years (literally, years) on a piece of writing (a very long piece of writing), for which you've sacrificed more than you ever thought you'd sacrifice for anything (your time, your freedom, sleep, relationships, and even, at times, your sanity), only to have it rejected. And worse, it's rejected for being "poorly written," which is like being booted off of a pro-league baseball team for not being able to tie your shoes properly. We're talking basics here, or so we (writers) like to think. And yet, if writing were nothing more than "practicing the basics," why's it so hard—hard even for one of the best of the best in my field?

It's alarming how many great scholars have admitted to struggling with writing. Bartholomae is not the only one. In a rather famous admission, one of the "fathers" of the field of Rhetoric and Composition, Peter Elbow—the guy who put freewriting on the map, wrote one of the first book-length studies of the writing process, and has been the virtual MLK, Jr. for voice-in-writing (yeah, that guy)—dropped out of graduate school because he suffered so badly from writer's block.[1]

My own story of my frustrated struggle with writing is not nearly so heroic as Elbow's or Bartholomae's. I did not fight the dragon beasts of poor writing skills or writer's block, return to the (writing) field as the victorious knight, and then settle in for a long, successful reign as one of the rulers of the land of Rhetoric and Composition. Rather, mine was (and, sometimes, still is) more Hamlet-like, more like a battle with a ghost—the ghost being the "Inspired Writer."

The Inspired Writer, as I understand her/him, is a figure for whom writing comes easily—the sort of Romantic hero who writes purely out of an awe-full state, generating perfect prose without the frustrated process of revision (or failure). This Inspired Writer is everywhere, in all the great stories of great writers who were so full of "writerliness" that they were tormented by their need to write; they were relentlessly pursued by their muses ... as was evidenced by their inked hands, tangled hair, ringed eyes, and profoundly watchful stares. They did not have to go crawling about in the muck of what-everybody's-already-written, across the desert of what-could-I-possibly-say, and over the mountain of an-audience-who-probably-knows-a-lot-more-than-I-do.

10   Of course, the great irony of this figure's story is that the Inspired Writer is really the transcendent distortion of real-life writers. It's much more likely that most of those great, real-life writers got their inked hands from gripping too hard their quills or pens in frustration, as they hovered over pages with more slashes, margin-notes, and edits than clean, untouched sentences set in perfect lines. They probably got their tangled hair from wrenching it; their ringed eyes from spending too many hours staring at black squiggles over white pages; and their profoundly watchful stares from their consequent, bad eyesight.

The fact is that they, too, had to answer to the great works that had been written before them; they, too, had to struggle with their own fears about sounding stupid; and they, too, had to answer to an often discerning and demanding audience. Yet, despite reality, the awesome figure of the Inspired Writer still holds sway, hovering over us like bad lighting, blinding us to our own work.

The pervasiveness of this myth of the Inspired Writer and the continued celebration of her/him works against us, as writers, for we often assume that if writing does not come easily, then our writing is not good—and in turn, that we cannot be good writers. Consequently, we believe that the writing that comes easily is the only good writing, so we will turn in papers that have been drafted quickly and without revision, hoping for the best (grade).

Now, in the days when I was clawing my way through classes as an English major, literature teachers didn't spend much time on revision. I don't ever remember being told anything about strategies for revision. I remember doing peer reviews, where we read each other's drafts and marked punctuation problems, having no idea how to examine—much less comment on—structure and analysis. Other than the five-paragraph formula I'd learned in high school,

I had no idea what a paper should or could look like. In other words, when I was learning to write college papers some fifteen years ago, I was totally on my own. The most useful strategy in my bag of tricks? Trial and error. And believe me, good grades or no, having had the opportunity recently (thanks to my mother moving and insisting, "take your STUFF!") to look at the papers I wrote back then, I see an awful lot of the latter.

You see, the awful, honest truth is that I'm no rabbit, no natural digger, no lover of thick, tangled messes, and I had no idea how to find my way through the knotted ideas at work in any first drafts, much less how to dig my way into more root (e.g. to go further with my claims, to push the analysis, to discover the "so what" of my work). I didn't find this place (the page) to be a comfy, hide-out-worthy home. In fact, I confess that I still don't. I have always loved to read, but writing has been much more work than I ever anticipated. And even after so many years of graduate school, and even more years of teaching writing and of writing scholarship, when one might think I should have fully embraced and embodied the status of "veteran" digger, I still, very often feel like I'm trudging through some thick of hard branches and harder roots to find my way down a page.

15   After years of reflecting on this trudging and of talking with students about how they, too, often feel as though they are trudging down a page—through ideas, among the cacophony of words (our own and others')—I've come to this (admittedly, unimpressive) realization: this is, for many of us, an alien discourse. I'm not like my two closest friends from graduate school, whose parents were academics. We didn't talk at breakfast about "the problematic representations of race in the media." Instead, my father told racist jokes that my sisters and I didn't recognize—until later—were racist. We didn't talk at dinner about "the mass oppression of 'other(ed)' cultures by corporate/national tyrants." My sisters and I talked about how the cheerleaders were way cooler than we were because they had better clothes, cars, hair, bodies, and boyfriends, and that we would, consequently, be losers for the rest of our lives.

Again, this is an alien discourse, even now. Well, not this. This is more like a personal essay, but the papers I was supposed to write for my literature classes, those were strange. I didn't normally think in the order that a paper would suggest—first broadly, then moving to specifics, which are treated as isolated entities, brought together in transitions and at the end of the paper. I didn't understand, much less use, words like "Marxism," "feminism," or even "close reading." I didn't know that Shakespeare may not have been Shakespeare. I didn't know that Hemingway was a drunk. I didn't know that really smart people spent their entire careers duking it out about who Shakespeare really was and whether Hemingway's alcoholism influenced his work.

I didn't know the vocabulary; I didn't know the issues; I didn't think in the right order; I didn't quote properly; and I was far too interested in the sinking, spinning feeling that writing—and reading—sometimes gave me, instead of being interested in the rigorousness of scholarly work, in modeling that work, and in becoming a member of this strange discourse community. Consequently, when a teacher finally sat me down to explain that this was, in fact, a community—one that occurred on pages, at conferences, in coffee shops, and over listservs—and that if I wanted to stay on the court, I'd have to learn the rules of the game, I was both intrigued and terrified. And no surprise, writing then became not just a way to induce the sinking, spinning thing of which I spoke earlier, but a way to think, a way to act—e.g. a way to figure out little things, like who "Mr. W.H." is in Shakespeare's dedication to his Sonnets, as well as big things, like how we can better fight the "isms" of this world.

No doubt, the sinking, spinning feeling that I experience when I write or read comes and goes now, but it always did. I feel it alternately, as it shares time with the "trudging" feeling I described earlier. But, please don't think that this trudging comes from having to learn and practice the writing conventions of an alien community. Rather, the feeling of "trudging" is a consequence, again, of that haunting specter, the Inspired Writer. The feeling comes from the expectation that writing should come from "the gods" or natural talent, and it is a consequence, too, of the expectation that this inspiration or talent should be always available to us—always there, though sometimes hidden, in some reservoir of our beings.

Thus, even now, when I hit a blank spot and the sentence stumbles off into white space, I feel … inadequate … or worse, like a fraud, like I'm playing a game that I've got no business playing. The reader is gonna red-card me. And what makes it worse: I have to write. Writing teacher and scholar or not, I have to write memos and emails and resumes and reports and thank you notes and on and on.

20   But the upshot of all of this is that you'd be amazed what talking about this frustration (and all of the attendant fears) will do for a writer, once she/he opens up and shares this frustration with other writers, other students, teachers … with

anyone who has to write. For example, once my students see that everyone sitting in this classroom has a gnawing fear about their work failing, about how they don't have "it," about how they don't feel justified calling themselves "writers," because most of them are "regular folks" required to take a writing class, well … then we can have ourselves a getting-down-to-it, honest and productive writing classroom. Then, we can talk about writer's block—what it is, what causes it, and what overcomes it. We can talk about how to develop "thick skins"—about how to listen to readers' commentaries and critiques without simultaneously wanting to rip our writings into tiny pieces, stomp them into a trashcan, and then set fire to them. And most importantly, then, we can talk about writing as a practice, not a reflection of some innate quality of the writer.

My work, for example, is more a reflection of the scholarship I spend the most time with than it is a reflection of me, per se. One strategy I learned in graduate school (and I swear, I picked it up by watching my first year composition students) is to imitate other, successful pieces of writing. By "imitate," of course I don't mean plagiarize. I mean that I imitate the form of those texts, e.g. the organization, and the ways that they engage with, explore, and extend ideas.

For example, a Rhetoric and Composition scholar named Patricia Bizzell has written scholarship that I use a lot in my own work. In fact, even when I don't use her work directly, I can see her influence on my thinking. A couple of years ago, after reading one of her books for about the hundredth time (seriously), I noticed that her articles and chapters are organized in predictable kinds of ways (not predictable as in boring, but predictable as in she's-a-pro). She seems to have a formula down, and it works. Her work is consistently solid— i.e. convincing, important—and using that formula, she's able to tackle really dense material and make it accessible to readers.

To be more specific, she tends to start with an introduction that demonstrates, right away, why the coming work is so important. For example, in "Foundationalism and Anti-Foundationalism in Composition Studies," she starts off the article by reminding us, basically (I'm paraphrasing here), that everybody's down with "the social," that we are all invested in examining how language—and writing—occurs in a context and how that context dictates meaning. So, for example, the word "we" in the previous sentence is a reference to Rhetoric and Composition teachers and scholars; however, in this sentence, it's not a reference to a group of people, but to the word "we," as it occurs in the previous sentence. See? Meaning changes according to context.

So, Bizzell starts with this premise: that everybody's down with the social, that we're invested in examining contexts, that we know that meaning happens in those contexts. Then, she introduces the problem: that we still want something pre-contextual (e.g. I know what "we" means because I can step outside of any contexts—including this one—and examine it objectively). Then, she gives two in-depth examples of where she sees the problem at work in the field. She then examines how we've tried to address that problem, then how we've failed at addressing it, and then she poses another/new perspective on the problem and, consequently, another/new way of addressing it.

25   This is her formula, and I imitate it, frequently, in my own work. It's rigorous, thorough, and like I said earlier, accessible. It works. But, sometimes I'm working on something totally different, something new (to me), and that formula starts to box me in too much; the formula becomes a tomb instead of a foundation. That's when I turn to outside readers.

Now, this one, actually, is a tougher strategy to use … because it requires that you share a piece of work that looks like a train wreck to you with another human being—ideally, another smart, patient, open-minded human being. I have four people I send my work out to consistently. One is my boss; one my mentor; one a (very successful) peer; and the other, a senior colleague I come dangerously close to worshipping. In other words, I don't send my stuff to my mom. I don't give it to my best friend, my boyfriend, my dance teacher, or my sisters. I only send my stuff to people who seem to be a lot better at writing scholarship than I feel like I am.

Again, it's hard to do, but I can't tell you how many students I'll see in my office over the course of a semester who will say, "But my mom read my paper, and she says it looks great"—while gripping a paper marked with a D or F. Mom may have been the final authority when you were negotiating curfews and driving and dating, but unless Mom's a (college-level) writing teacher, she'll be no more of an expert in college-level writing than your dentist will. Send it to her if you want an outside reader, but don't expect her final word to be similar to your teacher's final word. And while I'm on my soapbox … don't let anyone edit your papers … including your mom. It's called "collusion"—a kind of plagiarism—and it's really easy to spot, especially if you were the Comma Splice King in the first paper and use commas flawlessly in the second.

More importantly, keep in mind that if you only use your mom, or your coach, or some other person who's not in the same class, then you may be making the revision process (and the reading for that person) more difficult than necessary, since that reader will have no idea what you've read in class, what you've talked about in class, or what the assignment guidelines and grading criteria are. Writing occurs—and is assessed—in a context, remember?

The best strategy for finding and using readers is to start with the teacher (no, it's not cheating). Ask him/her to read a draft before you submit the final. Then, share the paper with a classmate, as well as someone who's not in the class. That way, you'll get an "insider's" perspective as well as an "outsider's."[2] I've heard students say that using anyone but the teacher for feedback seems to be a waste of time. However, I find that when a student brings me a draft, I (and most writing professors) read it in terms of how it should be revised, not how I'd grade it. So, after you revise based on the teacher's feedback, get other readers to take a look, again, at the newly revised version and have them read it as a finished product. This will help you get a better sense of how it's working as a text that will be graded.

30   The best piece of advice I can give you, though, is to tell the Inspired Writer to shut up and let you write. If you have to, find out about a few of your favorite writers. I guarantee that they struggle, too. If not them, try talking to your classmates and/or your teacher. Again, if they have written anything in their lives worth writing, then it took some effort to do so. And, once the insecurities are out there, so to speak, and not trapped in Pandora's little box to drive us mad with their "what if" whispers, you may discover that there's more to the writing process than just getting lost in branches and stumbling over roots.

There's nothing quite like finding that the black squiggles you typed onto that white page actually invoke a feeling in or change the mind of your reader(s). Of course, too, there's the emotion, revelation, clench of teeth, slackening of shoulders, or any other response, that a text elicits from even its own writer. The latter is, for my part, the biggest reason why I write—even now, and even and especially as I write scholarship. For me, the text is like a fire in the room. And I am often awed by the way it moves, sleeps, devours, and sustains, while I am simultaneously trying to master it (knowing full well that if I let it go, it will run riot, but knowing, too, that I can't push too hard or it will disappear altogether).

For what I've found in my own relationship to writing, and in talking to my students about theirs, is that it's about the connection, really—even if the connection is an antagonistic one. We like to think that thinking isn't for nothing; that communicating with another (even and especially with ourselves) is never entirely in vain; that what we have to say is perhaps/probably not brilliant but is, still, worth the attempt of saying, of writing, and of considering/being considered. No doubt, a whole lot of practice can give us the means to write in such a way that not only we, the writers, but others will want to listen, will want to read. And in that listening-talking, reading-writing relation, a collision, the inevitable momentary connection, happens.

Maybe we smack the dirt and roots; maybe we smack white space. Maybe a reader's jaw drops at the "gets it" insight of some obscure line in your paper that you don't even remember writing because you spent forty-five minutes working on the line right after it. Maybe you make someone stop and think for just a moment about something they've never considered before. Maybe you make friends with a bunch of classmates because of that story you wrote about the road trip you took last summer to a music festival. Maybe you inspired a heated class debate because of that paper you wrote about your personal project for saving the world.

But for all the misunderstandings, all the fears and so-called failings that happen among writer and paper and reader, there's always another white page, and there's always more to say. This is why we must write, why we must continue to practice: to keep talking, keep thinking, keep revising. Nobody's ever got the final word, not even on the page. We've all got the will to write: it's called "communication." Maybe you do so in music or in paint or in graphics or, even, in gossip. But here, in these black squiggles on this white page, you've listened to something I've had to say. Maybe you've not listened closely; maybe you're yawning or rolling your eyes. But if this is a decent piece of writing, you're giving some response right now—a smile? An exasperated sigh? A tensed shoulder? A clenched fist? Whatever the case, here, response is happening. And that's at least a (good) start.

Works Cited

Bartholomae, David. "Against the Grain." *Writers on Writing.* Ed. Tom Waldrep. New York, NY: Random House, 1985. 19–29.

Bizzell, Patricia. "Foundationalism and Anti-Foundationalism in Composition Studies." *Academic Discourse and Critical Consciousness.* Pittsburgh, PA: U of Pittsburgh P, 1992. 202–221.

Elbow, Peter. *Writing without Teachers.* New York, NY: Oxford UP, 1973.

Credit ——————————————————————————————————————

Allen, Sarah. "The Inspired Writer vs. The Real Writer." From *Writing Spaces: Readings on Writing Vol. 1.* Charles Lowe and Pavel Zemliansky, Eds. West Lafayette: Parlor Press, 2010: 34–44. Reprinted with the author's permission.

How to Tame a Wild Tongue

GLORIA ANZALDÚA

"We're going to have to control your tongue," the dentist says, pulling out all the metal from my mouth. Silver bits plop and tinkle into the basin. My mouth is a motherlode.

The dentist is cleaning out my roots. I get a whiff of the stench when I gasp. "I can't cap that tooth yet, you're still draining," he says.

"We're going to have to do something about your tongue," I hear the anger rising in his voice. My tongue keeps pushing out the wads of cotton, pushing back the drills, the long thin needles. "I've never seen anything as strong or as stubborn," he says. And I think, how do you tame a wild tongue, train it to be quiet, how do you bridle and saddle it? How do you make it lie down?

> "Who is to say that robbing a people of
> its language is less violent than war?"
>
> —Ray Gwyn Smith[1]

I remember being caught speaking Spanish at recess—that was good for three licks on the knuckles with a sharp ruler. I remember being sent to the corner of the classroom for "talking back" to the Anglo teacher when all I was trying to do was tell her how to pronounce my name. "If you want to be American, speak 'American.' If you don't like it, go back to Mexico where you belong."

5   "I want you to speak English. *Pa' hallar buen trabajo tienes que saber hablar el inglés bien. Qué vale toda tu educación sí todavía hablas inglés con un 'accent,'*" my mother would say, mortified that I spoke English like a Mexican. At Pan American University, I and all Chicano students were required to take two speech classes. Their purpose: to get rid of our accents.

Attacks on one's form of expression with the intent to censor are a violation of the First Amendment. *El Anglo con cara de inocentene nos arrancó la lengua.* Wild tongues can't be tamed, they can only be cut out.

Overcoming the Tradition of Silence

> *Ahogadas, escupimos el oscuro.*
> *Peleando con nuestra propia sombra*
> *el silencio nos sepulta.*

En boca cerrada no entran moscas. "Flies don't enter a closed mouth" is a saying I kept hearing when I was a child. *Ser habladora* was to be a gossip and a liar, to talk too much. *Muchachitas bien criadas,* well-bred girls don't answer back. *Es una falta de respeto* to talk back to one's mother or father. I remember one of the sins I'd recite to the priest in the confession box the few times I went to confession: talking back to my mother, *hablar pa' 'tras, repelar. Hocicona, repelona, chismosa,* having a big mouth, questioning, carrying tales are all signs of being *mal criada.* In my culture they are all words that are derogatory if applied to women—I've never heard them applied to men.

The first time I heard two women, a Puerto Rican and a Cuban, say the word *"nosotras,"* I was shocked. I had not known the word existed. Chicanas use *nosotros* whether we're male or female. We are robbed of our female being by the masculine plural. Language is a male discourse.

> And our tongues have become
> dry the wilderness has
> dried out our tongues
> and we have forgotten speech.

> —Irena Klepfisz[2]

Even our own people, other Spanish speakers *nos quieren poner candados en la boca.* They would hold us back with their bag of *reglas de academia.*

Oyé coma ladra: el lenguaje de la frontera.

> *Quien tiene boca se equivoca.*

> —Mexican Saying

10 *"Pacho,* cultural traitor, you're speaking the oppressor's language by speaking English, you're ruining the Spanish language," I have been accused by various Latinos and Latinas. Chicano Spanish is considered by the purist and by most Latinos deficient, a mutilation of Spanish.

But Chicano Spanish is a border tongue which developed naturally. Change, *evolución, enriquecimiento de palabras nuevas por invención o adopción* have created variants of Chicano Spanish, *un nuevo lenguaje. Un lenguaje que corresponde a un modo de vivir.* Chicano Spanish is not incorrect, it is a living language.

For a people who are neither Spanish nor live in a country in which Spanish is the first language; for a people who live in a country in which English is the reigning tongue but who are not Anglo; for a people who cannot entirely identify with either standard (formal, Castillian) Spanish nor standard English, what recourse is left to them but to create their own language? A language which they can connect their identity to, one capable of communicating the realities and values true to themselves—a language with terms that are neither *español ni inglés,* but both. We speak a patois, a forked tongue, a variation of two languages.

Chicano Spanish sprang out of the Chicanos' need to identify ourselves as a distinct people. We needed a language with which we could communicate with ourselves, a secret language. For some of us, language is a homeland closer than the Southwest—for many Chicanos today live in the Midwest and the East. And because we are a complex, heterogeneous people, we speak many languages. Some of the languages we speak are:

1. Standard English
2. Working class and slang English
3. Standard Spanish
4. Standard Mexican Spanish
5. North Mexican Spanish dialect.
6. Chicano Spanish (Texas, New Mexico, Arizona, and California have regional variations)
7. Tex-Mex
8. *Pachuco* (called *caló*)

My "home" tongues are the languages I speak with my sister and brothers, with my friends. They are the last five listed, with 6 and 7 being closest to my heart. From school, the media, and job situations, I've picked up standard and working class English. From Mamagrande Locha and from reading Spanish and Mexican literature, I've picked up Standard Spanish and Standard Mexican Spanish. From *los recién llegados,* Mexican immigrants, and *braceros,* I learned the North Mexican dialect. With Mexicans I'll try to speak either Standard Mexican Spanish or the North Mexican dialect. From my parents and Chicanos living in the Valley, I picked up Chicano Texas Spanish, and I speak it with my mom, younger brother (who married a Mexican and who rarely mixes Spanish with English), aunts, and older relatives.

15   With Chicanas from *Nuevo México* or *Arizona* I will speak Chicano Spanish a little, but often they don't understand what I'm saying. With most California Chicanas I speak entirely in English (unless I forget). When I first moved to San Francisco, I'd rattle off something in Spanish, unintentionally embarrassing them. Often it is only with another Chicana *tejana* that I can talk freely.

Words distorted by English are known as anglicisms or *pochismos.* The *pocho* is an anglicized Mexican or American of Mexican origin who speaks Spanish with an accent characteristic of North Americans and who distorts and reconstructs the language according to the influence of English.[3] Tex-Mex, or Spanglish, comes most naturally to me. I may switch back and forth from English to Spanish in the same sentence or in the same word. With my sister and my brother Nune and with Chicano *tejano* contemporaries I speak in Tex-Mex.

From kids and people my own age I picked up *Pachuco*. *Pachuco* (the language of the zoot suiters) is a language of rebellion, both against Standard Spanish and Standard English. It is a secret language. Adults of the culture and outsiders cannot understand it. It is made up of slang words from both English and Spanish. *Ruca* means girl or woman, *vato* means guy or dude, *chale* means no, *simón* means yes, *churro* is sure, talk is *periquiar*, *pigionear* means petting, *que gacho* means how nerdy, *ponte águila* means watch out, death is called *la pelona*. Through lack of practice and not having others who can speak it, I've lost most of the *Pachuco* tongue.

Chicano Spanish

Chicanos, after 250 years of Spanish/Anglo colonization, have developed significant differences in the Spanish we speak. We collapse two adjacent vowels into a single syllable and sometimes shift the stress in certain words such as *maíz/maiz, cohete/cuete*. We leave out certain consonants when they appear between vowels: *lado/lao, mojado/mojao*. Chicanos from South Texas pronounce *f* as *j* as in *jue* (*fue*). Chicanos use "archaisms," words that are no longer in the Spanish language, words that have been evolved out. We say *semos, truje, haiga, ansina, and naiden*. We retain the "archaic" *j*, as in *jalar*, that derives from an earlier *h*, (the French *halar* or the Germanic *halon* which was lost to standard Spanish in the 16th century), but which is still found in several regional dialects such as the one spoken in South Texas. (Due to geography, Chicanos from the Valley of South Texas were cut off linguistically from other Spanish speakers. We tend to use words that the Spaniards brought over from Medieval Spain. The majority of the Spanish colonizers in Mexico and the Southwest came from Extremadura—Hernán Cortés was one of them—and Andalucía. Andalucians pronounce *ll* like a *y*, and their *d's* tend to be absorbed by adjacent vowels: *tirado* becomes *tirao*. They brought *el lenguaje popular, dialectos y regionalismos*.[4])

Chicanos and other Spanish speakers also shift *ll* to *y* and *z* to *s*.[5] We leave out initial syllables, saying *tar* for *estar; toy* for *estoy, hora* for *ahora* (*cubanos* and *puertorriqueños* also leave out initial letters of some words). We also leave out the final syllable such as *pa* for *para*. The intervocalic *y*, the *ll* as in *tortilla, ella, botella*, gets replaced by *tortia* or *tortiya, ea, botea*. We add an additional syllable at the beginning of certain words: *atocar* for *tocar, agastar* for *gastar*. Sometimes we'll say *lavaste las vacijas*, other times *lavates* (substituting the *ates* verb endings for the *aste*).

20   We use anglicisms, words borrowed from English: *bola* from ball, *carpeta* from carpet, *máchina de lavar* (instead of *lavadora*) from washing machine. Tex-Mex argot, created by adding a Spanish sound at the beginning or end of an English word such as *cookiar* for cook, *watchar* for watch, *parkiar* for park, and *rapiar* for rape, is the result of the pressures on Spanish speakers to adapt to English.

We don't use the word *vosotros/as* or its accompanying verb form. We don't say *claro* (to mean yes), *imagínate,* or *me emociona,* unless we picked up Spanish from Latinas, out of a book, or in a classroom. Other Spanish-speaking groups are going through the same, or similar development in their Spanish.

Linguistic Terrorism

> *Deslenguadas. Somos los del español deficiente.* We are your linguistic nightmare, your linguistic aberration, your linguistic *mestisaje,* the subject of your *burla.* Because we speak with tongues of fire we are culturally crucified. Racially, culturally, and linguistically *somos huérfanos*—we speak an orphan tongue.

Chicanas who grew up speaking Chicano Spanish have internalized the belief that we speak poor Spanish. It is illegitimate, a bastard language. And because we internalize how our language has been used against us by the dominant culture, we use our language differences against each other.

Chicana feminists often skirt around each other with suspicion and hesitation. For the longest time I couldn't figure it out. Then it dawned on me. To be close to another Chicana is like looking into the mirror. We are afraid of what we'll see there. *Pena.* Shame. Low estimation of self. In childhood we are told that our language is wrong. Repeated attacks on our native tongue diminish our sense of self. The attacks continue throughout our lives.

Chicanas feel uncomfortable talking in Spanish to Latinas, afraid of their censure. Their language was not outlawed in their countries. They had a whole lifetime of being immersed in their native tongue; generations, centuries in which Spanish was a first language, taught in school, heard on radio and TV, and read in the newspaper.

25   If a person, Chicana or Latina, has a low estimation of my native tongue, she also has a low estimation of me. Often with *mexicanas y latinas* we'll speak English as a neutral language. Even among Chicanas we tend to speak English at parties or conferences. Yet, at the same time, we're afraid the other will think we're *agringadas* because we don't speak Chicano Spanish. We oppress each other trying to out-Chicano each other, vying to be the "real" Chicanas, to speak like Chicanos. There is no one Chicano language just as there is no one Chicano experience. A monolingual Chicana whose first language is English or Spanish is just as much a Chicana as one who speaks several variants of Spanish. A Chicana from Michigan or Chicago or Detroit is just as much a Chicana as one from the Southwest. Chicano Spanish is as diverse linguistically as it is regionally.

By the end of this century, Spanish speakers will comprise the biggest minority group in the U.S., a country where students in high schools and colleges are encouraged to take French classes because French is considered more "cultured." But for a language to remain alive it must be used.[6] By the end of this century English, and not Spanish, will be the mother tongue of most Chicanos and Latinos.

So, if you want to really hurt me, talk badly about my language. Ethnic identity is twin skin to linguistic identity—I am my language. Until I can take pride in my language, I cannot take pride in myself. Until I can accept as legitimate Chicano Texas Spanish, Tex-Mex, and all the other languages I speak, I cannot accept the legitimacy of myself. Until I am free to write bilingually and to switch codes without having always to translate, while I still have to speak English or Spanish when I would rather speak Spanglish, and as long as I have to accommodate the English speakers rather than having them accommodate me, my tongue will be illegitimate.

I will no longer be made to feel ashamed of existing. I will have my voice: Indian, Spanish, white, I will have my serpent's tongue—my woman's voice, my sexual voice, my poet's voice. I will overcome the tradition of silence.

> My fingers
> move sly against your palm
> Like women everywhere, we speak in code. ...
>
> —Malanie Kaye/Kantrowitz[7]

"Vistas," corridos, y conzida: My Native Tongue

In the 1960s, I read my first Chicano novel. It was *City of Night* by John Rechy, a gay Texan, son of a Scottish father and a Mexican mother. For days I walked around in stunned amazement that a Chicano could write and could get published. When I read *I Am Joaquín*[8] I was surprised to see a bilingual book by a Chicano in print. When I saw poetry written in Tex-Mex for the first time, a feeling of pure joy flashed through me. I felt like we really existed as a people. In 1971, when I started teaching High School English to Chicano students, I tried to supplement the required texts with works by Chicanos, only to be reprimanded and forbidden to do so by the principal. He claimed that I was supposed to teach "American" and English literature. At the risk of being fired,

I swore my students to secrecy and slipped in Chicano short stories, poems, a play. In graduate school, while working toward a Ph.D., I had to "argue" with one advisor after the other; semester after semester, before I was allowed to make Chicano literature an area of focus.

30   Even before I read books by Chicanos or Mexicans, it was the Mexican movies I saw at the drive-in—the Thursday night special of $1.00 a carload— that gave me a sense of belonging. *"Vámonos a las vistas,"* my mother would call out and we'd all—grandmother, brothers, sister, and cousins—squeeze into the car. We'd wolf down cheese and bologna white bread sandwiches while watching Pedro Infante in melodramatic tearjerkers like *Nosotros los pobres.* the first "real" Mexican movie (that was not an imitation of European movies). I remember seeing *Cuando los hijos se van* and surmising that all Mexican movies played up the love a mother has for her children and what ungrateful sons and daughters suffer when they are not devoted to their mothers. I remember the singing-type "westerns" of Jorge Negrete and Miquel Aceves Mejía. When watching Mexican movies, I felt a sense of homecoming as well as alienation. People who were to amount to something didn't go to Mexican movies, or *bailes,* or tune their radios to *bolero, rancherita,* and *corrido* music.

The whole time I was growing up, there was *norteño* music sometimes called North Mexican border music, or Tex-Mex music, or Chicano music, or *cantina* (bar) music. I grew up listening to *conjuntos,* three- or four-piece bands made up of folk musicians playing guitair, *bajo sexto,* drums, and button accordion, which Chicanos had borrowed from the German immigrants who had come to Central Texas and Mexico to farm and build breweries. In the Rio Grande Valley, Steve Jordan and Little Joe Hernández were popular, and Flaco Jiménez was the accordion king. The rhythms of Tex-Mex music are those of the polka, also adapted from the Germans, who in turn had borrowed the polka from the Czechs and Bohemians.

I remember the hot, sultry evenings when *corridos*—songs of love and death on the Texas-Mexican borderlands—reverberated out of cheap amplifiers from the local *cantinas* and wafted in through my bedroom window.

Corridos first became widely used along the South Texas/Mexican border uring the early conflict between Chicanos and Anglos. The *corridos* are usually about Mexican heroes who do valiant deeds against the Anglo oppressors. Pancho Villa's song, *"La cucaracha,"* is the most famous one. *Corridos* of John F. Kennedy and his death are still very popular in the Valley. Older Chicanos remember Lydia Mendoza, one of the great border *corrido* singers who was called *la Gloria de Tejas.* Her *"El tango negro,"* sung during the

Great Depression, made her a singer of the people. The everpresent *corridos* narrated one hundred years of border history, bringing news of events as well as entertaining. These folk musicians and folk songs are our chief cultural mythmakers, and they made our hard lives seem bearable.

I grew up feeling ambivalent about our music. Country-western and rock-and-roll had more status. In the 50s and 60s, for the slightly educated and *agringado* Chicanos, there existed a sense of shame at being caught listening to our music. Yet I couldn't stop my feet from thumping to the music, could not stop humming the words, nor hide from myself the exhilaration I felt when I heard it.

35   There are more subtle ways that we internalize identification, especially in the forms of images and emotions. For me food and certain smells are tied to my identity, to my homeland. Woodsmoke curling up to an immense blue sky; woodsmoke perfuming my grandmother's clothes, her skin. The stench of cow manure and the yellow patches on the ground; the crack of a .22 rifle and the reek of cordite. Homemade white cheese sizzling in a pan, melting inside a folded *tortilla*. My sister Hilda's hot, spicy *menudo, chile colorado* making it deep red, pieces of *panza* and hominy floating on top. My brother Carito barbequing *fajitas* in the backyard. Even now and 3,000 miles away, I can see my mother spicing the ground beef, pork, and venison with *chile*. My mouth salivates at the thought of the hot steaming *tamales* I would be eating if I were home.

Si le preguntas a mi mamá, "¿Qué eres?"

> "Identity is the essential core of who
> We are as individuals, the conscious
> expelience of the self inside."

—Gershen Kaufman[9]

Nosotros los Chicanos straddle the borderlands. On one side of us, we are constantly exposed to the Spanish of the Mexicans, on the other side we hear the Anglos' incessant clamoring so that we forget our language. Among ourselves we don't say *nosotros los americanos, o nosotros los españoles, o nosotros los hispanos.* We say *nosotros los mexicanos* (by *mexicanos* we do not mean citizens of Mexico; we do not mean a national identity, but a racial one). We distinguish between *mexicanos del otro lado* and *mexicanos de este lado.* Deep in our hearts we believe that being Mexican has nothing to do with which country one lives in. Being Mexican is a state of soul—not one of mind, not one of citizenship. Neither eagle nor serpent, but both. And like the ocean, neither animal respects borders.

Dime con quien andas y te diré quien eres.
(Tell me who your friends are and I'll tell you who you are.)

—Mexican Saying

Si le preguntas a mi mamá, "¿Oué eres?" te dirá, "Soy mexicana." My brothers and sister say the same. I sometimes will answer *"soy mexicana"* and at others will say *"soy Chicana" o "soy tejana."* But I identified as *"Raza"* before I ever identified as *"mexicana"* or "Chicana."

As a culture, we call ourselves Spanish when referring to ourselves as a linguistic group and when copping out. It is then that we forget our predominant Indian genes. We are 70–80 percent Indian.[10] We call ourselves Hispanic[11] or Spanish-American or Latin American or Latin when linking ourselves to other Spanish speaking peoples of the Western hemisphere and when copping out. We call ourselves Mexican-American[12] to signify we are neither Mexican nor American, but more the noun "American" than the adjective "Mexican" (and when copping out).

Chicanos and other people of color suffer economically for not acculturating. This voluntary (yet forced) alienation makes for psychological conflict, a kind of dual identity—we don't identify with the Anglo-American cultural values and we don't totally identify with the Mexican cultural values. We are a synergy of two cultures with various degrees of Mexicanness or Angloness. I have so internalized the borderland conflict that sometimes I feel like one cancels out the other and we are zero, nothing, no one. *A veces no soy nada ni nadie. Pero hasta cuando no lo soy, lo soy.*

40   When not copping out, when we know we are more than nothing, we call ourselves Mexican, referring to race and ancestry; *mestizo* when affirming both our Indian and Spanish (but we hardly ever own our Black ancestry); Chicano when referring to a politically aware people born and/or raised in the U.S.; *Raza* when referring to Chicanos; *tejanos* when we are Chicanos from Texas.

Chicanos did not know we were a people until 1965 when Ceasar Chavez and the farmworkers united and *I Am Joaquín* was published and *la Raza Unida* party was formed in Texas. With that recognition, we became a distinct people. Something momentous happened to the Chicano soul—we became aware of our reality and acquired a name and a language (Chicano Spanish) that reflected that reality. Now that we had a name, some of the fragmented pieces began to fall together—who we were, what we were, how we had evolved. We began to gel glimpses of what we might eventually become.

Yet the struggle of identities continues, the struggle of borders is our reality still. One day the inner struggle will cease and a true integration take place. In the meantime, *tenémos que hacer la lucha. ¿Quien está protegiendo los ranchos de mi gente? ¿Quién está tratando de cerrar la fisura entre la india y el blanco en nuestra sangre? El Chicano, si, el Chicano que anda como un ladrón en su propia casa.*

Los Chicanos, how patient we seem, how very patient. There is the quiet of the Indian about us.[13] We know how to survive. When other races have given up their tongue, we've kept ours. We know what it is to live under the hammer blow of the dominant *norte-americano* culture. But more than we count the blows, we count the days the weeks the years the centuries the eons until the white laws and commerce and customs will rot in the deserts they've created, lie bleached. *Humildes* yet proud, *quietos* yet wild, *nosotros losmexicanos-Chicanos* will walk by the crumbling ashes as we go about our business. Stubborn, persevering, impenetrable as stone, yet possessing a malleability that renders us unbreakable, we, the *mestizas* and *mestizos* will remain.

Credit ———————————————————————————————
Anzaldúa, Gloria. *Borderlands/La Frontera: The New Mestiza.* San Francisco: Aunt Lute Books, 1987.

Between Acceptance and Rejection:
Muslim Americans and the Legacies of September 11

MOUSTAFA BAYOUMI

On September 11, 2010, the ninth anniversary of the terrorist attacks on the World Trade Center, I headed to Lower Manhattan to observe two demonstrations that had been called for that day. One was at City Hall Park, where people were assembling not only to remember the fallen but also to voice their support for the burning issue of the summer, namely the construction of a Muslim Cultural Center. First called Cordoba House, the center was later renamed Park51 and became popularly known as "the Ground Zero mosque" (although it is neither at Ground Zero nor is it a mosque). Two long city blocks—and a world—away was an anti-Park51 protest. The enormous difference between the two demonstrations pointedly illustrates how Muslim American life has precariously swung, and continues to swing, between poles of acceptance and rejection since 2001.

The pro-Park51 demo was peopled by a cross-section of New York City. It was noisy, disorganized, and apparently ad-hoc. A quickly constructed stage anchored one end of the demonstration and speakers for a wide variety of political causes took the microphone to proclaim their belief in a multicultural America, opposition to bigotry and racism, criticisms of American imperialism, and support for workers' struggles in the city and around the world. The mood here was one of solidarity through people's differences (Figure 2). Multiethnic, multireligious, multiracial, young and old, the assembled group was made up of a wide swath of people who had all kinds of creative ways of wearing their jewelry, scarves, and piercings. In its multiplicity of people and causes, the demonstration seemed to be a pretty fair representation of New York City.

The anti-Park51 demonstration was something else entirely. News accounts estimated it was fifty percent larger than the pro-Park51 rally.[1] Organized by the rightwing group Stop the Islamization of America, this assembly was completely high-tech, with a large stage and a massive television monitor above that beamed in satellite feeds of former U.S. Ambassador to the U.N. John Bolton and other staunch conservatives to offer their "anti-Ground Zero Mosque" message. Men with suits and walkie-talkies were shuffling people and speakers around. The money behind the event was plainly evident, as was the difference in constituency. This group was overwhelmingly white and mostly older. American flags were everywhere, along with signs expressing the sentiment of the demonstration. Some were directed against the religion: "Hey Islam, we

Figure 1: Anti-Park51 protestors against the so-called "Ground-Zero Mosque" during a demonstration on September 11, 2010. Some conservatives speak of their fear of a "stealth jihad" that will usurp the U.S. Constitution and impose Shari'a law on the U.S. These types of narratives are not uncommon during charged ideological times. (Courtesy of Wikimedia Commons)

will never submit," read one. Another asked, "What would Jesus Do?" answering, "Have his throat slit by Mohammed." Many people held the same sign—the word "Sharia" written in bloodlike letters (Figure 1). Other signs attacked immigration policy: "Why give terrorists the rights of US citizens they are sworn to kill," "Terrorist Sleeping [sic] Cells in America are Muslims! Wake Up America!!!!" and "Illegal Aliens were Responsible for the 9/11 Attacks. The Solution is Simple. Close the Borders. No Immigration=No Terrorism" (in fact, none of the 9/11 hijackers entered the country illegally). Then there were the simple three-word signs: "No Victory Mosque," "No Obama Mosque," and "No Bloomberg Mosque." At the height of the demonstration were thousands of people yelling, "No Mosque! No Mosque!"

I've lived in New York City for twenty years and have attended my share of demonstrations, but this anti-Park51 demonstration felt different. It was raw and completely in-your-face. Directed not only at Muslims, the demonstrators' animus was also aimed at the few political leaders, such as Mayor Bloomberg, who had come out publicly in support of Park51 by defending the constitutional principle of the free exercise of religion. Opponents of Park51, however, weren't buying it, and the zeal of their passions against Muslims illustrated how much being a Muslim in America today is to embody, quite literally, some of America's most contested political and cultural debates. I came home depressed.

Sociological Dilemma

5   Before 9/11, most Americans probably thought very little about their Muslim neighbors. Despite a history that stretches back to the days of slavery—sizeable numbers of Africans enslaved in the United States were Muslim—Islam was rarely considered an American religion. The rise of the Nation of Islam and the

Figure 2: A demonstrator at a rally on September 11, 2010 in support of Park51. Note the sign's ecumenical message, which was common during this demonstration. (Photograph by Bud Korotzer; Courtesy of Next Left Notes)

spectacular life and death of Malcolm X notwithstanding, Muslim Americans barely registered on the American psyche.[2] Today, everything is different. Muslim Americans have become regular topics of conversation on television news and talk radio shows, subjects of investigation by research institutes, reasons for people to organize and demonstrate, and the concern of law enforcement and government policymakers. In short, Muslims in America have become a sociological dilemma.

As troubling as it is for a religious community to become scientifically interesting, it is equally true that Muslim Americans have also been warmly received by many of their fellow Americans, who have often sought them out to understand their faith and predicaments and to protect their civil liberties when threatened. Muslim Americans too, from young people to the major national organizations, have understood the responsibilities of communicating who they are to the wider public and have since September 11 spoken in a more American idiom about their dilemmas (including loudly condemning terrorism, despite protestations to the contrary).[3] They now often seek alliances and coalitions with other religious and minority groups in the country. They regularly hold open house at their mosques and Islamic centers to facilitate communication with non-Muslims. And campus-based Muslim Student Associations around the country sponsor Islam Awareness Weeks to represent themselves—rather than be represented by the media—to larger publics. Since 9/11, the general public has also shown an interest in understanding Islam and Muslims. For a while, the Qur'an was even a best seller.

Despite these fine efforts on the part of both Muslim and non-Muslim Americans, full acceptance of Muslim Americans seems less assured today than ever. According to an annual Washington Post–ABC News poll, approximately thirty-nine percent of Americans held unfavorable opinions of Islam in 2001. Dipping for a few years, the number rose to forty-six percent in 2006. In 2010, it reached forty-nine percent.[4] *The Economist* took a poll when the Park51 debates hit their stride, finding that fifty-five percent of Americans held negative opinions of Islam.[5]

This growing animosity surprises many Muslim Americans, since for many years following 9/11 popular anger was not the primary problem confronting their communities; religious and national-origin profiling was their true concern. While it is true that the number of reported hate crimes against Muslim Americans skyrocketed in the first six months after 9/11 (and still have not returned to pre-9/11 levels), the greatest reverberation for Muslim Americans came from the sweep arrests across the nation. Hundreds of immigrants were rounded up in the months after the terrorist attacks, often on flimsy evidence or simply on the basis of national origin. Law professor David Cole estimates that more than 5,000 individuals were arrested, the vast majority of them deported after spending months in detention.[6] One Palestinian man was arrested while driving four miles over the speed limit. He spent four months in jail before being deported.[7] Another Algerian man, arrested in September 2001 and cleared of any terrorism connection by November 2001, spent nearly five years in detention.[8] Eighty days was the average, according to the Justice Department's Inspector General, who criticized post-9/11 detention practices in two lengthy reports.[9]

As difficult as this was for the community, it could have been worse. David Ayers, U.S. Attorney General John Ashcroft's Chief of Staff, had proposed house-to-house searches in parts of the country with large Muslim communities. He was opposed by James Ziglar, then commissioner of the Immigration and Naturalization Service, who stood his ground by reportedly telling Ayres, "I know you're not a lawyer, but we do have this thing called the Constitution."[10] Without Ziglar's support, the proposal died in the water.

10   Other law enforcement initiatives that specifically targeted Muslim immigrants in the United States did survive. These included the Special Registration program, which required all adult male visitors to the country from twenty-four Muslim-majority countries (and North Korea) to register their whereabouts with the government, and the Absconder Apprehension Initiative, where the government sought to deport immigrants who had absconded on a deportation

order and and, in doing so, prioritized immigrants from Muslim-majority nations. Additional initiatives included "voluntary" interviews with Arab and Muslim immigrants in the country, warrantless wiretaps, extended use of the material witness statute (that many in the legal community see as an abuse of the law), the deployment of spies and informants into Muslim communities, and microscopic scrutiny of charities and charitable giving.[11]

These various initiatives, strung together in a short span of time, led often to feelings of being under siege by the authorities in many Muslim American communities. In 2006, the Vera Institute of Justice, an independent non-profit organization dedicated to examining law enforcement strategies, was commissioned by the Department of Justice to study how changes in policing since 9/11 had affected Arab American communities (the conclusions would apply generally to many Muslim American communities). Their report "confirmed that September 11 had a substantial impact on Arab American communities," drawing attention to worries about overzealous policing. "Although community members also reported increases in hate victimization," the report stated, "they expressed greater concern about being victimized by federal policies and practices than by individual acts of harassment or violence."[12]

Since the inception of these discriminatory policies, the Muslim American community has also found many allies and defenders of their rights, including the American Civil Liberties Union, the Center for Constitutional Rights, Amnesty International, Human Rights Watch, and other local organizations and individual attorneys. The support offered to the community illustrated a divided reaction on the part of the country. On the one hand, government initiatives, specific immigration policies, and law enforcement strategies were aimed directly at the larger Muslim American community. On the other hand, significant sectors of civil society offered substantial resistance to the targeting of Muslims on the basis of due process and equal treatment under the law.

Divided Cultural Front

The cultural front is similarly bifurcated. Wildly successful television shows like *24* showed a nation spellbound by the threat of homegrown terrorism. In season four, *24* depicted a harsh, duplicitous world where an ordinary Muslim Middle Eastern family in Southern California is called into action as a "sleeper cell" to perform a terrorist act in the United States. The Showtime series *Sleeper Cell* also depicted ordinary Muslims, this time from various backgrounds, ready and willing to follow their charismatic leader in attacking United States citizens. The film *Traitor* (2008), starring Don Cheadle, had a similar storyline.

Figure 3: Pastor Terry Jones, the fringe Florida preacher who gained international notoriety for his proposed "Burn the Qur'an Day" on September 11, 2010. Though he was persuaded to cancel those plans, on March 20, 2011, he taped himself burning a Qur'an, which sparked violent protests in Afghanistan. (Photograph by Stephen M. Dowell; Courtesy of Orlando Sentinel/MCT)

But films with other narratives also succeeded in portraying Muslim life in the United States through broader lenses. In a film about the friendship between an aging college professor and a young Arab immigrant drummer, the 2007 independent feature *The Visitor* sensitively depicted the realities of immigration detention, something rarely explored through film. Also in 2007, the WB Network carried the comedy show *Aliens in America* for one season, which rather brilliantly chronicled a Pakistani exchange student's life in Wisconsin during the age of terror. And in February 2010, Bill Cosby endorsed Katie Couric's call to model a television show about a Muslim American family after *The Cosby Show,* a popular sitcom that aired in the mid-eighties and greatly contributed to the decrease in discriminatory attitudes aimed at African Americans.[13]

15   These are positive signs of acceptance, but it may be too soon to rejoice; anger and suspicion against Muslim Americans is growing, and the dominant narrative about Muslim Americans seems to be changing. The American Muslim community had often been compared favorably to its European counterparts. American Muslims were seen as well assimilated and not a threat to public order (unlike recent Muslim immigrants, the story went), feeding the United States' image of itself as a successful immigrant-absorbing nation and notions of American superiority over Europe. A 2007 study by the Pew Research Center, called *Muslim Americans: Middle Class and Mostly Mainstream,* confirmed the idea of Muslim American integration, both by its title and its findings.[14]

But that story is receding while another—the fabulous story that American Muslims are on a "stealth jihad" to usurp the U.S. Constitution and impose Islamic law on the land—is quickly taking its place. This most recent narrative about Muslim Americans, which fuels the opposition to Park51, is expressed much less in the language of national security and far more through the language of cultural domination. In 2010, for example, the Texas State Board of Education alleged that high-school textbooks "whitewash" Islam while vilifying Christianity, and that Arab investors are taking over the American publishing industry, which is demonstrably untrue. They voted to limit references to Islam in their high-school textbooks, even though, as the Associated Press noted, "the resolution cites world-history books no longer used in Texas schools."[15] Oklahomans meanwhile voted overwhelmingly in November 2010 in favor of a state constitutional amendment that would ban the use of Sharia law in their courts (another non-issue). Voters there were reacting to a well-funded campaign and to what Republican State Representative Rex Duncan has called "a war for the survival of the United States."[16] Even though a federal judge has temporarily blocked this amendment as unconstitutional, a dozen other states have followed Oklahoma in introducing anti-Sharia legislation.

Similarly, recent antagonism to mosques is not limited to the area around Ground Zero. The Pew Center on Religion published a report in September 2010 that found that at least thirty-five mosques around the country have faced opposition over the past two years.[17] In one California case, mosque opponents were advised to bring dogs to their demonstration since, as the leader of their group stated, Muslims "hate dogs."[18] Meanwhile, Terry Jones, a fringe religious leader in Florida, garnered international coverage for his plans to burn Qur'ans on September 11, 2010 and was talked out of the idea by Secretary of Defense Robert Gates, no less (Figure 3). In March 2011, however, Jones staged a "mock trial" of the Qur'an which culminated in his public burning of the holy book, igniting deadly protests in Afghanistan.[19] Conservative talk-show host Bill O'Reilly appeared on the popular daytime television show *The View* on October 14, 2010, where he stated that "Muslims killed us on 9/11," causing two of the hosts, Whoopi Goldberg and Joy Behar, to walk off stage in anger. During the 2010 election season, the Tea Party Nation called on its supporters to oust African American Congressman Keith Ellison from his seat because he is Muslim.[20]

It would seem that the fear of terrorism, commonly (and regrettably) associated with Islam, is being usurped by a very popular fear of Muslims in general. Acceptance of Muslim Americans, a counterweight to these suspicions for many years, may also be receding. The questions are not just why this has happened, but why it has taken nine years for this dramatic change to occur and if it will remain.

One answer could be that the Muslim American community has itself become increasingly radical. The lunatic ravings of Yemeni-American firebrand Anwar Awlaki, telling Muslim Americans to rise up against their government, certainly don't help (Figure 4). Popular suspicion may also be stoked by recent, high-profile arrests of "homegrown" terrorists. (Many, though not all, of these cases are "sting" operations run by the FBI.) Representative Peter King (R-N.Y.) has gone so far as to hold congressional hearings about the radicalization of American Muslims.

20   Yet, a 2010 study by the Triangle Center on Terrorism and Homeland Security found that the number of Muslim Americans involved in terrorist activities is miniscule compared to the size of the community, labeling the problem of Muslim American homegrown terrorism "a serious, but limited, problem."[21] Forty percent of Muslim domestic terrorism suspects since 2001 have been turned in by fellow Muslims,[22] and law enforcement officials from around the country vocally contradict King's claim of Muslim non-cooperation.[23] Greg Sargent, a *Washington Post* columnist, calls King's hearings "buffoonery."[24]

Nativism and Paranoia

There may be better places to search for explanations for today's climate, including American traditions of nativism. As John Higham's classic work *Strangers in the Land: Patterns of American Nativism, 1860–1925* makes abundantly clear, Catholics, Germans, Blacks, Jews, Asians, political radicals, and immigrants of all sorts have all been vilified by a doctrine known variously as Know-Nothingism, 100 Percent Americanism, or the Anglo-Saxon ideal. "Nativism," Higham writes, "was a defensive type of nationalism, but the defense varied as the nativist lashed out sometimes against a religious peril, sometimes against a revolutionary peril, sometimes against a racial peril."[25]

Muslim Americans today are cast as the latest villains in the grand nativist epic about the downfall of the United States. And while nativism offers a clue into explaining anti-Muslim feeling in the United States today, we can better understand the situation by turning to a related phenomenon that Richard Hofstadter identified in 1964. In his classic essay on political paranoia, Hofstadter argues that a recurring motif in American conservative discourse is a "paranoid style" of politics. He uses the term "paranoid" because he believes it best describes "the heated exaggeration, suspiciousness, and conspiratorial fantasies" of the Right.[26] As Higham does, Hofstadter reaches back into the nineteenth century to provide a genealogy of his subject, but he is most interested in the Cold War politics of his age. The "paranoid style" was evident everywhere Hofstadter turned. He quotes Joseph McCarthy, who believed he was surrounded by "a conspiracy on a scale so immense as to dwarf any previous such venture in the history of man."[27] This paranoid disposition is driven by "catastrophe or the fear of catastrophe," which "is most likely to elicit the syndrome of paranoid rhetoric."[28] The paranoid style of American politics propels the fear and loathing of American Muslims today. The irrational panic

Figure 4: Anwar al-Awlaki, a radical Muslim firebrand and U.S. citizen, who had worked as an imam before relocating from the United States to his ancestral homeland of Yemen in 2004. Al-Awlaki's lectures have been cited by law-enforcement officials as sources of inspiration for several perpetrators and would-be perpetrators of terrorist acts. (Courtesy of Wikimedia Commons)

that Sharia law is on the cusp of conquering the nation has its roots in the Cold War conservative belief that the minions of the Soviet Union were deeply entrenched in the American ruling class and ready to turn on a ruble.

The modern anti-Muslim crusader in the United States believes that Islam is on the march in the country, and they are the last resistance. Just as immigration in the past left the nation nearly defenseless to the true and existential threats of the hour, so too does politically correct multiculturalism today. They believe that the conspiracy itself reaches high into the upper echelons of the ruling class, sometimes including President Obama himself. This may help explain why twenty-four percent of the electorate (and forty-six percent of the GOP), according to *Time,* believes that the president is a Muslim.[29] There is certainly a kind of implied racial coding going on here— being Muslim also means that Obama is simply not one of "us"—but the feeling that a cabal of international socialists and Muslims have or are ready to take over the country is implicit in much right-wing rhetoric today, from Republican leader Sarah Palin's exhortation to "take our country back" (from what, one might ask?) to the demands to see Barack Obama's birth certificate and the labeling of Park51 as the "Obama Mosque."

Hofstadter's words sometimes sound eerily contemporary, making the connection between past paranoia and today's sentiments even clearer. "The modern right wing," he writes,

> feels dispossessed: America has been taken away from them and their kind, though they are determined to try to repossess it and to prevent the final act of subversion. The old American virtues have already been eaten away by cosmopolitans and intellectuals; the old competitive capitalism has been gradually undermined by socialist and communist schemers;

the old national security and independence have been destroyed by treasonous plots, having as their most powerful agents not merely outsiders and foreigners but major statesmen seated at the very centers of American power. Their predecessors discovered foreign conspiracies; the modern radical right finds that conspiracy also embraces betrayal at home.[30]

25   It has lately become commonplace to argue that former President George W. Bush had been more respectful towards Islam than Obama, explaining why passions against Muslims only recently exploded. But this misses the point. Conservatives are driving today's anti-Muslim agenda, but under Bush's leadership, their notion of an imminent takeover of the United States government made little sense (that was left to Michael Moore's film *Fahrenheit 911* [2004], which illustrated a kind of paranoia of the left). On those few occasions when Bush did speak out for Muslim Americans and against hate crimes, the underlying point, as influential sociologist Max Weber would see it, was the state's monopoly on violence. The fact is that until recently, the American Muslim community was most concerned about state repression and racial profiling. Now, they have racial profiling *and* inflamed populist fear and anger to worry about.

It's possible, however, that a decade after the September 11 attacks, we have now hit bottom and better days are finally ahead of us. In his 2010 State of the Union Address President Obama proclaimed that "American Muslims are part of the American family," to loud, bi-partisan applause. Then again, doesn't the fact that the president felt the need to state the obvious mean that some—too many, really—do not yet believe it?

Credit

Bayoumi, Moustafa. "Between Acceptance and Rejection: Muslim Americans and the Legacies of September 11." *Magazine of History by Organization of American Historians 25.3* (2011): 15–19. Reproduced with permission of Organization of American Historians.

Backpacks vs. Briefcases: Steps toward Rhetorical Analysis

LAURA BOLIN CARROLL

First Impressions

Imagine the first day of class in first year composition at your university.* The moment your professor walked in the room, you likely began analyzing her and making assumptions about what kind of teacher she will be. You might have noticed what kind of bag she is carrying—a tattered leather satchel? a hot pink polka-dotted backpack? a burgundy brief case? You probably also noticed what she is wearing—trendy slacks and an untucked striped shirt? a skirted suit? jeans and a tee shirt?

It is likely that the above observations were only a few of the observations you made as your professor walked in the room. You might have also noticed her shoes, her jewelry, whether she wears a wedding ring, how her hair is styled, whether she stands tall or slumps, how quickly she walks, or maybe even if her nails are done. If you don't tend to notice any of these things about your professors, you certainly do about the people around you—your roommate, others in your residence hall, students you are assigned to work with in groups, or a prospective date. For most of us, many of the people we encounter in a given day are subject to this kind of quick analysis.

Now as you performed this kind of analysis, you likely didn't walk through each of these questions one by one, write out the answer, and add up the responses to see what kind of person you are interacting with. Instead, you quickly took in the information and made an informed, and likely somewhat accurate, decision about that person. Over the years, as you have interacted with others, you have built a mental database that you can draw on to make conclusions about what a person's looks tell you about their personality. You have become able to analyze quickly what people are saying about themselves through the way they choose to dress, accessorize, or wear their hair.

We have, of course, heard that you "can't judge a book by its cover," but, in fact, we do it all the time. Daily we find ourselves in situations where we are forced to make snap judgments. Each day we meet different people, encounter

---

unfamiliar situations, and see media that asks us to do, think, buy, and act in all sorts of ways. In fact, our saturation in media and its images is one of the reasons why learning to do rhetorical analysis is so important. The more we know about how to analyze situations and draw informed conclusions, the better we can become about making savvy judgments about the people, situations and media we encounter.

Implications of Rhetorical Analysis

5   Media is one of the most important places where this kind of analysis needs to happen. Rhetoric—the way we use language and images to persuade—is what makes media work. Think of all the media you see and hear every day: Twitter, television shows, web pages, billboards, text messages, podcasts. Even as you read this chapter, more ways to get those messages to you quickly and in a persuasive manner are being developed. Media is constantly asking you to buy something, act in some way, believe something to be true, or interact with others in a specific manner. Understanding rhetorical messages is essential to help us to become informed consumers, but it also helps evaluate the ethics of messages, how they affect us personally, and how they affect society.

Take, for example, a commercial for men's deodorant that tells you that you'll be irresistible to women if you use their product. This campaign doesn't just ask you to buy the product, though. It also asks you to trust the company's credibility, or ethos, and to believe the messages they send about how men and women interact, about sexuality, and about what constitutes a healthy body. You have to decide whether or not you will choose to buy the product and how you will choose to respond to the messages that the commercial sends.

Or, in another situation, a Facebook group asks you to support health care reform. The rhetoric in this group uses people's stories of their struggles to obtain affordable health care. These stories, which are often heart-wrenching, use emotion to persuade you—also called pathos. You are asked to believe that health care reform is necessary and urgent, and you are asked to act on these beliefs by calling your congresspersons and asking them to support the reforms as well.

Because media rhetoric surrounds us, it is important to understand how rhetoric works. If we refuse to stop and think about how and why it persuades us, we can become mindless consumers who buy into arguments about what makes us value ourselves and what makes us happy. For example, research has shown that only 2% of women consider themselves beautiful ("Campaign"), which has been linked to the way that the fashion industry defines beauty. We are also told by the media that buying more stuff can make us happy, but historical surveys show that US happiness peaked in the 1950s, when people saw as many advertisements in their lifetime as the average American sees in one year (Leonard).

Our worlds are full of these kinds of social influences. As we interact with other people and with media, we are continually creating and interpreting rhetoric. In the same way that you decide how to process, analyze or ignore these messages, you create them. You probably think about what your clothing will communicate as you go to a job interview or get ready for a date. You are also using rhetoric when you try to persuade your parents to send you money or your friends to see the movie that interests you. When you post to your blog or tweet you are using rhetoric. In fact, according to rhetorician Kenneth Burke, rhetoric is everywhere: "wherever there is persuasion, there is rhetoric. And wherever there is 'meaning,' there is 'persuasion.' Food eaten and digested is not rhetoric. But in the meaning of food there is much rhetoric, the meaning being persuasive enough for the idea of food to be used, like the ideas of religion, as a rhetorical device of statesmen" (71–72). In other words, most of our actions are persuasive in nature. What we choose to wear (tennis shoes vs. flip flops), where we shop (Whole Foods Market vs. Wal-Mart), what we eat (organic vs. fast food), or even the way we send information (snail mail vs. text message) can work to persuade others.

10   Chances are you have grown up learning to interpret and analyze these types of rhetoric. They become so commonplace that we don't realize how often and how quickly we are able to perform this kind of rhetorical analysis. When your teacher walked in on the first day of class, you probably didn't think to yourself, "I think I'll do some rhetorical analysis on her clothing and draw some conclusions about what kind of personality she might have and whether I think I'll like her." And, yet, you probably were able to come up with some conclusions based on the evidence you had.

However, when this same teacher hands you an advertisement, photograph or article and asks you to write a rhetorical analysis of it, you might have been baffled or felt a little overwhelmed. The good news is that many of the analytical processes that you already use to interpret the rhetoric around you are the same ones that you'll use for these assignments.

The Rhetorical Situation, Or Discerning Context

One of the first places to start is context. Rhetorical messages always occur in a specific situation or context. The president's speech might respond to a specific global event, like an economic summit; that's part of the context. You choose your clothing depending on where you are going or what you are doing; that's context. A television commercial comes on during specific programs and at specific points of the day; that's context. A billboard is placed in a specific part of the community; that's context, too.

In an article called "The Rhetorical Situation," Lloyd Bitzer argues that there are three parts to understanding the context of a rhetorical moment: exigence, audience and constraints. Exigence is the circumstance or condition that invites a response; "imperfection marked by urgency; it is a defect, an obstacle, something waiting to be done, a thing which is other than it should be" (Bitzer 304). In other words, rhetorical discourse is usually responding to some kind of problem. You can begin to understand a piece's exigence by asking, "What is this rhetoric responding to?" "What might have happened to make the rhetor (the person who creates the rhetoric) respond in this way?"

The exigence can be extremely complex, like the need for a new Supreme Court justice, or it can be much simpler, like receiving an email that asks you where you and your friends should go for your road trip this weekend. Understanding the exigence is important because it helps you begin to discover the purpose of the rhetoric. It helps you understand what the discourse is trying to accomplish.

15   Another part of the rhetorical context is audience, those who are the (intended or unintended) recipients of the rhetorical message. The audience should be able to respond to the exigence. In other words, the audience should be able to help address the problem. You might be very frustrated with your campus's requirement that all first-year students purchase a meal plan for on-campus dining. You might even send an email to a good friend back home voicing that frustration. However, if you want to address the exigence of the meal plans, the most appropriate audience would be the person/office on campus that oversees meal plans. Your friend back home cannot solve the problem (though she may be able to offer sympathy or give you some good suggestions), but the person who can change the meal plan requirements is probably on campus. Rhetors make all sorts of choices based on their audience. Audience can determine the type of language used, the formality of the discourse, the medium or delivery of the rhetoric, and even the types of reasons used the make the rhetor's argument. Understanding the audience helps you begin to see and understand the rhetorical moves that the rhetor makes.

The last piece of the rhetorical situation is the constraints. The constraints of the rhetorical situation are those things that have the power to "constrain decision and action needed to modify the exigence" (Bitzer 306). Constraints have a lot to do with how the rhetoric is presented. Constraints can be "beliefs, attitudes, documents, facts, traditions, images, interests, motives" (Bitzer 306). Constraints limit the way the discourse is delivered or communicated. Constraints may be something as simple as your instructor limiting your proposal to one thousand words, or they may be far more complex like the kinds of language you need to use to persuade a certain community.

So how do you apply this to a piece of rhetoric? Let's say you are flipping through a magazine, and you come across an advertisement that has a large headline that reads "Why Some People Say 'D'OH' When You Say 'Homer'" ("Why"). This ad is an Ad Council public service announcement (PSA) to promote arts education and is sponsored by Americans for the Arts and NAMM, the trade association of the international music products industry.

Since you want to understand more about what this ad means and what it wants you to believe or do, you begin to think about the rhetorical situation. You first might ask, "what is the ad responding to? What problem does it hope to address?" That's the exigence. In this case, the exigence is the cutting of arts funding and children's lack of exposure to the arts. According to the Ad Council's website, "the average kid is provided insufficient time to learn and experience the arts. This PSA campaign was created to increase involvement in championing arts education both in and out of school" ("Arts"). The PSA is responding directly to the fact that kids are not getting enough arts education.

Then you might begin to think about to whom the Ad Council targeted the ad. Unless you're a parent, you are probably not the primary audience. If you continued reading the text of the ad, you'd notice that there is information to persuade parents that the arts are helpful to their children and to let them know how to help their children become more involved with the arts. The ad tells parents that "the experience will for sure do more than entertain them. It'll build their capacity to learn more. In fact, the more art kids get, the smarter they become in subjects like math and science. And that's reason enough to make a parent say, 'D'oh!,' For Ten Simple Ways to instill art in your kids' lives visit AmericansForTheArts.org" ("Why"). Throughout the text of the ad, parents are told both what to believe about arts education and how to act in response to the belief.

20   There also might be a secondary audience for this ad—people who are not the main audience of the ad but might also be able to respond to the exigence. For example, philanthropists who could raise money for arts education or legislators who might pass laws for arts funding or to require arts education in public schools could also be intended audiences for this ad.

Finally, you might want to think about the constraints or the limitations on the ad. Sometimes these are harder to get at, but we can guess a few things. One constraint might be the cost of the ad. Different magazines charge differently for ad space as well as placement within the magazine, so the Ad Council could have been constrained by how much money they wanted to spend to circulate the ad. The ad is also only one page long, so there might have been a limitation on the amount of space for the ad. Finally, on the Ad Council's webpage, they list the requirements for organizations seeking the funding and support of the Ad Council. There are twelve criteria, but here are a few:

1. The sponsor organization must be a private non-profit 501(c)3 organization, private foundation, government agency or coalition of such groups.

2. The issue must address the Ad Council's focus on Health & Safety, Education, or Community. Applications which benefit children are viewed with favor—as part of the Ad Council's Commitment to Children.

3. The issue must offer a solution through an individual action.

4. The effort must be national in scope, so that the message has relevance to media audiences in communities throughout the nation. ("Become")

Each of these criteria helps to understand the limitations on both who can participate as rhetor and what can be said.

The exigence, audience and constraints are only one way to understand the context of a piece of rhetoric, and, of course, there are other ways to get at context. Some rhetoricians look at subject, purpose, audience and occasion. Others might look at the "rhetorical triangle" of writer, reader, and purpose.

An analysis using the rhetorical triangle would ask similar questions about audience as one using the rhetorical situation, but it would also ask questions about the writer and the purpose of the document. Asking questions about the writer helps the reader determine whether she or he is credible and knowledgeable. For example, the Ad Council has been creating public service announcements since 1942 ("Loose Lips Sink Ships," anyone?) and is a non-profit agency. They also document their credibility by showing the impact of their campaigns in several ways: "Destruction of our forests by wildfires has been reduced from 22 million acres to less than 8.4 million acres per year, since our Forest Fire Prevention campaign began" and "6,000 Children were paired with a mentor in just the first 18 months of our mentoring campaign" ("About"). Based on this information, we can assume that the Ad Council is a credible rhetor, and whether or not we agree with the rhetoric they produce, we can probably assume it contains reliable information. Asking questions about the next part of the rhetorical triangle, the purpose of a piece of rhetoric, helps you understand what the rhetor is trying to achieve through the discourse. We can discern the purpose by asking questions like "what does the rhetor want me to believe after seeing this message?" or "what does the rhetor want me to do?" In some ways, the purpose takes the exigence to the next step. If the exigence frames the problem, the purpose frames the response to that problem.

The rhetorical situation and rhetorical triangle are two ways to begin to understand how the rhetoric functions within the context you find it. The key idea is to understand that no rhetorical performance takes place in a vacuum. One of the first steps to understanding a piece of rhetoric is to look at the context in which it takes place. Whatever terminology you (or your instructor) choose, it is a good idea to start by locating your analysis within a rhetorical situation.

The Heart of the Matter—The Argument

25 The rhetorical situation is just the beginning of your analysis, though. What you really want to understand is the argument—what the rhetor wants you to believe or do and how he or she goes about that persuasion. Effective argumentation has been talked about for centuries. In the fourth century BCE, Aristotle was teaching the men of Athens how to persuade different kinds of audiences in different kinds of rhetorical situations. Aristotle articulated three "artistic appeals" that a rhetor could draw on to make a case—logos, pathos, and ethos.

Logos is commonly defined as argument from reason, and it usually appeals to an audience's intellectual side. As audiences we want to know the "facts of the matter," and logos helps present these—statistics, data, and logical statements. For example, on our Homer ad for the arts, the text tells parents that the arts will "build their capacity to learn more. In fact, the more art kids get, the smarter they become in subjects like math and science" ("Why"). You might notice that there aren't numbers or charts here, but giving this information appeals to the audience's intellectual side.

That audience can see a continuation of the argument on the Ad Council's webpage, and again much of the argument appeals to logos and draws on extensive research that shows that the arts do these things:

- Allow kids to express themselves creatively and bolster their self-confidence.
- Teach kids to be more tolerant and open.
- Improve kids' overall academic performance.

- Show that kids actively engaged in arts education are likely to have higher SAT scores than those with little to no arts involvement.

- Develop skills needed by the 21st century workforce: critical thinking, creative problem solving, effective communication, teamwork and more.

- Keep students engaged in school and less likely to drop out. ("Arts")

Each bullet above is meant to intellectually persuade parents that they need to be more intentional in providing arts education for their children.

Few of us are persuaded only with our mind, though. Even if we intellectually agree with something, it is difficult to get us to act unless we are also persuaded in our heart. This kind of appeal to emotion is called pathos. Pathetic appeals (as rhetoric that draws on pathos is called) used alone without logos and ethos can come across as emotionally manipulative or overly sentimental, but are very powerful when used in conjunction with the other two appeals.

Emotional appeals can come in many forms—an anecdote or narrative, an image such as a photograph, or even humor. For example, on their web campaign, People for the Ethical Treatment of Animals (PETA) uses an image of a baby chick and of Ronald McDonald wielding a knife to draw attention to their Chicken McCruely Un-Happy Meal. These images are meant to evoke an emotional response in the viewer and, along with a logos appeal with the statistics about how cruelly chickens are treated, persuade the viewer to boycott McDonalds.

30   Pathos can also be a very effective appeal if the rhetor has to persuade the audience in a very short amount of time, which is why it is used heavily in print advertisements, billboards, or television commercials. An investment company will fill a 30-second commercial with images of families and couples enjoying each other, seeming happy, and surrounded by wealth to persuade you to do business with them. The 30-second time spot does not allow them to give the 15-year growth of each of their funds, and pathetic appeals will often hold our interest much longer than intellectual appeals.

The ad promoting the importance of art uses humor to appeal to the audience's emotional side. By comparing the epic poet Homer to Homer Simpson and his classic "d'oh!" the ad uses humor to draw people into their argument about the arts. The humor continues as they ask parents if their kids know the difference between the Homers, "The only Homer some kids know is the one who can't write his own last name" ("Why"). The ad also appeals to emotion through its language use (diction), describing Homer as "one very ancient dude," and describing The Odyssey as "the sequel" to The Iliad. In this case, the humor of the ad, which occurs in the first few lines, is meant to draw the reader in and help them become interested in the argument before the ad gets to the logos, which is in the last few lines of the ad.

The humor also makes the organization seem real and approachable, contributing to the ethos. The humor might lead you to think that Americans for the Arts is not a stuffy bunch of suits, but an organization you can relate to or one that has a realistic understanding of the world. Ethos refers to the credibility of the rhetor—which can be a person or an organization. A rhetor can develop credibility in many ways. The tone of the writing and whether that tone is appropriate for the context helps build a writer's ethos, as does the accuracy of the information or the visual presentation of the rhetoric.

In the Homer ad, the ethos is built in several ways. The simple, humorous and engaging language, such as "Greek Gods. Achilles Heel. Trojan Horse. All of these icons are brought to us by one very ancient dude—Homer. In The Iliad and its sequel, The Odyssey, he presented Greek mythology in everyday language" ("Why") draws the audience in and helps the tone of the ad seem very approachable. Also, the knowledge of Greek mythology and the information about how the arts help children—which also contribute to the logos appeal—make the ad seem credible and authoritative. However, the fact that the ad does not use too many statistics or overly technical language also contributes to the ethos of the ad because often sounding too intellectual can come across as pompous or stuffy.

Aristotle's artistic appeals are not the only way to understand the argument of rhetoric. You might choose to look at the claim or the unstated assumptions of a piece; someone else might consider the visual appeal of the rhetoric, like the font, page layout, types of paper, or images; another person might focus on the language use and the specific word choice and sentence structure of a piece. Logos, pathos, and ethos can provide a nice framework for analysis, but there are numerous ways to understand how a piece of rhetoric persuades (or fails to persuade).

35   Looking at the context and components of a piece of rhetoric often isn't enough, though, because it is important to draw conclusions about the rhetoric—does it successfully respond to the exigence? Is it an ethical approach?

Is it persuasive? These kinds of questions let you begin to create your own claims, your own rhetoric, as you take a stand on what other people say, do, or write.

Beginning to Analyze

Once you have established the context for the rhetoric you are analyzing, you can begin to think about how well it fits into that context. You've probably been in a situation where you arrived way underdressed for an occasion. You thought that the dinner was just a casual get together with friends; it turned out to be a far more formal affair, and you felt very out of place. There are also times when discourse fails to respond to the situation well—it doesn't fit. On the other hand, successful discourses often respond very well to the context. They address the problem, consider the audience's needs, provide accurate information, and have a compelling claim. One of the reasons you work to determine the rhetorical situation for a piece of discourse is to consider whether it works within that context. You can begin this process by asking questions like:

- Does the rhetoric address the problem it claims to address?

- Is the rhetoric targeted at an audience who has the power to make change?

- Are the appeals appropriate to the audience?

- Does the rhetor give enough information to make an informed decision?

- Does the rhetoric attempt to manipulate in any way (by giving incomplete/inaccurate information or abusing the audience's emotions)?

- What other sub-claims do you have to accept to understand the rhetor's main claim? (For example, in order to accept the Ad Council's claim that the arts boost math and science scores, you first have to value the boosting of those scores.)

- What possible negative effects might come from this rhetoric?

Rhetorical analysis asks how discourse functions in the setting in which it is found. In the same way that a commercial for denture cream seems very out of place when aired during a reality television show aimed at teenagers, rhetoric that does not respond well to its context often fails to persuade. In order to perform analysis, you must understand the context and then you must carefully study the ways that the discourse does and does not respond appropriately to that context.

The bottom line is that the same basic principles apply when you look at any piece of rhetoric (your instructor's clothing, an advertisement, the president's speech): you need to consider the context and the argument. As you begin to analyze rhetoric, there are lots of different types of rhetoric you might encounter in a college classroom, such as

- Political cartoon
- Wikipedia entry
- Scholarly article
- Bar graph
- Op-Ed piece in the newspaper
- Speech
- YouTube video
- Book chapter
- Photograph
- PowerPoint presentation

All of the above types of discourse try to persuade you. They may ask you to accept a certain kind of knowledge as valid, they may ask you to believe a certain way, or they may ask you to act. It is important to understand what a piece of rhetoric is asking of you, how it tries to persuade you, and whether that persuasion fits within the context you encounter it in. Rhetorical analysis helps you answer those questions.

Implications of Rhetorical Analysis, Or Why Do This Stuff Anyway?

So you might be wondering if you know how to do this analysis already—you can tell what kind of person someone is by their clothing, or what a commercial wants you to buy without carefully listening to it—why do you need to know how to do more formal analysis? How does this matter outside a college classroom?

Well, first of all, much of the reading and learning in college requires some level of rhetorical analysis: as you read a textbook chapter to prepare for a quiz, it is helpful to be able to distill the main points quickly; when you read a journal article for a research paper, it is necessary to understand the scholar's thesis; when you watch a video in class, it is useful to be able to understand how the creator is trying to persuade you. But college is not the only place where an understanding of how rhetoric works is important. You will find yourself in many situations—from boardrooms to your children's classrooms or churches to city council meetings where you need to understand the heart of the arguments being presented.

40   One final example: in November 2000, Campbell's Soup Company launched a campaign to show that many of their soups were low in calories and showed pre-pubescent girls refusing to eat because they were "watching their weight." A very small organization called Dads and Daughters, a group that fights advertising that targets girls with negative body images, contacted Campbell's explaining the problems they saw in an ad that encouraged young girls to be self-conscious about their weight, and asked Campbell's to pull the ad. A few days later, Campbell's Vice President for Marketing and Corporate Communications called. One of the dads says, "the Vice President acknowledged he had received their letter, reviewed the ad again, saw their point, and was pulling the ad," responding to a "couple of guys writing a letter" ("Media"). Individuals who understand rhetorical analysis and act to make change can have a tremendous influence on their world.

Works Cited

"About Ad Council" *Ad Council.* Ad Council. n.d. Web. 11 March 2010.

"Arts Education." *Ad Council: Arts Education.* Ad Council. n.d. Web. 27 July 2009.

"Become an Ad Council Campaign." *Ad Council.* Ad Council. n.d. Web. 27 July 2009.

Bitzer, Lloyd. "The Rhetorical Situation." *Philosophy and Rhetoric* 1 (1968): 1–14. Rpt. in Martin J. Medhurst and Thomas W. Benson, eds. *Rhetorical Dimensions in Media.* Dubuque, IA: Kendall/Hunt, 1991. 300–10. Print.

Burke, Kenneth. *A Rhetoric of Motives.* Berkeley: U of California P, 1969. Print.

"Campaign for Real Beauty Mission." *Dove Campaign for Real Beauty.* 2008. Web. 27 July 2009.

Leonard, Annie. "Fact Sheet." *The Story of Stuff with Annie Leonard.* n.d. Web. 27 July 2009.

"The Media's Influence." *Perfect Illusions: Eating Disorders and the Family.* PBS. 2003. Web. 27 July 2009.

"Why Some People Say 'D'oh' When You Say 'Homer.'" *Ad Council: Arts Education.* Ad Council. n.d. Web. 27 July 2009.

Credit ──

Carroll, Laura Bolin. "Backpacks vs. Briefcases: Steps toward Rhetorical Analysis." Ed. Charles Lowe and Pavel Zemliansky. 1st ed. Anderson: Parlor Press, 2010. 45–58. Reprinted with the author's permission.

Trans Media Moments: Tumblr, 2011–2013

MARTY FINK AND QUINN MILLER

Abstract

For transgender, transsexual, genderqueer, and gender nonconforming people, emergent media technologies offer new outlets for self-representation, outlets that often last for only a brief moment. This article examines trans culture on the website Tumblr during the period from March 2011, when the authors began researching the platform, to May 2013, when Yahoo! paid creator David Karp over a billion dollars for the site. Through auto-ethnographic dialogue about the loose social networks within Tumblr to which the authors contributed during this phase, the article explores ephemeral aspects of self-representation at the intersection of postmodern art practice, sexual politics, and queer subjectivities. From at least 2011 to 2013, people collectively oriented in opposition to dominant discourses of gender and sexuality used Tumblr to refashion straight cisgender norms and to create everyday art in a hybrid media space.

Keywords

Transgender, Tumblr, new media, sexuality, queer, blog

ᘏᘄᘏᘄᘏᘄ

Introduction

Quinlan Miller (QM): Since debuting in 2007, the website Tumblr has fostered cultural exchange among people who identify as queer and transgender. The imageoriented pages of transgender, transsexual, genderqueer, and gender nonconforming people have created intricate networks of digital self-representation. These networks connect Tumblr users who collectively oppose traditional systems of gender distinction and who are also queer in terms of their sexual practices and conceptions of sexuality. Through the site, these users, like others, circulate everything from fashion, pornography, and life updates to theory, protest, and event publicity. Tumblr began acknowledging its integrated advertising last year. Then the company changed hands in May 2013, when Yahoo! paid 1.65 billion dollars for the site. As we discuss our research into and active participation in tumblr enclaves, I suggest that, as a way of channeling tensions between queer trans people and corporate interests, we use "Tumblr," with a capital "T," to refer to the company and the lowercase "tumblr" to mark resistant networks on the site, as well as specific users' tumblrs (i.e., their tumblr pages). The format encourages customization at many levels. Templates recur, but one tumblr generally looks much different from the next. Even more so than platforms like WordPress or Blogger, Tumblr allows users to cultivate a personal style at the level of design, which many users orient toward an aesthetic of formal experimentation, irony, historiography, or technophilia.

Marty Fink (MF): To start, we should describe the form and mechanisms of Tumblr for people unfamiliar with the site.

QM: Right. Tumblrs typically consist of a long chain of uncontextualized short entries, which may include images, recordings, links, and text in various combinations. For example, an entry consisting of a link to a song embeds an image of an album cover or other associated art. Posts aggregate visually, creating a portrait of each user that resembles the experience of web browsing—which is, in self-reflexive fashion, what generates content. Some users include explanatory descriptions with posts, while others do not. Some repost ("reblog") information included at the source of an entry, while others leave it up to the reader to track back to the original for citational information and an indication of the content and its authenticity or fabrication. Posts generally include a link, via the users' handles, to the original tumblr on which they appeared, along with the tumblr from which the user reblogged the entry. This platform creates a record of every image's circulation through "notes," which list each user who has posted an item to their tumblr. A post's notes reflect the order in which users reblogged the entry and include any commentary they added. I commonly use notes to check if I have accurately identified classic Hollywood era actors. On some occasions, I've supplied information or corrected misinformation about my favorite performers. Others use notes to engage in activist and intellectual conversation.

MF: It is these specific elements of the Tumblr interface that have allowed the site to host the "disidentificatory" (Muñoz 1999) work of queer users wrestling trans sexualities out of a white, middle-class, cisgender (non-trans), mass-consumption paradigm and toward an individually tailored, polyvocal, margin-based, and personalized form of distribution.

5 QM: Yes. The genderqueer and queer trans expression this environment has fostered crystalizes a lot of recent innovations in offline queer culture. I've been especially interested in examining the ways in which tumblrs focused on art, fashion, and activist culture feature objects of desire and/or identification. Many people, especially fat trans femme snarksters of color, are at the forefront of a field of inquiry Kate Bornstein and S. Bear Bergman (2010) discuss as "looks studies," one focused on interrupting and restructuring dominant modes of perception.

MF: My own use of Tumblr has helped to connect me to radical pockets of queer and trans heroes sharing their daily struggles, experiences, and art. My time on Tumblr—which I mostly spend reblogging queer/trans art, archival documents, and artifacts inspired by poodles, as well as my own web-based art—has majorly influenced my thinking about disabled queer/trans bodies, about fatness and fat queer/trans fashion, as well as the scope and breadth of possibility for queer/transsexual representation and pornography. Like any popular and accessible Internet medium, I do find it unstartling that Tumblr has been sold. Even before the sale, I have wondered about what content (for instance, the extreme jubilation and testimonials for certain brands of sex toys) is secretly just advertising and content motivated by corporate sponsorship. This sneaky fake user-generated content proliferates on other corporate owned sites like Facebook, and issues of where content comes from and in whose interests content grows now comes further to the fore. As with issues of privacy and image permanence on Facebook, the idyllic Tumblr of yore is going to be increasingly encroached on by corporate attention. One hopes, however, that Tumblr's increasing popularity will preserve its status as a continued outlet for original artwork and an additional channel of expression for events that transpire offline, or IRL ("In Real Life").

QM: At the time of the Yahoo! acquisition, I was fully engrossed in my own queer trans tumblr microcosm, which I cultivated by surfing the fringe elements of cinephiles, TV archivists, poststructuralists, and camp producers. For the past year, I had been actively reblogging film, telefilm, and queer trans art to my tumblr at an average of 100 posts per week.

MF: Our own ways of using Tumblr indicate the wide range of different forms queer trans content takes on the site. Certainly, there is an even broader range of forms and content beyond this one site. Yet the use of Tumblr has been especially revealing of collective online queer trans creativity, particularly around sexual expression, everyday coalitional politics, and genderqueer culture. I came to the site to connect to a community of queer introverts in my daily "real" life who spend much of their time building digital cultures online. I wanted to be part of these communities as well as the (often far less accessible) ones we were building offline. At present, Tumblr plays a unique role as a particular digital forum for disseminating self-representations of trans experience beyond local contexts and spatial boundaries.

QM: I created a tumblr account to follow (i.e., subscribe to) other people's tumblrs not anticipating I would post anything myself. The entries of each person you follow appear on your dash (the dashboard or "home" page), in a composite of current activity. An archival impulse has motivated my increasing participation in the site, as I reblog images for the record. These include images from my dashboard and also many I discover by intuitively tracing interesting activity through the thread of posts' notes. Reblogging involves one or two strokes. Soon after creating an account, I was adding original content in the form of scans, screen captures, links, audio, and photos.

10 MF: Outsiders typically understand Tumblr through the discourse of the blog, as a "microblog" platform. Whereas blogging implies prose, microblogging, or "tumblelogging" (aka "Tumblogging" on Tumblr), mostly involves marking and annotating, or simply reposting, content encountered on other sites. Showing some similarities but also striking differences from interfaces like Pintrest and Reddit, Tumblr sparks image-centered conversations about topics including art, fashion, race, disability, popular culture, and the obligatory cats. Radical and sex-positive queer and trans culture proliferates on Tumblr.

QM: That proliferation makes Tumblr an interesting venue for addressing cultural politics and questions of intersectionality together with topics in new media theory, like intertextuality and medium specificity. Tumblr can be more erratic than other sites in that certain subcultural practices foster unfamiliar modes of temporal engagement.

MF: Right. For example, people use Tumblr's specific temporal possibilities to register style and sexuality in relation to lived experiences of gender, race, class, diaspora, and ability with which they critically and creatively engage.

QM: Exactly. The recent merger has really shown the limitations of using the "blog" concept to understand Tumblr. As media critic Howard Rheingold points out, "Tumblr differs from first-wave blogging … by enabling people to express themselves by reblogging material they see elsewhere in a kind of collage of found social objects that reflect their vision or taste" (2012, 140). Yet, as part of the acquisition coverage, journalists suggested sites like WordPress and Twitter as alternatives to Tumblr, oblivious to the medium-specific structures of feeling that have made Tumblr appealing to queer trans dissidents. In an emblematic misconstrual of Tumblr, Yahoo! CEO Marissa Mayer described the Tumblr dashboard as "the inbox for the blogs you follow" (Lunden 2013). While this is in some ways a useful analogy, it overlooks Tumblr's own messaging systems. The reference to email domesticates many significant features that infuse instability and idiosyncrasy into the platform. In practice, Tumblr's aesthetics reference a mode of engagement distinct to the site—a mode that may be contingent on the combination of its relative accessibility, in terms of interface and network transparency, and its simultaneous obscurity, in terms of the intensive specialization of the subcultures and insular fandoms the site supported prior to its FaceBook-ification.

Cultural production in the pre-Yahoo! buyout period raises important questions about how innovative modes of social networking spark new media practices resistant to the corporate monetization of cultural production driving the development and dissemination of web 2.0 technology.

Trans Cultural Production

15   MF: Given the silences and fetishistic misrepresentations in public culture around trans existence, the Internet facilitates information exchange and self-exploration for many trans people. Vastly different types of trans people with vastly different self-understandings and sexual identities create a broad range of communities online. Tumblr has been a prolific outlet for queer trans people, in particular. On any given day, one might, whether according to whim or design, post a series of photos found elsewhere, images from one's own digital camera; a popular meme; and some brief comments or hashtags annotating the popularity or significance of the posted content.

QM: Yes. Tumblr is a system of simultaneous consumption and production within which pleasures of juxtaposition, repetition, and recurrence are frequent and fast-paced. Its temporal and spatial dimensions are fascinating. Depending on the time of day, day of the week, and a host of other variables, including how many pages you follow—I'm currently at 475—there may be several new posts or there may be hundreds every time you refresh your dash. Every moment is a provocative illustration of the Benjaminian concept of "now-time," or the revolutionary possibility in the present. Through posts and commentary, I can sometimes see which people, of those I follow, follow each other. I often explore new networks by viewing the pages of people who reblog or like something I post and cruising their seemingly most tangential connections. These elements make tumblr's taste-based subcultures different from the profiles on a site like FaceBook in that, to thrive within Tumblr's format, you need to labor and gain credibility according to particularly intense systems of distinction. Within this system, genderqueer and queer trans tumblr users can displace the pernicious norms conditioning representations of trans people within the constraints of mainstream spaces (online and off). Spaces of antinormative trans self-representation within the Tumblr network compel a nuancing of current scholarly understandings of trans and genderqueer sexualities, identities, and representations.

MF: To appreciate the impact of queer trans tumblr production, it is important to consider the acute need for new media spaces for trans cultural production, given the long history of obstacles to self-representation that transgender, gender nonconforming, and gender variant people have faced. Trans identities have been recurrently coopted, oversimplified, fetishized, and erased by mainstream media outlets and cultural productions.

QM: Without a doubt, even with the increase in exposure over the past decades, mainstream media productions focus on middle-class, professional trans people, compelling them to provide personal stories of anatomy and physical transformation. The biographical focus on gender norms within the transition narrative—rather than on pressing issues of access to documentation, education, housing, employment, and health care—forecloses an analysis of the social and economic factors that shape trans lives (Namaste 2005, 49).

Journalists are paying increasing attention to transsexual and transgender people, but as Viviane Namaste's writings show, their reports rarely allow us to speak in our own terms about our own lives (2005, 47). Namaste's work explains how news media frame trans experience as something for the interest and entertainment of cis viewers, while failing to address the legal and financial barriers that trans people face. Julia Serano's analysis of mainstream media representations of trans people identifies a reductive focus on the physical aspects of transition, in particular (2007, 54). Serano argues that the cultural obsession with anatomy and appearance results in prevalent tropes of transition (from an endless barrage of before-and-after pictures to overwrought sequences of "putting on" one's gender), particularly for women, that ultimately produce a class-based differentiation between trans and cis people, overemphasizing gender difference and undervaluing the role of sexism and misogyny in shaping trans experience (2007, 57).

20　　*In illuminating connections between gender binaries and the maintenance of patriarchy, Serano's work demonstrates how we can combat gender-based violence on a wider scale by challenging myopic images of trans-ness and transition. Dominant discourses of sexuality and gender limit how trans people and our sexual practices are defined and understood. The dominant representational system reduces trans sexuality (i.e., the sexuality of trans people) to gender performance or to fetishized images of trans bodies. As Eve Kosofsky Sedgwick (1990) established, sexuality and sexual practice are "known" through gender. In contexts overdetermined by a hetero/homosexual opposition, a person's gender and the gender of their partners is seen to determine their sexual identity. As Sedgwick's work reveals, this system of organizing sexuality follows from severe discursive constraints on what signifies as "sexuality" and what "sexuality" can entail. The epistemological framework that grants credence to homo/ hetero distinctions overshadows an abundance of objects, subject positions, and practices—all relatively independent of gender—around which we might organize erotic life.*

QM: Clusters of cultural production across individual tumblrs showcase this abundance of sexual objects, one reason it remains unclear whether Tumblr's queer trans constituency will survive Yahoo! ownership. These networks are particularly vulnerable to and potentially jeopardized by the advertising-marketing-demographics interests signaled by the sale. In Tumblr's early period, at least, queer trans tumblr production has often foreshadowed scholarship in academic trans studies.

MF: True. Without much institutional support, trans studies of sexuality have sought to make distinctions of sexual practice beyond homo/hetero knowable and representable. For instance, Patrick Califia's ([1994] 2001) classic essay on anal fisting in BDSM argues for hand/wrist size and not gender or genitals as the object of cruising and sexual attention. Jack Halberstam's analysis of subcultural media similarly repositions sexuality not as an outcome of gender identity but rather in relation to other factors like building friendships, resisting gender-based violence, surviving mental illness, and battling poverty (2005, 95). As Serano and Namaste caution, crucial daily aspects of trans lives that are seemingly unrelated to gender or sexuality must be self-represented to encompass the ways in which transness intersects with a host of other factors that inform sexual desire where and when it does arise.

QM: This is why the merger, however unsurprising, is so unsettling to me. Mayer and Tumblr founder David Karp have stated commitments to protect Tumblr and not "screw it up" (Mayer 2013). In particular, the owners claim they will limit the incursion of advertising on the site to avoid censoring pornography and other content that might turn off mass audiences and thus big ticket investments in ad space. Yet the very fact of Yahoo! control changes the information and everyday art production that appears on Tumblr. The site's aesthetics and the possible meanings of its content are shaped by discursive and economic contexts.

MF: Up to this point, Tumblr has circulated important aspects of queer trans imaginaries through a catalog of images reminiscent of earlier eras but suited to the constantly shifting new media landscape. In the digital realm, vectors of racial, disabled, activist, artistic, and transnational identity complicate conventional expectations of trans identity and experience. Tumblr has facilitated the online emergence of a "callout culture" where people of color can draw awareness to and effectively critique daily practices of racism and cultural appropriation that often go unchecked.

25   *Tumblr's systems of trans self-representation thereby call into question both the freedoms and the limitations of digital production as an emerging cultural force. Issues of distribution indicate the importance of remaining aware of how the Internet tends to reinforce cultural norms of whiteness. Even within digital spaces aiming—or at least claiming—to represent diversity and the work of artists of color, structural racism prevails.*

MF: Elisha Lim comes to mind. Since 2010, Lim has used their tumblr as an installation space for their illustrated interviews with trans, butch, sissy, and other queerly identified people of color. These portraits link genderqueer self-presentation with queer modes of sexual expression through discussions of flirtation, dandyism, racialization, diaspora, and fashion.

Lim's (2010) *100 Butches* circulates digitally and in print, countering white and heterodominant norms influencing media representations of gender presentation, sexual practice, and queer erotics. In one comic from this series, the speaker asks, "Do people read me as masculine? Do they see my Chinese race first? And what does that do to their perception of masculinity?" The illustrations accompanying such commentary draw on a mix of transnational references. Through candidly relating the experience of the subjects who sit for portraits, Lim creates a queer diasporic space for the self-fashioning and self-representation of gender nonconforming and racialized bodies. Rendered with delicate but stark ink lines and bright demonstrative colors that complement the earnestness of the text, the speaker reflects, "I've decided to create my own show. I dress for myself and I imitate my own East Asian role models like Andy Lau and Bi … [with] fur coats, sunglasses indoors, and bleached tips."

Online, Lim's representations circulate within media outlets that replicate the dominant privileging of whiteness within media production. We can trace this process by looking at Lim's tumblr from their 2011 calendar comic *The Illustrated Gentleman*. This piece features queer and trans people of color in equestrian menswear, yet the most circulated image was the one month out of twelve whose subject was white. *The Illustrated Gentleman* offers an anecdotal exploration of how style and clothing can express the intricacies of gender, sexual, and racial identification. In this context, the disproportionate reblogging of the one white model recuperates Lim's artistic world, in which queer people of color outnumber white queers by 11:1.

QM: I saw something similar play out with a post on "Experiments in Legitimacy." When Quentin Tarantino's *Django Unchained* (2012) came out, I reblogged a number of images from relevant unacknowledged intertexts—of Julius Carry's Lord Bowler, for example, a black bounty hunter character in the mid-1990s scifi buddy western TV series *The Adventures of Brisco County Jr.* (FOX, 1993–1994). I was particularly interested in presenting Melvin Van Peebles's *Sweet Sweetback's Baadasssss Song*, an experimental feature from 1971, as uncited source material. Of the three *Sweetback* stills I made, one person reblogged the image of the film's epigraph and one other person reblogged an intertitle proclaiming the protagonist's aim to "collect some dues" from the racist structures of U.S. power. Far more users—sixty-five and counting—have circulated the text that prefaces the "dues" shot, which reads simply, "watch out."

30   While the reblogging of the least politicized *Sweetback* image seems to have slowed to a steady pace, a spike in its recirculation came after someone erased Van Peebles's name and the name of his film, radically decontextualizing the image. In the time since I made that post, Tumblr has introduced photosets, a feature that allows you to present multiple images as a single post. This feature might have prevented the "watch out" slide from circulating independently of

the "dues" placard that follows it in the film, but there is no way to intervene. I can delete the image from my tumblr, but it won't be extracted from the tumblrs of other users, and people may continue to reblog it from the other pages on which it appears.

In the case of these *Sweetback* posts, as with Lim's *Illustrated Gentleman*, the notes feature presents a record of cultural appropriation and white-centrism even as the actual process of reblogging and liking posts reinscribes cycles of misrepresentation. Given the regeneration of social hierarchies through market logics, Yahoo!'s acquisition of Tumblr will likely only exacerbate the inequities that generate such nuances at the level of representation.

MF: It is useful here to turn to Alexandra Juhasz's (2010) critique of the corporate and mainstream structure of online spaces in "YouTube at Five." Juhasz, who is interested in the use of Internet video for activism, notes that users produce YouTube videos at a rate of twenty-four hours per minute. As far as those videos that might contribute to wide-scale resistance to dominant ideology go, "It is just as hard to find them (again) as it's always been."

QM: Juhasz presents the lack of archiving, standardization, and general orderliness of information in online social networks as evidence that sites like YouTube are less democratic than they purport to be. However, it is often this state of disarray in digital media that allows for a sense of freedom beyond traditional representational politics.

MF: According to Juhasz, the higher production values of YouTube's "official" videos allocate real ownership over cultural production to better-funded projects (usually advertisements), while rendering low budget and homemade videos marginal or inferior. Independent and radical queer trans media makers like Rae Spoon and Lim are therefore juxtaposed in digital venues against the shiny, easier to find corporate images of mainstream media. While cultural makers like Spoon and Lim use musical covers and queer art to speak back to and engage critically with these media, their position is still always rendered against dominant images that proliferate online. As the circulation of Lim's work demonstrates, though it may seem like the digital world offers a larger range of representation than cable or Hollywood, the entrenched hierarchies of "old" media continue to characterize online space.

35　　QM: As skeptical as I am of a Yahoo! owned and operated Tumblr, I question Juhasz's read of the YouTube situation. Juhasz implies that YouTube content coincides with corporate media productions. However, representations of the kind Raymond Williams describes as oppositional and unincorporated also proliferate. On Tumblr, the disparity between dominant ideology and resistant discursive production is amplified by the fast pace of intensely referential practices. The combination of impermanence, anonymity, visual imagery, cultivated ambiguity, and the idiosyncrasies of specific spaces of interaction allows venues of self-celebration by queers critical of what Rubin (1992) has called the consecration of a "charmed circle" of sexuality. If you do find your subcultural niche within a network like Tumblr, it is a very sweet spot.

MF: Trans cultural makers' use of Tumblr complements that of earlier media forms. At the same time, there are significant differences between contemporary online social networks and the systems of media circulation in earlier eras.

QM: The online work of queer trans producers often showcases the overlaps of different platforms. Since 2008, for example, "Not Another Aiden" has used many different sites for self-representation and anonymous queer trans visibility. The moniker "Not Aiden" and its author's blog subtitle, "Life of A Non-Standard Gay (trans) Guy," reference white hetero norms among trans men. Not Aiden, a Jewish Latino effeminate fanboy top and a "gay guy who happens to be trans," disabuses readers who may have assumed he was white of their error in the entry "Why I don't post about being a man of color." Addressing effeminate gay trans men like himself, he writes, "I remember what it was like for me when I thought you could only be trans if you were straight." Not Aiden started a tumblr, as he recalls, sometime around the first season of *Glee*. He now has three tumblrs: notaidenarchive presents a static record of his initial foray on the site, while his personal tumblr offers the "ramblings of a compact, overly analytical, often cranky fan geek." Notaiden, which dates back to early 2012 and continues the work of his original blog, providing outreach to trans men and boys who are neither straight nor butch, has replaced the discussion forum he used to host with the open source software phpBB and rendered the posts of his WordPress blog less frequent and more introspective. Tumblr's "ask" mechanism allows him to correspond quickly about trans topics while reblogging Harry Potter and porn posts on his primary tumblr. That tumblr, like his trans related tumblrs, counters the misperception that all trans people are either genderqueer or straight and gender conforming, effectively centering and unsensationalizing this public intellectual's camp orientation and flaming gender expression—characteristics that, in dominant mainstream and trans contexts, would be seen as anomalous if recognized at all.

MF: This type of self-representation in digital venues powerfully recalls a rich history of trans cultural production in print. Tumblr, in particular, inspires me to return to radical trans cultural production predating the Internet. Historical connections that might link Tumblr to earlier moments of DIY zine production and fan culture are also especially compelling.

Queer trans people have a strong tradition of using peripheral forms of cultural production to break isolation and establish community. Analyzing objects preserved at the Kinsey Institute, Joanne Meyerowitz shows how, in the post-World War II era, trans people scrapbooked and collaged images of Christine Jorgenson, the blonde bombshell poster woman for American access to gender affirming surgeries (1998, 175). The collective potential for recirculation of Jorgenson's image was in many ways confined by the tropes of racial, national, and gender identity that critics and journalists deployed. Nevertheless, as trans people reimagined Jorgenson's image through their own cut-and-paste archives, she came to represent new possibilities for trans representation, as well as for previously unrepresented embodiments and desires.

40 *As Meyerowitz suggests, popular media and trans people's responses to it allow us to retrieve trans history from the lexicon of the medical industry through a re-circulation of dominant media production by trans people themselves (1998, 177). Cultural production is especially important because it brings representations of transness out of the single-issue focus of medical realm where it often appears and into intersectional dialogue with daily experiences of access to factors like employment, housing, community supports, and education.*

MF: Other blueprints for today's trans tumblrs are evident in A. J. Withers's (2012) "If I Can't Dance, Is it Still My Revolution" and Micah Bazant's (1999) *Timtum: A Trans Jew Zine*. Like the Jorgenson scrapbooks, *Timtum* uses cut-and-paste collaging, in this case to represent Claude Cahun, a photographer and performance artist in 1930's Germany, as a trans ancestor and object of desire. Through a decoupaging of image and text, typewritten and handwritten fonts, and a code mixing of English, Hebrew, and French, Bazant declares his *"crush sur Claude,"* whom he historicizes as a "Jewish genderfreak artfag anti-Nazi resistance fighter."

QM: Cahun is one of many historical figures that critics thoughtlessly characterize according to cis norms. Through an emphasis on first given names and familiar sexual identity categories, this normative framing overwrites more complex trans sensibilities and queer dynamics. Artists like Cahun should inspire new ways of representing the possibility of trans experience in past eras. So far, we see this work happening in marginalized queer trans and genderqueer cultural production—especially on Tumblr—but not in the academy.

MF: *Timtum* addresses this very tension between a history of trans aesthetics and the cisnormative process of scholarly canonization. Bazant's work is indicative of a broader range of new media in that, through a rendering of scars, ambiguities, and other bodily signifiers of radical gender identity, it celebrates a Yiddish feygeleh history from which the contemporary trans body can evolve by rooting itself in Jewish cultural diaspora and in dialogue with the past. This work contests the official historicization of cultural figures with a participatory and transient DIY aesthetic. Onto a historical publication of Cahun's legacy, Bazant visually inscribes the textual ambiguities that signify radical gender identity through the body. The text annotates official accounts of Cahun, manually changing all of Cahun's pronouns to render him a trans hero and predecessor to Bazant's own identity. Rather than rewriting history, *Timtum* reabsorbs it, framing trans sexuality as a site that seeks pleasure from embodied uncertainties and marks of transition.

QM: Queer trans tumblrs capitalizing on Tumblr's capabilities initiate and proliferate this process of reabsorption.

45   MF: That brings me back to A. J. Withers's "If I Can't Dance, Is it Still My Revolution," a notable zine that speaks back to dominant cultural practices in ways that we can now read as an important precursor to trans production on Tumblr. Withers's zine frames trans desire along lines of access. Trans bodies are bodies in protest—at being barred by the restrictions of physically inaccessible spaces as well as by the inaccessibility of the nation-state and its economic, educational, militarized, bordered, and administrative zones. With gender signified through one's location in medical arenas, and sexuality expressed through the cruising of hospital spaces such as the prostate cancer ward, Withers's writing represents trans desire beyond conventional narratives of hetero, monogamous, and able-bodied trans people.

Through the intermixing of personal anecdotes and political call outs, tumblrs explore trans sexuality in the context of discrimination, health care, housing access, migration struggles, and street protests, moving out of an assimilationist paradigm and into a multi-issue, antinationalist, and queer framework. Rather than locating the trans body as a site exclusively of medicalization, tumblrs present access to medical services as interconnected to broader types of access from citizenship to the need to increase welfare rates and minimum wage. Linking Tumblr use, zines spotlight collaborative trans production of a wide range of queer political practices and sexual expressions. Historical research into different phases of self-representation shows how shifts in social norms are bound up with new media as one of many shifts in conditions of cultural production.

Media, Gender, and Sexuality Theory

MF: As a venue for self-representation, Tumblr points to the potential as well as to the limitations of digital cultures in moving sexuality out of the fetishized realm of the obscene and into more productive conversations of how desire functions alongside daily experiences of factors like racism, disability, and gender-based violence that converge to influence offline lives.

QM: Queer trans tumblrs have facilitated collective departures from cis and trans norms in ways that illuminate the range of possibilities online. People's use of Tumblr has emphasized some of the ways in which many trans people contribute to queer culture through cultural practices related to sexuality—and to sexuality by way of gender—rather than simply in direct relation to gender. Through the juxtaposition of aesthetics and social critique, tumblr archives evoke the complexity of queer, trans, and genderqueer cultural history. In the context of specific Tumblr users, images of people making art, charting transitions, having sex, hanging out—or doing anything, really—communicate specific users' interests, states of mind, erotic sensibilities, and political commitments. In the intertextual spaces carved out by the links between tumblrs, genderqueer and queer trans self-representations integrate seamlessly with lesbian, gay, bi, pan, poly, and asexual culture. As subsets of trans people develop queer gender and genderqueer identities within gay, lesbian, and bisexual lexicons, new media representations undermine cis norms in accordance with—and sometimes beyond—offline social practices.

Sets of images organized through individual curatorial work and through collective reblogging draw attention to complex realms of identity, experience, and power relations, including those addressing: the relational production of queer gender, the role of sex in non- and anti-binary gender expression, and the multiplicity of meanings attached to what the dominant culture views as "secondary sex characteristics."

50 QM: Genderqueer tumblrs commonly create a context within which people can interpret photographs—whether celebrities and models or "selfies" (self-portraits)— in a space apart from binary gender constructions. These contexts, alternately disparate and interwoven, complicate assumed distinctions between trans and non-trans people. On the whole, these tumblrs further real-time

practices of self-determination in which people gender body parts and sexual behavior based on self-understandings rather than essentialist or preconceived understandings of how bodies signify.

MF: Through tumblrs, people are expressing their sexual desires *as trans* or as organized around seemingly nonsexual facets of identity including race ("fuckyeahftmsofcolor"), black culture ("allaboutstuds"), ability ("cripqueer"), or fashion ("deeplezstonerwitch") (Tumblr). "Baking Butches," for instance, offers a welcome for butches of all genders and identifications to post. The site welcomes users with the tagline: "Butch, Dyke, Trans, Genderqueer, Inbetween, Boi, Sissyboi, Tomboy, Wotever ... it does not matter about your identity, we still want your pictures. Baking Butches is inclusive of EVERYTHING." A similar trend has emerged on Tumblr's trans porn and "xxx" blogs. The content of many of these tumblrs transgresses the limitations within rigidly gendered categories of "female" and "male." In addition to providing a forum for the juxtaposition of bodies often reductively fetishized or desexualized by mainstream prescriptions of sexual beauty, these tumblrs also counter biological essentialism by rescripting the possibilities assigned to gendered bodied parts within cis frameworks. Posts featuring self-shot porn are routinely accompanied by commentary that creates new discursive terrain for trans subjectivity, through kinky and gender queer reconfigurations of dominant discourses. Naked portraits posted by a "lesbian identified, homoromantic gray asexual, fat (fuck the haters!), nerdy trans-chick," for example, appear with the comments: "I love all of you here on tumblr, it has been your support and encouragement that has helped me truly accept my body as beautiful and have the pride enough to share it with the world!" The mixing of cisgendered and trans bodies within tumblrs that run off of submissions from users such as this rejects ideological distinctions between cis and gender nonconforming embodiment, as bodies formerly marked as gender normative signify, in these contexts, as trans and/or queer.

QM: Tumblr's dashboard feature can contribute to this rejection, further enhancing the variety of bodies displayed onscreen—together, adjacent, and in juxtaposition.

MF: Yes, while some blogs cater specifically to images categorized by only one gender grouping or sexual bent, Tumblr's specific homepage function congregates images from multiple sites into one stream of images reflecting each individual user's interests, tastes, and history on the site. This format blends together sexual images that otherwise lack commonalities because they range from modest to hardcore, schoolgirls to bears, professional to cameraphone, vampire to vanilla, sentimental to humorous, long shots to close ups, male to female, and beyond. Such a format also resists categorizing postings by only one rubric, such as gender or transgender per se.

QM: Postings become even further removed from classificatory strongholds once they are shuffled and collaged together by reblogs and by creative interlocutors who merge materials from multiple and sometimes initially disconnected sources.

55   MF: Within these spaces, gendered body parts are transformed to assume new meanings; breasts can become an extension of masculinity and cocks can become feminine accessories or toys. Tumblr, furthermore, refuses to distinguish between pornographic (18+) and "regular" websites, instead using the classification NSFW (Not Safe For Work) to mark those blogs that may alternate indiscriminately between posts of cupcakes, fashion, kittens, and cocks of the flesh, synthetic, and illustrated varieties. One pornstar and poster on transqueersxxx.tumblr.com writes, under a professional photograph of his muscular and tattooed shirtless body, "For the life of me, I don't know how we're led to believe that breasts don't look good on men." Another anonymous amateur poster likewise reflects, "I used to hate my cock, but I'm gradually learning to have fun with it. I don't think it will ever feel 'right' to have one. But it's a fun toy I can play with in the meantime!"

QM: That reminds me of an image that was liked and reblogged over a hundred times in under a month of circulation—a hand-drawn sketch of a person sporting a polka dotted bra and an erection. Accompanying the image is hand-drawn text that reads: "I don't care if you're FTM ["female-to-male"] or MTF ["male-to-female"], just as long as you're DTF" ["down to fuck"]. In coupling MTF and FTM with DTF, the image interweaves digital idioms of sexual expression with genderqueer and trans lingo that, whether invoked as contemporary classification or vintage slang, emphasizes self-representation. The image's bra-and-no-panties device renders MTF and FTM in a space of overlap, expanding cultural meanings of IRL trans subjectivities by way of digital image circulation.

MF: The FTM-MTF-DTF post is indicative of the way queer trans and genderqueer tumblrs transgress the boundaries between the mundane and obscene, between gender normativity and gender variance, and between male and female loci of desire. Trans tumblr communities, unlike many radical queer and transsexual spaces IRL, call into question definitions of sexuality that rely on categories of assigned or essentialized sex. In conceptualizing sexual content not as globally inappropriate but as situationally NSFW, the conversations that can happen between sexualized and quotidian images online take new forms. Thanks to the NSFW conceptualization, erotic images can be juxtaposed and put into conversation with the other seemingly desexualized aspects of daily existence that shape and inform sexual identity, desire, and its affirming expression across contexts and forms.

In refusing binary logic that equates body parts with certain genders, queer trans tumblrs organize sexuality around a variety of desires that extend beyond gender identity alone or by confining meanings of transgender as represented in the mainstream. While some tumblrs are dedicated specifically to trans porn, most alternate between sexual images of trans and cis bodies; scrolling down the page one would likely encounter a range of body parts, gender presentations, and genitalia, hormonally/ surgically altered and not. These venues, however, are not without the limits of new media of which Juhasz warns, as sites like "transqueersxxx" have been critiqued by readers for the overrepresentation of whiteness and the failure to connect with racialized communities online. New media open up exciting venues for self-representation, yet these venues continue to reflect representational barriers typical of older and offline platforms.

Conclusion

QM: Within a historical perspective that includes radical media predating and premeditating the Internet, attention to Tumblr illuminates a broad range of queer practices and everyday cultural production by trans people.

60   MF: Sexuality and sexual experience are central to contemporary iterations of the queer media traditions in which trans people participate. Across this range of sexual formations, vectors of racial, disabled, transnational, and genderqueer identity influence trans people's sexual practices and self-expressions. A lineage of resistance to dominant media suggests that oppositional trans representations evolve and shift as media access and technology change. Based on our discussion here, I would argue against reducing trans sexuality (or any sexuality) to a biology-based equation of gender identity and object choice.

QM: Again, a historical view is crucial to understanding the aesthetics of tumblr's pre-Yahoo! moment and its facilitation of queer trans creativity. As people migrate to Tumblr, the spaces they create take on many forms. The website becomes a laboratory for erotic experimentation, a canvas for the collective depiction of trans desires, and a living archive of sexual attraction.

MF: Queer trans sex cultures online broaden and expand the available range of embodied representations of transness. Online queer praxis informed by trans experience creates new possibilities for the articulation of complex sexual desires, as well as for the radical gendering of trans bodies. In the period we studied, sexuality materialized not as a sequestered physical occurrence but as an extension of the daily and broader experiences of gender, disability, race, class, age, colonialism, medicalization, and media representation that converge to inform trans people's complex daily lives. I was especially intrigued by the ways in which, on the site, broad facets of everyday experience and personal expression countered the fetishizing practices of dominant media by expanding the conceptual scope of what trans sexual representation might entail.

QM: Issues of aesthetics and medium specificity have been equally striking. Lately, I have been preoccupied by the question of how long the queer trans Tumblr renaissance will last—or if it is already over. From a queer trans perspective, the threat of Tumblr's monetization is situated within ongoing legacies of misrepresentation, corporation-driven cultural appropriation, and assimilation by way of media conglomeration.

MF: Right. While digital sites demonstrate the potential for broadening the already expansive worlds of queer, trans, and genderqueer cultures, dominant structures continue to dictate what we can search for and find online. This is Juhasz's whole point. In my view, digital culture is a duplicitous space; the Internet maintains the primacy of dominant voices even as it offers exciting possibilities for expanding trans self-representations. Overall, gendered and sexual norms prevail even online, where technological access and anonymity often fuels gender and sexual policing, as well as outpours of racism, ableism, and classism that obscure the cultural presence of already marginalized voices. Yet, as tumblr would suggest, moving beyond stable constructions of gender, sexuality, ability, racial, national, and trans categories is partly what renders many of us DTF IRL.

65 QM: Whether or not the site continues to be a central venue for such a queer ethos, trans tumblr use pre-Yahoo! offers a glimpse into a radically transformed set of possibilities for self-representation for people whose everyday lives and art practices are, although incomprehensible within dominant ideology, flourishing online and off.

From at least 2011 to 2013, people collectively oriented in opposition to dominant discourses of gender and sexuality used Tumblr to refashion straight cisgender norms and to create everyday art in a hybrid media space.

Declaration of Conflicting Interests

The authors declared no potential conflicts of interest with respect to the research, authorship, and/or publication of this article.

Funding

The authors received no financial support for the research, authorship, and/or publication of this article.

Works Cited

Bazant, M. 1999. *Timtum: A Trans Jew Zine*. Self Published.

Bornstein, K., and S. Bear Bergman. 2010. *Gender Outlaws: The Next Generation*. Berkeley, CA: Seal Press.

Califia, P. (1994) 2000. "Gay Men, Lesbians, and Sex: Doing It Together." In *Public Sex: The Culture Of Radical Sex*, edited by Pat Califia, 191–98. San Francisco, CA: Cleis.

Halberstam, J. 2005. *In a Queer Time and Place: Transgender Bodies, Subcultural Lives*. New York: New York University Press.

Juhasz, A. 2010. "YouTube at five: What's it to You?" *In Learning from YouTube (online videobook)*. Boston: MIT Press. http://vectors.usc.edu/projects/learningfromyoutube/texteo. php?composite=198&;tour=7&.

Lim, E. 2010. *100 Butches*. www.elishalim.com.

Lim, E. 2011. *The Illustrated Gentleman*. www.elishalim.com.

Lunden, I. 2013. "Yahoo: Expect Ads on Tumblr to Ramp Up Significantly in 2014." *Tech Crunch*, May 20. http://techcrunch.com/2013/05/20/yahoo-expect-ads-on-tumblr-to-ramp-up-significantly-in-2014/.

Mayer, M. 2013. *Now Panic and Freak Out*. http://marissamayr.tumblr.com/post/50902274591/ im-delighted-to-announce-that-weve-reached-an.

Meyerowitz, J. 1998. "'Sex Change' And The Popular Press: Historical Notes On Transsexuality in The Popular Press, 1930–1955." *GLQ* 4 (2): 159–87.

Muñoz, J. E. 1999. *Disidentifications: Queers of Color and the Performance of Politics*. Minneapolis: University of Minnesota Press.

Namaste, V. 2005. *Sex Change, Social Change: Reflections on Identity, Institutions and Imperialism*. Toronto, ON: Women's Press.

Rheingold, H. 2012. *Net Smart: How to Thrive Online*. Cambridge, MA: MIT Press.

Rubin, G. 1992. "Thinking Sex: Notes For a Radical Theory of the Politics of Sexuality." In *Pleasure and Danger: Exploring Female Sexuality*, edited by Carole S. Vance, 267–93. London: Pandora.

Sedgwick, E. K. 1990. *The Epistemology of the Closet*. Berkeley: University of California Press. Serano, J. 2007. *Whipping Girl: A Transsexual Woman on Sexism and the Scapegoating Of Femininity*. Emeryville, CA: Seal Press.

Tumblr (blogs). URLs cited include allaboutstuds; bakingbutches; cripqueer; deeplezstonerwitch; fuckyeahftmsofcolor; ndelphinus; notaiden; notaidenarchive (tumblr.com). Accessed August 22, 2011–July 20 2013.

Withers, A. J. 2012. "If I Can't Dance, Is It Still My Revolution." *Print Zine and Website*. http:// still.my.revolution.tao.ca.

Credit

Is He Boyfriend Material?
Representation of Males in Teenage Girls' Magazines

KIRSTEN B. FIRMINGER

Abstract

Teenage girls' magazines play an important role in shaping the norms of the millions of girls who read them. In this article, I examine, through the discursive analysis of two issues each of five different popular teenage girls' magazines (ten issues total), how males and male behavior are represented. Guided by the magazines, girls are "empowered" to be informed consumers of boys, who are written about as shallow, highly sexual, emotionally inexpressive, and insecure, but also as potential boyfriends, providing romance, intimacy, and love. Framed by fashion and beauty products in both the advertisement and magazine content, success in attracting the "right" boy and finding love is presented as a result of girls' self-regulation, personal responsibility, and good choices, with only their own lack of self-esteem and effort holding them back.

Keywords

Adolescents, gender norms, consumption, magazines, content analysis

༄༅༄༅༄༅

It seems like guys lock up their feelings tighter than Fort Knox, right? Well, here's the key to opening that emotional vault! … CG! Epiphany: When a guy finally opens up to you, you'll know he has set you apart from other girls.

—*CosmoGirl,* All About Guys Section, "Guy Magnet Cheat Sheet"

༄༅༄༅༄༅

On the pages of popular teenage girls' magazines, boys are presented (in)congruently as the providers of potential love, romance, and excitement and as highly sexual, attracted to the superficial, and emotionally inexpressive. The magazines guide female readers toward avoiding the "bad" male and male behavior (locking up their feelings tighter than Fort Knox) and obtaining the "good" male and male behavior (setting you apart from other girls). Within girls' magazines, success in life and (heterosexual) love is girls' responsibility, tied to their ability to self-regulate, make good choices, and present themselves in the "right"way. The only barriers are girls' own lack of self-esteem or limited effort (Harris 2004). While the "girl power" language of the feminist movement is used, its politics and questioning of patriarchal gender norms are not discussed. Instead, the magazines advocate relentless surveillance of self, boys, and peers. Embarrassing and confessional tales, quizzes, and opportunities to rate and judge boys and girls on the basis of their photos and profiles encourage young women to "fashion" identities through clothes, cosmetics, beauty items, and consumerism.

Popular teenage girls' magazines. In the United States, teenage girls' magazines are read by more than 75 percent of teenage girls (Market profile: Teenagers 2000). The magazines play an important role in shaping the norms and expectations during a crucial stage of identity and relationship development. Currie (1999) found that some readers consider the magazines' content to be more compelling than their own personal experiences and knowledge. Magazines are in the business of both selling themselves to their audience and selling their audience to advertisers (Kilborne 1999). Teenage girls are advertised as more loyal to their favorite magazines than to their favorite television programs, with magazines touted as "a sister and a friend rolled into one" (Market profile: Teenagers 2000). Magazines attract and keep advertisers by providing the right audience for their products and services, suppressing information that might offend the advertiser, and including editorial content saturated in advertiser-friendly advice (Kilborne 1999).

In this textual environment, consumerist and individualist attitudes and values are promoted to the exclusion of alternative perspectives. Across magazines, one relentless message is clear: "the road to happiness is attracting males for successful heterosexual life by way of physical beautification" (Evan et al. 1991; see also Carpenter 1998, Currie 1999, Signorelli 1997). Given the clarity of this message, little work has been done focusing on the portrayal of males that the girls are supposed to attract. I began my research examining this question: how are males and male behavior portrayed in popular teenage girls' magazines?

Method

To explore these questions, I designed a discursive analysis of a cross-section of adolescent girls' magazines, sampling a variety of magazines and analyzing across them for common portrayals of males. *Seventeen* and *YM* are long-running adolescent girls' magazines. *Seventeen* has a base circulation of 2.4 million while *YM* has a circulation of 2.2 million (*Advertising Age* 74: 21). As a result of the potential of the market, the magazines that are directed at adolescent girls have expanded to include the new *CosmoGirl* (launched in 1999) and *ELLEgirl* (in 2001). Very successful, *CosmoGirl* has a base circulation of 1 million. *ELLEgirl* reports a smaller circulation of 450,000 (*Advertising Age* 74: 21). Chosen as an alternative to the other adolescent girls' magazines, *Girls' Life* is directed at a younger female audience and is the winner of the 2000, 1999, and 1996 Parents' Choice Awards Medal and of the 2000 and 1998 Parents' Guide to Children's Media Association Award of Excellence. The magazine reports it is the number one magazine for girls ages 10 to 15, with a circulation of 3 million (http://www.girlslife.com/infopage.php, retrieved May 23, 2004).

5   I coded two issues each of *Seventeen, YM, CosmoGirl, ELLEgirl,* and *Girls' Life,* for a total of ten issues. Magazines build loyalty with their readers by presenting the same kinds of material, in a similar form, month after month (Duke 2002). To take into account seasonal differences in content, I purchased the magazines six months apart, once during December 2002 and once during July 2003. While the magazines range in their dates of publication (for instance, Holiday issue, December issue, January issue, etc.), all the magazines were together at the same newsstand at the singular time of purchase.

Results

Within the pages of the magazines, articles and photo layouts focus primarily on beauty, fashion, celebrities and entertainment, boys and love, health and sex, and self-development. The magazines specialize, with emphasis more or less on one of these topics over the other: *ElleGirl* presents itself as more fashion focused, while self-development is the emphasis for *Girls' Life*'s younger audience. Within the self-development sections, one can find articles focusing on topics such as activities, school, career aspirations, volunteering, sports, and politics. However, even in these articles, focus is on the social, interpersonal aspects of relationships and on consumption instead of the actual doing and mastery of activities.

Advertising permeates the magazines, accounting for 20.8 percent to 44.8 percent of the pages. Additionally, many of the editorial articles, presumably noncommercial, are written in ways that endorse specific products and services (see Currie 1999, for more information on "advertorials"). For instance, one advice column responded to a reader's inquiry about a first kiss by recommending " … [having] the following supplies [handy] for when the magical moment finally arrives: Sugarless mints, yummy flavored lip gloss (I dig Bonne Bell Lip Smackers) …"

Male-focused content. On average, 19.7 percent of the pages focused on males[1], ranging from a minimum of 13.6 percent in *ELLEGirl* to a maximum percent in *Seventeen*. Articles on boys delve into boys' culture, points of view, opinions, interests, and hobbies, while articles on girls' activities focus more pointedly on the pursuit of boys. Girls learn "Where the boys are," since the "next boyfriend could be right under your nose." They are told,

> Where to go: Minor-league ballparks. Why: Cute guys! … Who'll be there: The players are just for gazing at; your targets are the cuties in the stands. And don't forget the muscular types lugging soda trays up and down the aisles. What to say: Ask him what he thinks about designated hitters (they're paid just to bat). He'll be totally impressed that you even brought up the subject.

10

Figure 1: "The Rating Game" and "All About Eli"
SOURCE: Image 1 (left): ElleGirl May/June 2003, p. 136, "Fashion Lab,"
published by Hachette Filipacchi Media, New York, NY.

Males are offered up to readers in several different formats. First we read profiles, then we meet "examples," we are allowed question and answer, we are quizzed, and then we are asked to judge the males. Celebrity features contain in-depth interviews with male celebrities, while personal short profiles of celebrities or "regular" guys include a photo, biographical information, hobbies, interests, and inquiries such as his "three big requirements for a girl-friend" and "his perfect date." *CosmoGirl's* fold-out photo centerfold (see Figure 1) informs readers that the first thing 27-year-old Eli notices about a girl is "the way she carries herself," his turn-ons are "Confidence, intelligence, sense of humor, lips, eyes, and a sense of adventure," and his turn-offs are "insecurity, dishonesty, and anything fake." In question-and-answer articles, regular columnists answer selected questions that the readers have submitted.[2] Some columns consistently focus on boys, such as "GL Guys by Bill and Dave" and *YM's* "Love Q and A," while others focus on a variety of questions, for instance *ELLEgirl's* "Ask Jennifur" profiles of noncelebrity males are presented and judged in rating articles. The magazines publish their criteria for rating boys, via rhetorical devices such as "the magazine staffs' opinions" or the opinion polls of other teenage girls (see Figure 1).

Ratings include categories such as "his style," "dateable?," and "style factor." For example, in *CosmoGirl's* Boy-O-Meter article, "Dateable?: I usually go for dark hair, olive skin, and thick eyebrows. But his eyes make me feel like I could confide in him," or *ELLEgirl's* The Rating Game, "He's cute, but I don't dig the emo look and the hair in the face. It's girlie." Readers can then assess their opinions in relation to those of other girls' and the magazine staff.

Romantic stories and quotes enable readers to witness "real" romance and love and compare their "personal experiences" to those presented in the magazines. For instance, "Then one day I found a note tucked in my locker that said, 'You are different than everyone else. But that is why you are beautiful.' At the bottom of the note it said, 'From Matt—I'm in your science class. 'We started dating the next day." These can also be rated, as the magazine staff then responded, "Grade: A. He sounds like a very smart boy."

Finally, the readers can then test their knowledge and experiences through the quizzes in the magazines, such as *Seventeen's* quiz, "Can your summer love last?" with questions and multiple-choice answers:

> As he's leaving for a weeklong road trip with the guys, he: A) tells you at least 10 times how much he's going to miss you. B) promises to call you when he gets a chance. C) can't stop talking about how much fun it will be to "get away" with just his buddies for seven whole days.

15   Over the pages, boys as a "product" begin to merge with the [other] products and services being sold to girls in "training" as informed consumers, learning to feel "empowered" and make good "choices." While a good boy is a commodity of value, the young women readers learn that relationships with boys should be considered disposable and interchangeable like the other products being sold, "Remember, BFs come and go, but best friends are for- ever! Is he worth it? Didn't think so."

Embarrassing and confessional stories. Short embarrassing or confessional stories submitted by the readers for publication provide another textual window through which young women can view gender politics; one issue of *YM* included a special pull-out book focused exclusively on confessionals.[3] Kaplan and Cole (2003) found in their four focus groups that the girls enjoy the embarrassing and confessional stories because they reveal "what it is like to be a teenage girl."

On average, two-thirds of the confessional/embarrassing stories were male focused; in 42–100 percent of the stories males were the viewing audience for, or participant in, a girl's embarrassing/confessional moment. Often these stories involve a "cute boy," "my boyfriend," or "my crush." For example:

> My friends and I noticed these cute guys at the ice cream parlor. As we were leaving with our cones, the guys offered to walk with us. I was wearing my chunky-heeled shoes and feeling pretty awesome … until I tripped. My double scoop flew in the air and hit one of the guys. Oops.

Teenage girls within these stories are embarrassed about things that have happened, often accidentally, with males typically as the audience. While this may allow the female readers to see that they are not the only ones who have experienced embarrassing moments, it also reinforces the notion of self-surveillance as well as socializes girls to think of boys as the audience and judges of their behavior (Currie 1999).

20   *Representations of males.* To assess how males are represented, I coded content across male-focused feature articles and "question and answer" columns.[4] These articles contained the most general statements about boys and their behaviors, motivations, and characteristics (for example, "Guys are a few steps behind girls when it comes to maturity level"[5]).

A dominant tension in the representations of boys involves males' splitting of intimacy from sexuality (see Whitney Missildine's article in this issue). The magazine advises girls as they negotiate these different behaviors and situations, trying to choose the "right" guy (who will develop an intimate relationship with a girl), reject the "bad" guy (who is focused only on sex), or if possible, change the "bad" guy into the "good" guy (through a girl's decisions and interactions with the male).

> My boyfriend and I were together for 10 months when he said he wanted to take a break—he wasn't sure he was ready for such a commitment. The thought of him seeing other people tore me apart. So every day while we were broken up, I gave him something as a sign of my feelings for him: love sayings cut out from magazines, or cute comics from the paper. Eventually he confessed that he had just been confused and that he loved me more than ever.

As girls are represented as responsible for good shopping, they are represented also as responsible for selecting/changing/shaping male behavior. If girls learn to make the right choices, they can have the right relationship with the right guy, or convert a "bad"/confused boy into a good catch.

The tension is most evident in stories about males' high sex drive, attraction to superficial appearances, emotional inexpressiveness, and fear of rejection and contrasted with those males who are "keepers": who keep their sex drive in check, value more than just girls' appearances, and are able to open up. The articles and advice columns blend the traditional and the feminist; encompassing both new and old meanings and definitions of what it means to be female and male within today's culture (Harris 2004).

25   *The males' sex drive.* The "naturally" high sex drive of males rises as the most predominant theme across the magazines. Viewed as normal and unavoidable in teenage boys, girls write to ask for an explanation and advice, and they are told:

> You invited a guy you kind of like up to your room (just to talk!) and he got the wrong idea. This was not your fault. Guys—especially unchaperoned guys on school trips—will interpret any move by a girl as an invitation to get heavy. And I mean any move. You could have sat down next to him at a lab table and he would have taken that as a sign from God that you wanted his body.

When it comes to the topic of sexuality, traditional notions surround "appropriate behavior" for young women and men. Girls learn that males respect and date girls who are able to keep males' sex drive in check and who take time building a relationship. Girls were rarely shown as being highly sexual or interested only in a sexual relationship with a boy. Girls are supposed to avoid potentially dangerous situations (such as being alone with a boy) and draw the line (since the males frequently are unable to do so). If they don't, they can be labeled sluts.

> Don't even make out with someone until you're sure things are exclusive. When you hook up with him too early, you're giving him the message that you are something less than a goddess (because, as you know, a goddess is guarded in a temple, and it's not easy to get to her). Take it from me when I tell you that guys want to be with girls they consider goddesses. So treat your body as a temple—don't let just any one in.

> Most guys would probably assume that a girl who ditches guys after intimacy is slutty. I know, I know—there's a double standard. It seems like the "players" among us can date and dump as frequently as they please, but it's only a social no-no when you girls do it.

30   A guy in heat tried to take advantage of you and you wouldn't give in. That's all that matters. You may have kissed him, but, ultimately, the decision to draw the line was yours and you did it. That's nothing to feel slutty about.

Valuing superficial appearances. Driven by sex, males were shown as judging and valuing girls based on their appearance.

> That's bad, but it's scarier when combined with another sad male truth: They're a lot more into looks than we are.

> Okay, I'm the first to admit that guys can be shallow and insipid and *Baywatch* brainwashed to the point where the sight of two balloons on a string will turn them on.

Since males are thought to be interested in the superficial, girls sought advice on how to be most superficially appealing, asking what do guys prefer, including the size of a girl's breasts, hair color, eye color, height, and weight. Girls are portrayed as wanting to know how to present themselves to attract boys, demonstrating an interaction between girls' ideas and understanding of what males want and girls' own choices and behaviors.

35 *Boys are emotionally inexpressive.* Across features, readers learn about boys' inability or unwillingness to open up and share their feelings. However, the articles suggest also that if a girl is able to negotiate the relationship correctly, she could get a guy to trust her.

> Let's say you go to the pet store and see a really cute puppy you'd like to pet, but every time you try, he pulls away because he was treated badly in the past. People aren't much different. Move very slowly, and build up trust bit by bit. Show this guy you're into him for real, and he'll warm up to you. Puppy love is worth the wait.

Girls are responsible for doing the emotional work and maintenance and for being change agents in relationships, not allowing room for or even expecting males to take on any of these tasks (see also Chang 2000).

Boys' insecurity and fear of rejection. Boys are displayed as afraid of rejection. Reflecting the neoliberal ideology of "girl power," girls were urged by the magazines to take the initiative in seeking out and approaching boys. This way they are in control of and responsible for their fate, with only lack of confidence, self-esteem, and effort holding them back from finding romance and love.

> So in the next week (why waste more time?), write him a note, pull him aside at a party, or call him up with your best friend by your side for support. Hey, he could be psyched that you took the initiative.

40 > So I think you may have to do the work. If there's a certain guy you're feelin' and you think he's intimidated by you, make the first move. Say something to relax him, like, "What's up? My name is Chelsea." After that, he'll probably start completing sentences.

Males' potential—the "keepers." "Consider every guy to be on a level playing field—they all have potential." Boys were shown to have "potential" and girls were advised to search out the "right" guys.

> He does indeed sound dreamy. He also sounds like a total gentleman, considering he hasn't attempted to jump your bones yet, so the consensus is: He's a keeper.

Most guys are actually smarter than you think and are attracted to all sorts of things about the female species. Yes, big boobs definitely have their dedicated fan base, but so do musical taste, brains, a cute laugh, style and the ability to throw a spiral football (to name just a few). What's a turn-on or deal breaker for one guy is a nonevent for another.

The streets are filled with guys who are nice, hot, smart, fun, and half-naked (joking … sort of!). And they all want to spend some time with an unattached pumpkin like you.

45   These boys become the center of the romantic stories and quotes about love and relationships. Resulting from and sustained by girls' self-regulation, personal responsibility, effort, and good choices (as guided by the tools and advice provided by the magazines), these boys are for keeps.

Discussion

Within the magazines, girls are invited to explore boys as shallow, highly sexual, emotionally inexpressive, and insecure and boys who are potential boyfriends, providing romance, intimacy, and love. Males' high sex drive and interest in superficial appearances are naturalized and left unquestioned in the content of the magazines; within a "girl power" version of compulsory heterosexuality, girls should too learn the right way to approach a boy in order to get what they want—"the road to happiness is attracting males for successful heterosexual life by way of physical beautification" (Evans et al. 1991). Girls walk the fine line of taking advantage of males' interest in sex and appearance, without crossing over into being labeled a slut. Socialized to be purchasers of beauty and fashion products that promise to make them attractive to boys, girls are "in charge" of themselves and the boys they "choose." It's a competitive market so they better have the right understanding of boys, as well as the right body and outfit to go with it.

The magazines' portrayals, values, and opinions are shaped by their need to create an advertiser-friendly environment while attracting and appealing to the magazines' audience of teenage girls. Skewing the portrayal of males and females to their target audience, magazine editors, writers, and, though I have not highlighted it here—advertisers, take advantage of gender-specific fantasies, myths, and fears (Craig 1993). Boys become another product, status symbol, and identity choice. If girls' happiness requires finding romance and love, girls should learn to be informed consumers of boys. By purchasing the magazines, they have a guide to this process, guaranteed to help them understand "What his mixed signals really mean." In addition, if boys are concerned with superficial appearances, it is to the benefit of girls to buy the advertised products and learn "The best swimsuit for [their] bod[ies]."

As girls survey and judge themselves and others, possessions and consumption become the metric for assessing status (Rohlinger 2002; Salamon 2003), the cultural capital for teenagers in place of work, community, and other activities (Harris 2004). The feminist "girl empowerment" becomes personal, appropriated to sell products. The choice and purchase of products and services sold in the magazines promise recreation and transformation, of not only one's outward appearance but also of one's inner self, leading to happiness, satisfaction, and success (Kilborne 1999). Money is the underlying driving force in magazine content. However, while the magazines focus on doing good business, girls are being socialized by the magazines' norms and expectations.

"Bottom line: look at dating as a way to sample the menu before picking your entrée. In the end, you'll be much happier with the choice you make! Yum!"

Works Cited

Carpenter, L. M. 1998. From girls into women: Scripts for sexuality and romance in Seventeen Magazine, 1974–1994. *The Journal of Sex Research* 35: 158–168.

Chang, J. 2000. Agony-resolution pathways: How women perceive American men in Cosmopolitan's agony (advice) column. *The Journal of Men's Studies* 8: 285–308.

Currie, D. H. 1999. Girl talk: Adolescent magazines and their readers. Toronto: University of Toronto Press.

Craig, S. 1993. Selling masculinities, selling femininities: Multiple genders and the economics of television. *The Mid-Atlantic Almanack* 2: 15–27.

Duke, L. 2002. Get real!: Cultural relevance and resistance to the mediated feminine ideal. *Psychology and Marketing* 19: 211–233.

Evans, E., J. Rutberg, and C. Sather. 1991. Content analysis of contemporary teen magazines for adolescent females. *Youth and Society* 23: 99–120.

Girls' Life magazine: About us. Retrieved May 23, 2004 from http://www.girlslife.com/infopage.php.

Kaplan, E. B. and L. Cole. 2003. I want to read stuff on boys": White, Latina, and Black girls reading Seventeen magazine and encountering adolescence. *Adolescence* 38: 141–159.

Market profile: Teenagers. 2000. Magazine Publishers of America.

McRobbie, A. 1991. Feminism and Youth Culture. London: Macmillan.

Rohlinger, D. 2002. Eroticizing men: Cultural influences on advertising and male objectification. *Sex Roles: A Journal of Research* 46: 61–74.

Salamon, S. 2003. From hometown to nontown: Rural community effects of suburbanization. *Rural Sociology* 68: 1–24.

Signorelli, N. 1997. A content analysis: Reflections of girls in the media, a study of television shows and commercials, movies, music videos, and teen magazine articles and ads. Children Now and Kaiser Family Foundation Publication.

Tolman, D. L., R. Spencer, T. Harmon, M. Rosen-Reynoso, and M. Stripe. 2004. Getting close, staying cool: Early adolescent boys' experiences with romantic relationships, In *Adolescent boys: Exploring diverse cultures of boyhood,* edited by N.Way and J. Chu. New York: NYU Press.

Tolman, D. L., R. Spencer, M. Rosen-Reynoso, and M. Porche. 2002. Sowing the seeds of violence in heterosexual relationships: Early adolescents narrate compulsory heterosexuality. *Journal of Social Issues* 59: 159–178.

Van Roosmalen, E. 2000. Forces of patriarchy: Adolescent experiences of sexuality and conceptions of relationships. *Youth and Society* 32: 202–227.

Where the girls are. 2003. *Advertising Age* 74: 21.

Credit

Republished with permission of Sage Publications, from Men and Masculinities, pp. 298–308, Kirsten Firminger, vol. 8, no. 3, January 2006; permission conveyed through Copyright Clearance Center, Inc.

A Herstory of the #BlackLivesMatter Movement

ALICIA GARZA

I created #BlackLivesMatter with Patrisse Cullors and Opal Tometi, two of my sisters, as a call to action for Black people after 17-year-old Trayvon Martin was post-humously placed on trial for his own murder and the killer, George Zimmerman, was not held accountable for the crime he committed. It was a response to the anti-Black racism that permeates our society and also, unfortunately, our movements.

Black Lives Matter is an ideological and political intervention in a world where Black lives are systematically and intentionally targeted for demise. It is an affirmation of Black folks' contributions to this society, our humanity, and our resilience in the face of deadly oppression.

We were humbled when cultural workers,[1] artists,[2] designers[3] and techies offered their labor and love to expand #BlackLivesMatter beyond a social media hashtag. Opal, Patrisse, and I created the infrastructure for this movement project—moving the hashtag from social media to the streets. Our team grew through a very successful Black Lives Matter ride,[4] led and designed by Patrisse Cullors and Darnell L. Moore, organized to support the movement that is growing in St. Louis, MO, after 18-year old Mike Brown was killed at the hands of Ferguson Police Officer Darren Wilson. We've hosted national conference calls focused on issues of critical importance to Black people working hard for the liberation of our people. We've connected people across the country working to end the various forms of injustice impacting our people. We've created space for the celebration and humanization of Black lives.

The Theft of Black Queer Women's Work

As people took the #BlackLivesMatter demand into the streets, mainstream media and corporations also took up the call, #BlackLivesMatter appeared in an episode of *Law & Order: SVU* in a mash up[5] containing the Paula Deen racism scandal and the tragedy of the murder of Trayvon Martin.

5   Suddenly, we began to come across varied adaptations of our work—all lives matter, brown lives matter, migrant lives matter, women's lives matter, and on and on. While imitation is said to be the highest form of flattery, I was surprised when an organization called to ask if they could use "Black Lives Matter" in one of their campaigns. We agreed to it, with the caveat that a) as a team, we preferred that we not use the meme to celebrate the imprisonment of any individual and b) that it was important to us they acknowledged the genesis of #BlackLivesMatter. I was surprised when they did exactly the opposite and then justified their actions by saying they hadn't used the "exact" slogan and, therefore, they deemed it okay to take our work, use it as their own, fail to credit where it came from, and then use it to applaud incarceration.

I was surprised when a community institution wrote asking us to provide materials and action steps for an art show they were curating, entitled "Our Lives Matter." When questioned about who was involved and why they felt the need to change the very specific call and demand around Black lives to "our lives," I was told the artists decided it needed to be more inclusive of all people of color. I was even more surprised when, in the promotion of their event, one of the artists conducted an interview that completely erased the origins of their work–rooted in the labor and love of queer Black women.

Pause.

When you design an event/campaign/et cetera based on the work of queer Black women, don't invite them to participate in shaping it, but ask them to provide materials and ideas for next steps for said event, that is racism in practice. It's also hetero-patriarchal. Straight men, unintentionally or intentionally, have taken the work of queer Black women and erased our contributions. Perhaps if we were the charismatic Black men many are rallying around these days, it would have been a different story, but being Black queer women in this society (and apparently within these movements) tends to equal invisibility and nonrelevancy.

We completely expect those who benefit directly and improperly from White supremacy to try and erase our existence. We fight that every day. But when it happens amongst our allies, we are baffled, we are saddened, and we are enraged. And it's time to have the political conversation about why that's not okay.

10   We are grateful to our allies[6] who have stepped up to the call that Black lives matter, and taken it as an opportunity to not just stand in solidarity[7] with us, but to investigate the ways in which anti-Black racism is perpetuated in their own communities. We are also grateful to those allies who were willing to engage in critical dialogue with us about this unfortunate and problematic dynamic. And for those who we have not yet had the opportunity to engage with around the adaptations of the Black Lives Matter call, please consider the following points.

Broadening the Conversation to Include Black Life

Black Lives Matter is a unique contribution that goes beyond extrajudicial killings of Black people by police and vigilantes. It goes beyond the narrow nationalism that can be prevalent within some Black communities, which merely call on Black people to love Black, live Black and buy Black, keeping straight cis Black men in the front of the movement while our sisters, queer and trans and disabled folk take up roles in the background or not at all. Black Lives Matter affirms the lives of Black queer and trans folks, disabled folks, Black-undocumented folks, folks with records, women and all Black lives along the gender spectrum. It centers those that have been marginalized within Black liberation movements. It is a tactic to (re)build the Black liberation movement.

When we say Black Lives Matter, we are talking about the ways in which Black people are deprived of our basic human rights and dignity. It is an acknowledgement Black poverty and genocide is state violence. It is an acknowledgment that 1 million Black people are locked in cages in this country—one half of all people in prisons or jails—is an act of state violence. It is an acknowledgment that Black women continue to bear the burden of a relentless assault on our children and our families and that assault is an act of state violence. Black queer and trans folks bearing a unique burden in a hetero-patriarchal society that disposes of us like garbage and simultaneously fetishizes us and profits off of us is state violence; the fact that 500,000 Black people in the US are undocumented immigrants and relegated to the shadows is state violence; the fact that Black girls are used as negotiating chips during times of conflict and war is state violence; Black folks living with disabilities and different abilities bear the burden of state-sponsored Darwinian experiments that attempt to squeeze us into boxes of normality defined by White supremacy is state violence. And the fact is that the lives of Black people—not ALL people—exist within these conditions is consequence of state violence.

When Black people get free, everybody gets free.

#BlackLivesMatter doesn't mean your life isn't important—it means that Black lives, which are seen as without value within White supremacy, are important to your liberation. Given the disproportionate impact state violence has on Black lives, we understand that when Black people in this country get free, the benefits will be wide reaching and transformative for society as a whole. When we are able to end hypercriminalization and sexualization of Black people and end the poverty, control, and surveillance of Black people, every single person in this world has a better shot at getting and staying free. When Black people get free, everybody gets free. This is why we call on Black people and our allies to take up the call that Black lives matter. We're not saying Black lives are more important than other lives, or that other lives are not criminalized and oppressed in various ways. We remain in active solidarity with all oppressed people who are fighting for their liberation and we know that our destinies are intertwined.

And, to keep it real—it is appropriate and necessary to have strategy and action centered around Blackness without other non-Black communities of color, or White folks for that matter, needing to find a place and a way to center themselves within it. It is appropriate and necessary for us to acknowledge the critical role that Black lives and struggles for Black liberation have played in inspiring and anchoring, through practice and theory, social movements for the liberation of all people. The women's movement, the Chicano liberation movement, queer movements, and many more have adopted the strategies, tactics and theory of the Black liberation movement. And if we are committed to a world where all lives matter, we are called to support the very movement that inspired and activated so many more. That means supporting and acknowledging Black lives.

15   Progressive movements in the United States have made some unfortunate errors when they push for unity at the expense of really understanding the concrete differences in context, experience and oppression. In other words, some want unity without struggle. As people who have our minds stayed on freedom, we can learn to fight anti-Black racism by examining the ways in which we participate in it, even unintentionally, instead of the worn out and sloppy practice of drawing lazy parallels of unity between peoples with vastly different experiences and histories.

When we deploy "All Lives Matter" as to correct an intervention specifically created to address antiblackness, we lose the ways in which the state apparatus has built a program of genocide and repression mostly on the backs of Black people—beginning with the theft of millions of people for free labor—and then adapted it to control, murder, and profit off of other communities of color and immigrant communities. We perpetuate a level of White supremacist domination by reproducing a tired trope that we are all the same, rather than acknowledging that non-Black oppressed people in this country are both impacted by racism and domination, and simultaneously, BENEFIT from anti-black racism.

When you drop "Black" from the equation of whose lives matter, and then fail to acknowledge it came from somewhere, you further a legacy of erasing Black lives and Black contributions from our movement legacy. And consider whether or not when dropping the Black you are, intentionally or unintentionally, erasing Black folks from the conversation or homogenizing very different experiences. The legacy and prevalence of anti-Black racism and hetero-patriarchy is a lynch pin holding together this unsustainable economy. And that's not an accidental analogy.

In 2014, hetero-patriarchy and anti-Black racism within our movement is real and felt. It's killing us and it's killing our potential to build power for transformative social change. When you adopt the work of queer women of color, don't name or recognize it, and promote it as if it has no history of its own such actions are problematic. When I use Assata's powerful demand[8] in my organizing work, I always begin by sharing where it comes from, sharing about Assata's significance to the Black Liberation Movement, what its political purpose and message is, and why it's important in our context.

When you adopt Black Lives Matter and transform it into something else (if you feel you really need to do that—see above for the arguments not to), it's appropriate politically to credit the lineage from which your adapted work derived. It's important that we work together to build and acknowledge the legacy of Black contributions to the struggle for human rights. If you adapt Black Lives Matter, use the opportunity to talk about its inception and political framing. Lift up Black lives as an opportunity to connect struggles across race, class, gender, nationality, sexuality and disability.

20   And, perhaps more importantly, when Black people cry out in defense of our lives, which are uniquely, systematically, and savagely targeted by the state, we are asking you, our family, to stand with us in affirming Black lives. Not just all lives. Black lives. Please do not change the conversation by talking about how your life matters, too. It does, but we need less watered down unity and a more active solidarities with us, Black people, unwaveringly, in defense of our humanity. Our collective futures depend on it.

Credit ——

Garza, Alicia. "A Herstory of the #BlackLivesMatter Movement." *The Feminist Wire 7 Oct. 2014.*

Peculiar Benefits

ROXANE GAY

When I was young, my parents took our family to Haiti during the summers. For them, it was a homecoming. For my brothers and me it was an adventure, sometimes a chore, and always a necessary education on privilege and the grace of an American passport. Until visiting Haiti, I had no idea what poverty really was or the difference between relative and absolute poverty. To see poverty so plainly and pervasively left a profound mark on me.

To this day, I remember my first visit, and how at every intersection, men and women, shiny with sweat, would mob our car, their skinny arms stretched out, hoping for a few gourdes or American dollars. I saw the sprawling slums, the shanties housing entire families, the trash piled in the streets, and also the gorgeous beach and the young men in uniforms who brought us Coca-Cola in glass bottles and made us hats and boats out of palm fronds. It was hard for a child to begin to grasp the contrast of such inescapable poverty alongside almost repulsive luxury, and then the United States, a mere eight hundred miles away, with its gleaming cities rising out of the landscape and the well-maintained interstates stretching across the country, the running water and the electricity. It wasn't until many, many years later that I realized my education on privilege began long before I could appreciate it in any meaningful way.

Privilege is a right or immunity granted as a peculiar benefit, advantage, or favor. There is racial privilege, gender (and identity) privilege, heterosexual privilege, economic privilege, able-bodied privilege, educational privilege, religious privilege, and the list goes on and on. At some point, you have to surrender to the kinds of privilege you hold. Nearly everyone, particularly in the developed world, has something someone else doesn't, something someone else yearns for.

The problem is, cultural critics talk about privilege with such alarming frequency and in such empty ways, we have diluted the word's meaning. When people wield the word "privilege," it tends to fall on deaf ears because we hear that word so damn much it has become white noise.

5   One of the hardest things I've ever had to do is accept and acknowledge my privilege. It's an ongoing project. I'm a woman, a person of color, and the child of immigrants, but I also grew up middle class and then upper middle class. My parents raised my siblings and me in a strict but loving environment. They were and are happily married, so I didn't have to deal with divorce or crappy intramarital dynamics. I attended elite schools. My master's and doctoral degrees were funded. I got a tenure-track position my first time out. My bills are paid. I have the time and resources for frivolity. I am reasonably well published. I have an agent and books to my name. My life has been far from perfect, but it's somewhat embarrassing for me to accept just how much privilege I have.

It's also really difficult for me to consider the ways in which I lack privilege or the ways in which my privilege hasn't magically rescued me from a world of hurt. On my more difficult days, I'm not sure what's more of a pain in my ass—being black or being a woman. I'm happy to be both of these things, but the world keeps intervening. There are all kinds of infuriating reminders of my place in the world—random people questioning me in the parking lot at work as if it is unfathomable that I'm a faculty member, the persistence of lawmakers trying to legislate the female body, street harassment, strangers wanting to touch my hair.

We tend to believe that accusations of privilege imply we have it easy, which we resent because life is hard for nearly everyone. Of course we resent these accusations. Look at white men when they are accused of having privilege. They tend to be immediately defensive (and, at times, understandably so). They say, "It's not my fault I am a white man," or "I'm [insert other condition that discounts their privilege]," instead of simply accepting that, in this regard, yes, they benefit from certain privileges others do not. To have privilege in one or more areas does not mean you are wholly privileged. Surrendering to the acceptance of privilege is difficult, but it is really all that is expected. What I remind myself, regularly, is this: the acknowledgment of my privilege is not a denial of the ways I have been and am marginalized, the ways I have suffered.

You don't necessarily *have* to do anything once you acknowledge your privilege. You don't have to apologize for it. You need to understand the extent of your privilege, the consequences of your privilege, and remain aware that people who are different from you move through and experience the world in ways you might never know anything about. They might endure situations you can never know anything about. You could, however, use that privilege for the greater good—to try to level the playing field for everyone, to work for social justice, to bring attention to how those without certain privileges are disenfranchised. We've seen what the hoarding of privilege has done, and the results are shameful.

When we talk about privilege, some people start to play a very pointless and dangerous game where they try to mix and match various demographic characteristics to determine who wins at the Game of Privilege. Who would win in a privilege battle between a wealthy black woman and a wealthy white man? Who would win a privilege battle between a queer white man and a queer Asian woman? Who would win in a privilege battle between a working-class white man and a wealthy, differently abled Mexican woman? We could play this game all day and never find a winner. Playing the Game of Privilege is mental masturbation—it only feels good to those playing the game.

10   Too many people have become self-appointed privilege police, patrolling the halls of discourse, ready to remind people of their privilege whether those people have denied that privilege or not. In online discourse, in particular, the specter of privilege is always looming darkly. When someone writes from experience, there is often someone else, at the ready, pointing a trembling finger, accusing that writer of having various kinds of privilege. How dare someone speak to a personal experience without accounting for every possible configuration of privilege or the lack thereof? We would live in a world of silence if the only people who were allowed to write or speak from experience or about difference were those absolutely without privilege.

When people wield accusations of privilege, more often than not, they want to be heard and seen. Their need is acute, if not desperate, and that need rises out of the many historical and ongoing attempts to silence and render invisible marginalized groups. Must we satisfy our need to be heard and seen by preventing anyone else from being heard and seen? Does privilege automatically negate any merits of what a privilege holder has to say? Do we ignore everything, for example, that white men have to say?

We need to get to a place where we discuss privilege by way of observation and acknowledgment rather than accusation. We need to be able to argue beyond the threat of privilege. We need to stop playing Privilege or Oppression Olympics because we'll never get anywhere until we find more effective ways of talking through difference. We should be able to say, "This is my truth," and have that truth stand without a hundred clamoring voices shouting, giving the impression that multiple truths cannot coexist. Because at some point, doesn't privilege become beside the point?

Privilege is relative and contextual. Few people in the developed world, and particularly in the United States, have no privilege at all. Among those of us who participate in intellectual communities, privilege runs rampant. We have disposable time and the ability to access the Internet regularly. We have the freedom to express our opinions without the threat of retaliation. We have smartphones and iProducts and desktops and laptops. If you are reading this essay, you have some kind of privilege. It may be hard to hear that, I know, but if you cannot recognize your privilege, you have a lot of work to do; get started.

Argument as Conversation
The Role of Inquiry in Writing a Researched Argument

STUART GREENE

Argument is very much a part of what we do every day: We confront a public issue, something that is open to dispute, and we take a stand and support what we think and feel with what we believe are good reasons. Seen in this way, argument is very much like a conversation. By this, I mean that making an argument entails providing good reasons to support your viewpoint, as well as counterarguments, and recognizing how and why readers might object to your ideas. The metaphor of conversation emphasizes the social nature of writing. Thus inquiry, research, and writing arguments are intimately related. If, for example, you are to understand the different ways others have approached your subject, then you will need to do your "homework." This is what Doug Brent (1996) means when he says that research consists of "the looking-up of facts in the context of other worldviews, other ways of seeing" (78).

In learning to argue within an academic setting, such as the one you probably find yourself in now, it is useful to think about writing as a form of inquiry in which you convey your understanding of the claims people make, the questions they raise, and the conflicts they address. As a form of inquiry, then, writing begins with problems, conflicts, and questions that you identify as important. The questions that your teacher raises and that you raise should be questions that are open to dispute and for which there are not prepackaged answers. Readers within an academic setting expect that you will advance a scholarly conversation and not reproduce others' ideas. Therefore, it is important to find out who else has confronted these problems, conflicts, and questions in order to take a stand within some ongoing scholarly conversation. You will want to read with an eye toward the claims writers make, claims that they are making with respect to you, in the sense that writers want you to think and feel in a certain way. You will want to read others' work critically, seeing if the reasons writers use to support their arguments are what you would consider good reasons. And finally, you will want to consider the possible counterarguments to the claims writers make and the views that call your own ideas into question.

Like the verbal conversations you have with others, effective arguments never take place in a vacuum; they take into account previous conversations that have taken place about the subject under discussion. Seeing research as a means for advancing a conversation makes the research process more *real*, especially if you recognize that you will need to support your claims with evidence in order to persuade readers to agree with you. The concept and practice of research arises out of the specific social context of your readers' questions and skepticism.

Reading necessarily plays a prominent role in the many forms of writing that you do, but not simply as a process of gathering information. This is true whether you write personal essays, editorials, or original research based on library research. Instead, as James Crosswhite suggests in his book *The Rhetoric of Reason,* reading "means making judgments about which of the many voices one encounters can be brought together into productive conversation" (131).

5   When we sit down to write an argument intended to persuade someone to do or to believe something, we are never really the first to broach the topic about which we are writing. Thus, learning how to write a researched argument is a process of learning how to enter conversations that are already going on in written form. This idea of writing as dialogue—not only between author and reader but between the text and everything that has been said or written beforehand—is important. Writing is a process of balancing our goals with the history of similar kinds of communication, particularly others' arguments that have been made on the same subject. The conversations that have already been going on about a topic are the topic's historical context.

Perhaps the most eloquent statement of writing as conversation comes from Kenneth Burke (1941) in an oft-quoted passage:

> Imagine that you enter a parlor. You come late. When you arrive, others have long preceded you, and they are engaged in a heated discussion, a discussion too heated for them to pause and tell you exactly what it is about. In fact the discussion had already begun long before any of them got there, so that no one present is qualified to retrace for you all the steps that had gone before. You listen for a while, until you decide that you have caught the tenor of the argument; then you put in your oar. Someone answers; you answer him; another comes to your defense; another aligns himself against you, to either the embarrassment or gratification of your opponent, depending on the quality of your ally's assistance. However, the discussion is interminable. The hour grows late, you must depart, with the discussion still vigorously in progress. (110–111)

As this passage describes, every argument you make is connected to other arguments. Every time you write an argument, the way you position yourself will depend on three things: which previously stated arguments you share, which previously stated arguments you want to refute, and what new opinions and supporting information you are going to bring to the conversation. You may, for example, affirm others for raising important issues, but assert that they have not given those issues the thought or emphasis that they deserve. Or you may raise a related issue that has been ignored entirely.

Entering the Conversation

To develop an argument that is akin to a conversation, it is helpful to think of writing as a process of understanding conflicts, the claims others make, and the important questions to ask, not simply as the ability to tell a story that influences readers' ways of looking at the world or to find good reasons to support our own beliefs. The real work of writing a researched argument occurs when you try to figure out the answers to the following:

- What topics have people been talking about?
- What is a relevant problem?
- What kinds of evidence might persuade readers?
- What objections might readers have?
- What is at stake in this argument? (What if things change? What if things stay the same?)

10   In answering these questions, you will want to read with an eye toward identifying an *issue,* the *situation* that calls for some response in writing, and framing a *question*.

Identify an Issue

An issue is a fundamental tension that exists between two or more conflicting points of view. For example, imagine that I believe that the best approach to educational reform is to change the curriculum in schools. Another person might suggest that we need to address reform by considering social and economic concerns. One way to argue the point is for each writer to consider the goals of education that they share, how to best reach those goals, and the reasons why their approach might be the best one to follow. One part of the issue is (*a*) that some people believe that educational reform should occur through changes in the curriculum; the second part is (*b*) that some people believe that reform should occur at the socioeconomic level. Notice that in defining different parts of an issue, the conflicting claims may not necessarily invalidate each other. In fact, one could argue that reform at the levels of curriculum and socioeconomic change may both be effective measures.

Keep in mind that issues are dynamic and arguments are always evolving. One of my students felt that a book he was reading placed too much emphasis on school-based learning and not enough on real-world experience. He framed the issue in this way: "We are not just educated by concepts and facts that we learn in school. We are educated by the people around us and the environments that we live in every day." In writing his essay, he read a great deal in order to support his claims and did so in light of a position he was writing against: "that education in school is the most important type of education."

Identify the Situation

It is important to frame an issue in the context of some specific situation. Whether curricular changes make sense depends on how people view the problem. One kind of problem that E. D. Hirsch identified in his book *Cultural Literacy* is that students do not have sufficient knowledge of history and literature to communicate well. If that is true in a particular school, perhaps the curriculum might be changed. But there might be other factors involved that call for a different emphasis. Moreover, there are often many different ways to define an issue or frame a question. For example, we might observe that at a local high school, scores on standardized tests have steadily decreased during the past five years. This trend contrasts with scores during the ten years prior to any noticeable decline. Growing out of this situation is the broad question, "What factors have influenced the decline in standardized scores at this school?" Or one could ask this in a different way: "To what extent have scores declined as a result of the curriculum?"

The same principle applies to Anna Quindlen's argument about the homeless in her commentary "No Place Like Home," which illustrates the kinds of connections an author tries to make with readers. Writing her piece as an editorial in the *New York Times,* Quindlen addresses an issue that appears to plague New Yorkers. And yet many people have come to live with the presence of homelessness in New York and other cities. This is the situation that motivates Quindlen to write her editorial: People study the problem of homelessness, yet nothing gets done. Homelessness has become a way of life, a situation that seems to say to observers that officials have declared defeat when it comes to this problem.

Frame a Good Question

15 A good question can help you think through what you might be interested in writing; it is specific enough to guide inquiry and meets the following criteria:

- It can be answered with the tools you have.
- It conveys a clear idea of who you are answering the question for.
- It is organized around an issue.
- It explores "how," "why," or "whether," and the "extent to which."

A good question, then, is one that can be answered given the access we have to certain kinds of information. The tools we have at hand can be people or other texts. A good question also grows out of an issue, some fundamental tension that you identify within a conversation. Through identifying what is at issue, you should begin to understand for whom it is an issue—who you are answering the question for.

Framing as a Critical Strategy for Writing, Reading, and Doing Research

Thus far, I have presented a conversational model of argument, describing writing as a form of dialogue, with writers responding to the ways others have defined problems and anticipating possible counterarguments. In this section, I want to add another element that some people call framing. This is a strategy that can help you orchestrate different and conflicting voices in advancing your argument.

Framing is a metaphor for describing the lens, or perspective, from which writers present their arguments. Writers want us to see the world in one way as opposed to another, not unlike the way a photographer manipulates a camera lens to frame a picture. For example, if you were taking a picture of friends in front of the football stadium on campus, you would focus on what you would most like to remember, blurring the images of people in the background. How you set up the picture, or frame it, might entail using light and shade to make some images stand out more than others. Writers do the same with language (see also Chapter 4).

For instance, in writing about education in the United States, E. D. Hirsch uses the term *cultural literacy* as a way to understand a problem, in this case the decline of literacy. To say that there is a decline, Hirsch has to establish the criteria against which to measure whether some people are literate and some are not. Hirsch uses *cultural literacy* as a lens through which to discriminate between those who fulfill his criteria for literacy and those who do not. He defines *cultural literacy* as possessing certain kinds of information. Not all educators agree. Some oppose equating literacy and information, describing literacy as an *event* or as a *practice* to argue that literacy is not confined to acquiring bits of information; instead, the notion of literacy as an *event* or *practice* says something about how people use what they know to accomplish the work of a community. As you can see, any perspective or lens can limit readers' range of vision: readers will see some things and not others.

20   In my work as a writer, I have identified four reasons to use framing as a strategy for developing an argument. First, framing encourages you to name your position, distinguishing the way you think about the world from the ways others do. Naming also makes what you say memorable through key terms and theories. Readers may not remember every detail of Hirsch's argument, but they recall the principle—cultural literacy—around which he organizes his details. Second, framing forces you to offer both a definition and description of the principle around which your argument develops. For example, Hirsch defines *cultural literacy* as "the possession of basic information needed to thrive in the modern world." By defining your argument, you give readers something substantive to respond to. Third, framing specifies your argument, enabling others to respond to your argument and to generate counterarguments that you will want to engage in the spirit of conversation. Fourth, framing helps you organize your thoughts, and readers', in the same way that a title for an essay, a song, or a painting does.

To extend this argument, I would like you to think about framing as a strategy of critical inquiry when you read. By critical inquiry, I mean that reading entails understanding the framing strategies that writers use and using framing concepts in order to shed light on our own ideas or the ideas of others. Here I distinguish *reading as inquiry* from *reading as a search for information.* For example, you might consider your experiences as readers and writers through the lens of Hirsch's conception of cultural literacy. You might recognize that schooling for you was really about accumulating information and that such an approach to education served you well. It is also possible that it has not. Whatever you decide, you may begin to reflect upon your experiences in new ways in developing an argument about what the purpose of education might be.

Alternatively, you might think about your educational experiences through a very different conceptual frame in reading the following excerpt from Richard Rodriguez's memoir, *Hunger of Memory.* In this book, Rodriguez explains the conflicts he experienced as a nonnative speaker of English who desperately sought to enter mainstream culture, even if this meant sacrificing his identity as the son of Mexican immigrants. Notice how Rodriguez recalls his experience as a student through the framing concept of "scholarship boy" that he reads in Richard Hoggart's 1957 book, *The Uses of Literacy.* Using this notion of "scholarship boy" enables him to revisit his experience from a new perspective.

As you read this passage, consider what the notion of "scholarship boy" helps Rodriguez to understand about his life as a student. In turn, what does such a concept help you understand about your own experience as a student?

For weeks I read, speed-read, books by modern educational theorists, only to find infrequent and slight mention of students like me .... Then one day, leafing through Richard Hoggart's *The Uses of Literacy,* I found, in his description of the scholarship boy, myself. For the first time I realized that there were other students like me, and so I was able to frame the meaning of my academic success, its consequent price—the loss.

Motivated to reflect upon his life as a student, Rodriguez comes across Richard Hoggart's book and a description of "the scholarship boy."

25   Hoggart's description is distinguished, at least initially, by deep understanding. What he grasps very well is that the scholarship boy must move between environments, his home and the classroom, which are at cultural extremes, opposed. With his family, the boy has the intense pleasure of intimacy, the family's consolation in feeling public alienation. Lavish emotions texture home life. *Then,* at school, the instruction bids him to trust lonely reason primarily. Immediate needs set the pace of his parents' lives. From his mother and father the boy learns to trust spontaneity and nonrational ways of knowing. *Then,* at school, there is mental calm. Teachers emphasize the value of a reflectiveness that opens a space between thinking and immediate action.

His initial response is to identify with Hoggart's description. Notice that Rodriguez says he used what he read to "frame the meaning of my academic success."

The scholarship boy moves between school and home, between moments of spontaneity and reflectiveness.

Years of schooling must pass before the boy will be able to sketch the cultural differences in his day as abstractly as this. But he senses those differences early. Perhaps as early as the night he brings home an assignment from school and finds the house too noisy for study.

He has to be more and more alone, if he is going to 'get on.' He will have, probably unconsciously, to oppose the ethos of the hearth, the intense gregariousness of the working-class family group .... The boy has to cut himself off mentally, so as to do his homework, as well as he can. (47)

Rodriguez uses Hoggart's words and idea to advance his own understanding of the problem he identifies in his life: that he was unable to find solace at home and within his working-class roots.

In this excerpt, the idea of framing highlights the fact that other people's texts can serve as tools for helping you say more about your own ideas. If you were writing an essay using Hoggart's term *scholarship boy* as a lens through which to say something about education, you might ask how Hoggart's term illuminates new aspects of another writer's examples or your own—as opposed to asking, "How well does Hoggart's term *scholarship boy* apply to my experience?" (to which you could answer, "Not very well"). Further, you might ask, "To what extent does Hirsch's concept throw a more positive light on what Rodriguez and Haggart describe?" or "Do my experiences challenge, extend, or complicate such a term as *scholarship boy*?"

∞∞∞

Now that you have a sense of how framing works, let's look at an excerpt from a researched argument a first-year composition student wrote, titled "Learning 'American' in Spanish." The full text of this essay can be found at the end of this essay. The assignment to which she responded asked her to do the following:

30   Draw on your life experiences in developing an argument about education and what it has meant to you in your life. In writing your essay, use two of the four authors (Freire, Hirsch, Ladson-Billings, Pratt) included in this unit to frame your argument or any of the reading you may have done on your own. What key terms, phrases, or ideas from these texts help you teach your readers what you want them to learn from your experiences? How do your experiences extend or complicate your critical frames?

In the past, in responding to this assignment, some people have offered an overview of almost their entire lives, some have focused on a pivotal experience, and others have used descriptions of people who have influenced them. The important thing is that you use those experiences to argue a position: for example, that even the most well-meaning attempts to support students can actually hinder learning. This means going beyond narrating a simple list of experiences, or simply asserting an opinion. Instead you must use—and analyze your experiences, determining which will most effectively convince your audience that your argument has a solid basis.

∞∞∞

As you read the excerpt from this student's essay, ask yourself how the writer uses two framing concepts—"transculturation" and "contact zone"—from Mary Louise Pratt's article "Arts of the Contact Zone." What do these ideas help the writer bring into focus? What experience do these frames help her to name, define, and describe?

Exactly one week after graduating from high school, with thirteen years of American education behind me, I boarded a plane and headed for a Caribbean island. I had fifteen days to spend on an island surrounded with crystal blue waters, white sandy shores, and luxurious ocean resorts. With beaches to play on by day and casinos to play in during the night, I was told that this country was an exciting new tourist destination. My days in the Dominican Republic, however, were not filled with snorkeling lessons and my nights were not spent at the blackjack table. Instead of visiting the ritzy East Coast, I traveled inland to a mountain community with no running water and no electricity. The bus ride to this town, called Guayabal, was long, hot, and uncomfortable. The mountain roads were not paved and the bus had no air-conditioning. Surprisingly, the four-hour ride flew by. I had plenty to think about as my mind raced with thoughts of the next two weeks. I wondered if my host family would be welcoming, if the teenagers would be friendly, and if my work would be hard. I mentally prepared myself for life without the everyday luxuries of a flushing toilet, a hot shower, and a comfortable bed. Because Guayabal was without such basic commodities, I did not expect to see many reminders of home. I thought I was going to leave behind my American ways and immerse myself into another culture. These thoughts filled my head as the bus climbed the rocky hill toward Guayabal. When I finally got off the bus and stepped into the town square, I realized that I had thought wrong: There was no escaping the influence of the American culture.

The writer has not yet named her framing concept; but notice that the concrete details she gathers here set readers up to expect that she will juxtapose the culture of Guayabal and the Dominican Republic with that of the United States.

In a way, Guayabal was an example of what author Mary Louise Pratt refers to as a contact zone. Pratt defines a contact zone as "a place where cultures meet, clash, and grapple with each other, often in contexts of highly asymmetrical relations of power" (76). In Guayabal, American culture and American consumerism were clashing with the Hispanic and Caribbean culture of the Dominican Republic. The clash came from the Dominicans' desire to be American in every sense, and especially to be consumers of American products. This is nearly impossible for Dominicans to achieve due

The writer names her experience as an example of Pratt's conception of a "contact zone." Further, the writer expands on Pratt's quote by relating it to her own observations. And finally, she uses this frame as a way to organize the narrative (as opposed to ordering her narrative chronologically).

to their extreme poverty. Their poverty provided the "asymmetrical relation of power" found in contact zones, because it impeded not only the Dominican's ability to be consumers, but also their ability to learn, to work, and to live healthily. The effects of their poverty could be seen in the eyes of the seven-year-old boy who couldn't concentrate in school because all he had to eat the day before was an underripe mango. It could be seen in the brown, leathered hands of the tired old man who was still picking coffee beans at age seventy.

35   The moment I got off the bus I noticed the clash between the American culture, the Dominican culture, and the community's poverty. It was apparent in the Dominicans' fragmented representation of American pop culture. Everywhere I looked in Guayabal I saw little glimpses of America. I saw Coca-Cola ads painted on raggedy fences. I saw knockoff Tommy Hilfiger shirts. I heard little boys say, "I wanna be like Mike" in their best English, while playing basketball. I listened to merengue house, the American version of the traditional Dominican merengue music. In each instance the Dominicans had adopted an aspect of American culture, but with an added Dominican twist. Pratt calls this transculturation. This term is used to "describe processes whereby members of subordinated or marginal groups select and invent from materials transmitted by a dominant or metropolitan culture" (80). She claims that transculturation is an identifying feature of contact zones. In the contact zone of Guayabal, the marginal group, made up of impoverished Dominicans, selected aspects of the dominant American culture, and invented a unique expression of a culture combining both Dominican and American styles. My most vivid memory of this transculturalization was on a hot afternoon when I heard some children yelling, "Helado! Helado!" or "Ice cream! Ice cream!" I looked outside just in time to see a man ride by on a bicycle, ringing a hand bell and balancing a cooler full of ice cream in the front bicycle basket. The Dominican children eagerly chased after him, just as American children chase after the ice-cream truck.

The writer provides concrete evidence to support her point.

The writer offers an illustration of what she experienced, clarifying how this experience is similar to what Pratt describes. Note that Pratt's verb clash, *used in the definition of* contact zone, *reappears here as part of the author's observation.*

The author adds another layer to her description, introducing Pratt's framing concept of "transculturation." Here again she quotes Pratt in order to bring into focus her own context here. The writer offers another example of transculturation.

Although you will notice that the writer does not challenge the framing terms she uses in this paper, it is clear that rather than simply reproducing Pratt's ideas and using her as the Voice of Authority, she incorporates Pratt's understandings to enable her to say more about her own experiences and ideas. Moreover, she uses this frame to advance an argument in order to affect her readers' views of culture. In turn, when she mentions others' ideas, she does so in the service of what she wants to say.

Conclusion: Writing Researched Arguments

I want to conclude this chapter by making a distinction between two different views of research. On the one hand, research is often taught as a process of collecting information for its own sake. On the other hand, research can also be conceived as the discovery and purposeful use of information. The emphasis here is upon *use* and the ways you can shape information in ways that enable you to enter conversations. To do so, you need to demonstrate to readers that you understand the conversation: what others have said in the past, what the context is, and what you anticipate is the direction this conversation might take. Keep in mind, however, that contexts are neither found nor located. Rather, context, derived from the Latin *contexere,* denotes a process of weaving together. Thus your attempt to understand context is an active process of making connections among the different and conflicting views people present within a conversation. Your version of the context will vary from others' interpretations.

Your attempts to understand a given conversation may prompt you to do research, as will your attempts to define what is at issue. Your reading and inquiry can help you construct a question that is rooted in some issue that is open to dispute. In turn, you need to ask yourself what is at stake for you and your reader other than the fact that you might be interested in educational reform, homelessness, affirmative action, or any other subject. Finally, your research can provide a means for framing an argument in order to move a conversation along and to say something new.

If you see inquiry as a means of entering conversations, then you will understand research as a social process. It need not be the tedious task of collecting information for its own sake. Rather, research has the potential to change readers' worldviews and your own.

Acknowledgment

I wish to thank Robert Kachur and April Lidinsky for helping me think through the notions of argument as conversation and framing.

Works Cited

Bartholomae, David, and Anthony Petrosky. 1996. *Ways of Reading: An Anthology for Writers.* New York: Bedford Books.

Brent, Doug. 1996. "Rogerian Rhetoric: Ethical Growth Through Alternative Forms of Argumentation." In *Argument Revisited; Argument Redefined: Negotiating Meaning in a Composition Classroom,* 73–96. Edited by Barbara Emmel, Paula Resch, and Deborah Tenney. Thousand Oaks, CA: Sage Publications.

Burke, Kenneth. 1941. *The Philosophy of Literary Form.* Berkeley: University of California Press.

Crosswhite, James. 1996. *The Rhetoric of Reason: Writing and the Attractions of Argument.* Madison, WI: University of Wisconsin Press.

Freire, Paulo. 1970. *Pedagogy of the Oppressed.* New York: Continuum.

Hirsch, E. D. 1987. *Cultural Literacy.* New York: Vintage Books.

Ladson-Billings, Gloria. 1994. *The Dreamkeepers: Successful Teachers of African American Children.* New York: Teachers College Press.

Quindlen, Anna. 1993. "No Place Like Home." In *Thinking Out Loud: On the Personal, the Public, and the Private,* 42–44. New York: Random House.

Rodriguez, Richard. 1983. Hunger of Memory: *The Education of Richard Rodriguez.* New York: Bantam Books.

Credit ————————————————————————————————————
Stuart Greene, "Argument as Conversation: The Role of Inquiry in Writing a Researched Argument"
Reprinted with the permission of the author.

Understanding Patriarchy

BELL HOOKS

Patriarchy is the single most life-threatening social disease assaulting the male body and spirit in our nation. Yet most men do not use the word "patriarchy" in everyday life. Most men never think about patriarchy—what it means, how it is created and sustained. Many men in our nation would not be able to spell the word or pronounce it correctly. The word "patriarchy" just is not a part of their normal everyday thought or speech. Men who have heard and know the word usually associate it with women's liberation, with feminism, and therefore dismiss it as irrelevant to their own experiences. I have been standing at podiums talking about patriarchy for more than thirty years. It is a word I use daily, and men who hear me use it often ask me what I mean by it.

Nothing discounts the old antifeminist projection of men as all-powerful more than their basic ignorance of a major facet of the political system that shapes and informs male identity and sense of self from birth until death. I often use the phrase "imperialist white-supremacist capitalist patriarchy" to describe the interlocking political systems that are the foundation of our nation's politics. Of these systems the one that we all learn the most about growing up is the system of patriarchy, even if we never know the word, because patriarchal gender roles are assigned to us as children and we are given continual guidance about the ways we can best fulfill these roles.

Patriarchy is a political-social system that insists that males are inherently dominating, superior to everything and everyone deemed weak, especially females, and endowed with the right to dominate and rule over the weak and to maintain that dominance through various forms of psychological terrorism and violence. When my older brother and I were born with a year separating us in age, patriarchy determined how we would each be regarded by our parents. Both our parents believed in patriarchy; they had been taught patriarchal thinking through religion.

At church they had learned that God created man to rule the world and everything in it and that it was the work of women to help men perform these tasks, to obey, and to always assume a subordinate role in relation to a powerful man. They were taught that God was male. These teachings were reinforced in every institution they encountered—schools, courthouses, clubs, sports arenas, as well as churches. Embracing patriarchal thinking, like everyone else around them, they taught it to their children because it seemed like a "natural" way to organize life.

5   As their daughter I was taught that it was my role to serve, to be weak, to be free from the burden of thinking, to caretake and nurture others. My brother was taught that it was his role to be served; to provide; to be strong; to think, strategize, and plan; and to refuse to caretake or nurture others. I was taught that it was not proper for a female to be violent, that it was "unnatural." My brother was taught that his value would be determined by his will to do violence (albeit in appropriate settings). He was taught that for a boy, enjoying violence was a good thing (albeit in appropriate settings). He was taught that a boy should not express feelings. I was taught that girls could and should express feelings, or at least some of them. When I responded with rage at being denied a toy, I was taught as a girl in a patriarchal household that rage was not an appropriate feminine feeling, that it should not only not be expressed, but it should be eradicated. When my brother responded with rage at being denied a toy, he was taught as a boy in a patriarchal household that his ability to express rage was good but that he had to learn the best setting to unleash his hostility. It was not good for him to use his rage to oppose the wishes of his parents, but later, when he grew up, he was taught that rage was permitted and that allowing rage to provoke him to violence would help him protect home and nation.

We lived in farm country, isolated from other people. Our sense of gender roles was learned from our parents, from the ways we saw them behave. My brother and I remember our confusion about gender. In reality I was stronger and more violent than my brother, which we learned quickly was bad. And he was a gentle, peaceful boy, which we learned was really bad. Although we were often confused, we knew one fact for certain: we could not be and act the way we wanted to, doing what we felt like. It was clear to us that our behavior had to follow a predetermined, gendered script. We both learned the word "patriarchy" in our adult life, when we learned that the script that had determined what we should be, the identities we should make, was based on patriarchal values and beliefs about gender.

I was always more interested in challenging patriarchy than my brother was because it was the system that was always leaving me out of things that I wanted to be part of. In our family life of the fifties, marbles were a boy's game. My brother had inherited his marbles from men in the family; he had a tin box to keep them in. All sizes and shapes, marvelously colored, they were to my eye the most beautiful objects. We played together with them, often with me aggressively clinging to the marble I liked best, refusing to share. When Dad was at work, our stay-at-home mom was quite content to see us playing marbles together. Yet Dad, looking at our play from a patriarchal perspective, was disturbed by what he saw. His daughter, aggressive and competitive, was a better player than his son. His son was passive; the boy did not really seem to care who won and was willing to give over marbles on demand. Dad decided that this play had to end, that both my brother and I needed to learn a lesson about appropriate gender roles.

One evening my brother was given permission by Dad to bring out the tin of marbles. I announced my desire to play and was told by my brother that "girls did not play with marbles," that it was a boy's game. This made no sense to my four- or five-year-old mind, and I insisted on my right to play by picking up marbles and shooting them. Dad intervened to tell me to stop. I did not listen. His voice grew louder and louder. Then suddenly he snatched me up, broke a board from our screen door, and began to beat me with it, telling me, "You're just a little girl. When I tell you to do something, I mean for you to do it." He beat me and he beat me, wanting me to acknowledge that I understood what I had done. His rage, his violence captured everyone's attention. Our family sat spellbound, rapt before the pornography of patriarchal violence. After this beating I was banished—forced to stay alone in the dark. Mama came into the bedroom to soothe the pain, telling me in her soft southern voice, "I tried to warn you. You need to accept that you are just a little girl and girls can't do what boys do." In service to patriarchy her task was to reinforce that Dad had done the right thing by, putting me in my place, by restoring the natural social order.

I remember this traumatic event so well because it was a story told again and again within our family. No one cared that the constant retelling might trigger post-traumatic stress; the retelling was necessary to reinforce both the message and the remembered state of absolute powerlessness. The recollection of this brutal whipping of a little-girl daughter by a big strong man, served as more than just a reminder to me of my gendered place; it was a reminder to everyone watching/remembering, to all my siblings, male and female, and to our grownwoman mother that our patriarchal father was the ruler in our household. We were to remember that if we did not obey his rules, we would be punished, punished even unto death. This is the way we were experientially schooled in the art of patriarchy.

10   There is nothing unique or even exceptional about this experience. Listen to the voices of wounded grown children raised in patriarchal homes and you will hear different versions with the same underlying theme, the use of violence to reinforce our indoctrination and acceptance of patriarchy. In *How Can I Get Through to You?* family therapist Terrence Real tells how his sons were

initiated into patriarchal thinking even as their parents worked to create a loving home in which antipatriarchal values prevailed. He tells of how his young son Alexander enjoyed dressing as Barbie until boys playing with his older brother witnessed his Barbie persona and let him know by their gaze and their shocked, disapproving silence that his behavior was unacceptable:

> Without a shred of malevolence, the stare my son received transmitted a message. You are not to do this. And the medium that message was broadcast in was a potent emotion: shame. At three, Alexander was learning the rules. A ten second wordless transaction was powerful enough to dissuade my son from that instant forward from what had been a favorite activity. I call such moments of induction the "normal traumatization" of boys.

To indoctrinate boys into the rules of patriarchy, we force them to feel pain and to deny their feelings.

My stories took place in the fifties; the stories Real tells are recent. They all underscore the tyranny of patriarchal thinking, the power of patriarchal culture to hold us captive. Real is one of the most enlightened thinkers on the subject of patriarchal masculinity in our nation, and yet he lets readers know that he is not able to keep his boys out of patriarchy's reach. They suffer its assaults, as do all boys and girls, to a greater or lesser degree. No doubt by creating a loving home that is not patriarchal, Real at least offers his boys a choice: they can choose to be themselves or they can choose conformity with patriarchal roles. Real uses the phrase "psychological patriarchy" to describe the patriarchal thinking common to females and males. Despite the contemporary visionary feminist thinking that makes clear that a patriarchal thinker need not be a male, most folks continue to see men as the problem of patriarchy. This is simply not the case. Women can be as wedded to patriarchal thinking and action as men.

Psychotherapist John Bradshaw's clear-sighted definition of patriarchy in *Creating Love* is a useful one: "The dictionary defines 'patriarchy' as a 'social organization marked by the supremacy of the father in the clan or family in both domestic and religious functions'. "Patriarchy is characterized by male domination and power. He states further that "patriarchal rules still govern most of the world's religious, school systems, and family systems." Describing the most damaging of these rules, Bradshaw lists "blind obedience—the foundation upon which patriarchy stands; the repression of all emotions except fear; the destruction of individual willpower; and the repression of thinking whenever it departs from the authority figure's way of thinking." Patriarchal thinking shapes the values of our culture. We are socialized into this system, females as well as males. Most of us learned patriarchal attitudes in our family of origin, and they were usually taught to us by our mothers. These attitudes were reinforced in schools and religious institutions.

15   The contemporary presence of female-headed house holds has led many people to assume that children in these households are not learning patriarchal values because no male is present. They assume that men are the sole teachers of patriarchal thinking. Yet many female-headed households endorse and promote patriarchal thinking with far greater passion than two-parent households. Because they do not have an experiential reality to challenge false fantasies of gender roles, women in such households are far more likely to idealize the patriarchal male role and patriarchal men than are women who live with patriarchal men every day. We need to highlight the role women play in perpetuating and sustaining patriarchal culture so that we will recognize patriarchy as a system women and men support equally, even if men receive more rewards from that system. Dismantling and changing patriarchal culture is work that men and women must do together.

Clearly we cannot dismantle a system as long as we engage in collective denial about its impact on our lives. Patriarchy requires male dominance by any means necessary, hence it supports, promotes, and condones sexist violence. We hear the most about sexist violence in public discourses about rape and abuse by domestic partners. But the most common forms of patriarchal violence are those that take place in the home between patriarchal parents and children. The point of such violence is usually to reinforce a dominator model, in which the authority figure is deemed ruler over those without power and given the right to maintain that rule through practices of subjugation, subordination, and submission.

Keeping males and females from telling the truth about what happens to them in families is one way patriarchal culture is maintained. A great majority of individuals enforce an unspoken rule in the culture as a whole that demands we keep the secrets of patriarchy, thereby protecting the rule of the father. This rule of silence is upheld when the culture refuses everyone easy access even to the word "patriarchy." Most children do not learn what to call this system of institutionalized gender roles, so rarely do we name it in everyday speech. This silence promotes denial. And how can we organize to challenge and change a system that cannot be named?

It is no accident that feminists began to use the word "patriarchy" to replace the more commonly used "male chauvanism" and "sexism." These courageous voices wanted men and women to become more aware of the way patriarchy affects us all. In popular culture the word itself was hardly used during the heyday of contemporary feminism. Antimale activists were no more eager than their sexist male counterparts to emphasize the system of patriarchy and the way it works. For to do so would have automatically exposed the notion that men were all-powerful and women powerless, that all men were oppressive and women always and only victims. By placing the blame for the perpetuation of sexism solely on men, these women could maintain their own allegiance to patriarchy, their own lust for power. They masked their longing to be dominators by taking on the mantle of victimhood.

Like many visionary radical feminists I challenged the misguided notion, put forward by women who were simply fed up with male exploitation and oppression, that men were "the enemy." As early as 1984 I included a chapter with the title "Men: Comrades in Struggle" in my book *Feminist Theory: From Margin to Center* urging advocates of feminist politics to challenge any rhetoric which placed the sole blame for perpetuating patriarchy and male domination onto men:

20   Separatist ideology encourages women to ignore the negative impact of sexism on male personhood. It stresses polarization between the sexes. According to Joy Justice, separatists believe that there are "two basic perspectives" on the issue of naming the victims of sexism: "There is the perspective that men oppress women. And there is the perspective that people are people, and we are all hurt by rigid sex roles." ... Both perspectives accurately describe our predicament. Men do oppress women. People are hurt by rigid sexist role patterns, These two realities coexist. Male oppression of women cannot be excused by the recognition that there are ways men are hurt by rigid sexist roles. Feminist activists should acknowledge that hurt, and work to change it—it exists. It does not erase or lessen male responsibility for supporting and perpetuating their power under patriarchy to exploit and oppress women in a manner far more grievous than the serious psychological stress and emotional pain caused by male conformity to rigid sexist role patterns.

Throughout this essay I stressed that feminist advocates collude in the pain of men wounded by patriarchy when they falsely represent men as always and only powerful, as always and only gaining privileges from their blind obedience to patriarchy. I emphasized that patriarchal ideology brainwashes men to believe that their domination of women is beneficial when it is not:

Often feminist activists affirm this logic when we should be constantly naming these acts as expressions of perverted power relations, general lack of control of one's actions, emotional powerlessness, extreme irrationality, and in many cases, outright insanity. Passive male absorption of sexist ideology enables men to falsely interpret this disturbed behavior positively. As long as men are brainwashed to equate violent domination and abuse of women with privilege, they will have no understanding of the damage done to themselves or to others, and no motivation to change.

Patriarchy demands of men that they become and remain emotional cripples. Since it is a system that denies men full access to their freedom of will, it is difficult for any man of any class to rebel against patriarchy, to be disloyal to the patriarchal parent, be that parent female or male.

The man who has been my primary bond for more than twelve years was traumatized by the patriarchal dynamics in his family of origin. When I met him he was in his twenties. While his formative years had been spent in the company of a violent, alcoholic dad, his circumstances changed when he was twelve and he began to live alone with his mother. In the early years of our relationship he talked openly about his hostility and rage toward his abusing dad. He was not interested in forgiving him or understanding the circumstances that had shaped and influenced his dad's life, either in his childhood or in his working life as a military man.

25   In the early years of our relationship he was extremely critical of male domination of women and children. Although he did not use the word "patriarchy," he understood its meaning and he opposed it. His gentle, quiet manner often led folks to ignore him, counting him among the weak and the powerless. By the age of thirty he began to assume a more macho persona, embracing the dominator model that he had once critiqued. Donning the mantle of patriarch, he gained greater respect and visibility. More women were drawn to him. He was noticed more in public spheres. His criticism of male domination ceased. And indeed he begin to mouth patriarchal rhetoric, saying the kind of sexist stuff that would have appalled him in the past.

These changes in his thinking and behavior were triggered by his desire to be accepted and affirmed in a patriarchal workplace and rationalized by his desire to get ahead. His story is not unusual. Boys brutalized and victimized by patriarchy more often than not become patriarchal, embodying the abusive patriarchal masculinity that they once clearly recognized as evil. Few men brutally abused as boys in the name of patriarchal maleness courageously resist the brainwashing and remain true to themselves. Most males conform to patriarchy in one way or another.

Indeed, radical feminist critique of patriarchy has practically been silenced in our culture. It has become a subcultural discourse available only to well-educated elites. Even in those circles, using the word "patriarchy" is regarded as passé. Often in my lectures when I use the phrase "imperialist white-supremacist capitalist patriarchy" to describe our nation's political system, audiences laugh. No one has ever explained why accurately naming this system is funny. The laughter is itself a weapon of patriarchal terrorism. It functions as a disclaimer, discounting the significance of what is being named. It suggests that the words themselves are problematic and not the system they describe. I interpret this laughter as the audience's way of showing discomfort with being asked to ally themselves with an antipatriarchal disobedient critique. This laughter reminds me that if I dare to challenge patriarchy openly, I risk not being taken seriously.

Citizens in this nation fear challenging patriarchy even as they lack overt awareness that they are fearful, so deeply embedded in our collective unconscious are the rules of patriarchy. I often tell audiences that if we were to go door-to-door asking if we should end male violence against women, most people would give their unequivocal support. Then if you told them we can only stop male violence against women by ending male domination, by eradicating patriarchy, they would begin to hesitate, to change their position. Despite the many gains of contemporary feminist movement—greater equality for women in the workforce, more tolerance for the relinquishing of rigid gender roles— patriarchy as a system remains intact, and many people continue to believe that it is needed if humans are to survive as a species. This belief seems ironic, given that patriarchal methods of organizing nations, especially the insistence on violence as a means of social control, has actually led to the slaughter of millions of people on the planet.

Until we can collectively acknowledge the damage patriarchy causes and the suffering it creates, we cannot address male pain. We cannot demand for men the right to be whole, to be givers and sustainers of life. Obviously some patriarchal men are reliable and even benevolent caretakers and providers, but still they are imprisoned by a system that undermines their mental health.

30   Patriarchy promotes insanity. It is at the root of the psychological ills troubling men in our nation. Nevertheless there is no mass concern for the plight of men. In *Stiffed: The Betrayal of the American Man,* Susan Faludi includes very little discussion of patriarchy:

> Ask feminists to diagnose men's problems and you will often get a very clear explanation: men are in crisis because women are properly challenging male dominance. Women are asking men to share the public reins and men can't bear it. Ask antifeminists and you will get a diagnosis that is, in one respect, similar. Men are troubled, many conservative pundits say, because women have gone far beyond their demands for equal treatment and are now trying to take power and control away from men … The underlying message: men cannot be men, only eunuchs, if they are not in control. Both the feminist and antifeminist views are rooted in a peculiarly modern American perception that to be a man means to be at the controls and at all times to feel yourself in control.

Faludi never interrogates the notion of control. She never considers that the notion that men were somehow in control, in power, and satisfied with their lives before contemporary feminist movement is false.

Patriarchy as a system has denied males access to full emotional well-being, which is not the same as feeling rewarded, successful, or powerful because of one's capacity to assert control over others. To truly address male pain and male crisis we must as a nation be willing to expose the harsh reality that patriarchy has damaged men in the past and continues to damage them in the present. If patriarchy were truly rewarding to men, the violence and addiction in family life that is so all-pervasive would not exist. This violence was not created by feminism. If patriarchy were rewarding, the overwhelming dissatisfaction most men feel in their work lives—a dissatisfaction extensively documented in the work of Studs Terkel and echoed in Faludi's treatise—would not exist.

In many ways *Stiffed* was yet another betrayal of American men because Faludi spends so much time trying not to challenge patriarchy that she fails to highlight the necessity of ending patriarchy if we are to liberate men. Rather she writes:

35   Instead of wondering why men resist women's struggle for a freer and healthier life, I began to wonder why men refrain from engaging in their own struggle. Why, despite a crescendo of random tantrums, have they offered no methodical, reasoned response to their predicament: Given the untenable and insulting nature of the demands placed on men to prove themselves in our culture, why don't men revolt? … Why haven't men responded to the series of betrayals in their own lives—to the failures of their fathers to make good on their promises–with some thing coequal to feminism?

Note that Faludi does not dare risk either the ire of feminist females by suggesting that men can find salvation in feminist movement or rejection by potential male readers who are solidly antifeminist by suggesting that they have something to gain from engaging feminism.

So far in our nation visionary feminist movement is the only struggle for justice that emphasizes the need to end patriarchy. No mass body of women has challenged patriarchy and neither has any group of men come together to lead the struggle. The crisis facing men is not the crisis of masculinity; it is the crisis of patriarchal masculinity. Until we make this distinction clear, men will continue to fear that any critique of patriarchy represents a threat. Distinguishing political patriarchy, which he sees as largely committed to ending sexism, therapist Terrence Real makes clear that the patriarchy damaging us all is embedded in our psyches:

Psychological patriarchy is the dynamic between those qualities deemed "masculine" and "feminine" in which half of our human traits are exalted while the other half is devalued. Both men and women participate in this tortured value system. Psychological patriarchy is a "dance of contempt," a perverse form of connection that replaces true intimacy with complex, covert layers of dominance and submission, collusion and manipulation. It is the unacknowledged paradigm of relationships that has suffused Western civilization generation after generation, deforming both sexes, and destroying the passionate bond between them.

By highlighting psychological patriarchy, we see that everyone is implicated and we are freed from the misperception that men are the enemy. To end patriarchy we must challenge both its psychological and its concrete manifestations in daily life. There are folks who are able to critique patriarchy but unable to act in an antipatriarchal manner.

40 To end male pain, to respond effectively to male crisis, we have to name the problem. We have to both acknowledge that the problem is patriarchy and work to end patriarchy. Terrence Real offers this valuable insight: "The reclamation of wholeness is a process even more fraught for men than it has been for women, more difficult and more profoundly threatening to the culture at large." If men are to reclaim the essential goodness of male being, if they are to regain the space of openheartedness and emotional expressiveness that is the foundation of well-being, we must envision alternatives to patriarchal masculinity. We must all change.

Credit
Bell Hooks, "Understanding Patriarchy" http://imaginenoborders.org/pdf/zines/
UnderstandingPatriarchy.pdf

"Bros Before Hos": The Guy Code

MICHAEL KIMMEL

Whenever I ask young women what they think it means to be a woman, they look at me puzzled, and say, basically, "Whatever I want." "It doesn't mean anything at all to me," says Nicole, a junior at Colby College in Maine. "I can be Mia Hamm, I can be Britney Spears, I can be Madame Curie or Madonna. Nobody can tell me what it means to be a woman anymore."

For men, the question is still meaningful—and powerful. In countless workshops on college campuses and in high-school assemblies, I've asked young men what it means to be a man. I've asked guys from every state in the nation, as well as about fifteen other countries, what sorts of phrases and words come to mind when they hear someone say, "Be a man!"

The responses are rather predictable. The first thing someone usually says is "Don't cry," then other similar phrases and ideas—never show your feelings, never ask for directions, never give up, never give in, be strong, be aggressive, show no fear, show no mercy, get rich, get even, get laid, win—follow easily after that.

Here's what guys say, summarized into a set of current epigrams. Think of it as a "Real Guy's Top Ten List."

1. "Boys Don't Cry"

2. "It's Better to be Mad than Sad"

3. "Don't Get Mad—Get Even"

4. "Take It Like a Man"

5. "He Who has the Most Toys When he Dies, Wins"

6. "Just Do It," or "Ride or Die"

7. "Size Matters"

8. "I Don't Stop to Ask for Directions"

9. "Nice Guys Finish Last"

10. "It's All Good"

5   The unifying emotional subtext of all these aphorisms involves never showing emotions or admitting to weakness. The face you must show to the world insists that everything is going just fine, that everything is under control, that there's

nothing to be concerned about (a contemporary version of Alfred E. Neuman of *MAD* Magazine's "What, me worry?"). Winning is crucial, especially when the victory is over other men who have less amazing or smaller toys. Kindness is not an option, nor is compassion. Those sentiments are taboo.

This is "The Guy Code," the collection of attitudes, values, and traits that together composes what it means to be a man. These are the rules that govern behavior in Guyland, the criteria that will be used to evaluate whether any particular guy measures up. The Guy Code revisits what psychologist William Pollack called "the boy code" in his bestselling book *Real Boys*—just a couple of years older and with a lot more at stake. And just as Pollack and others have explored the dynamics of boyhood so well, we now need to extend the reach of that analysis to include late adolescence and young adulthood.

In 1976, social psychologist Robert Brannon summarized the four basic rules of masculinity:

1. "No Sissy Stuff!" Being a man means not being a sissy, not being perceived as weak, effeminate, or gay. Masculinity is the relentless repudiation of the feminine.

2. "Be a Big Wheel." This rule refers to the centrality of success and power in the definition of masculinity. Masculinity is measured more by wealth, power, and status than by any particular body part.

3. "Be a Sturdy Oak." What makes a man is that he is reliable in a crisis. And what makes him so reliable in a crisis is not that he is able to respond fully and appropriately to the situation at hand, but rather that he resembles an inanimate object. A rock, a pillar, a species of tree.

4. "Give 'em Hell." Exude an aura of daring and aggression. Live life out on the edge. Take risks. Go for it. Pay no attention to what others think.

Amazingly, these four rules have changed very little among successive generations of high-school and college-age men. James O'Neil, a developmental psychologist at the University of Connecticut, and Joseph Pleck, a social psychologist at the University of Illinois, have each been conducting studies of this normative definition of masculinity for decades. "One of the most surprising findings," O'Neil told me, "is how little these rules have changed."

Being a Man Among Men

Where do young men get these ideas? "Oh, definitely, my dad," says Mike, a 20-year-old sophomore at Wake Forest. "He was always riding my ass, telling me I had to be tough and strong to make it in this world."

10   "My older brothers were always on my case," says Drew, a 24-year-old University of Massachusetts grad. "They were like, always ragging on me, calling me a pussy, if I didn't want to play football or wrestle. If I just wanted to hang out and like play my Xbox, they were constantly in my face."

"It was subtle, sometimes," says Warren, a 21-year-old at Towson, "and other times really out front. In school, it was the male teachers, saying stuff about how explorers or scientists were so courageous and braving the elements and all that. Then, other times, it was phys-ed class, and everyone was all over everyone else talking about 'He's so gay' and 'He's a wuss.'"

"The first thing I think of is my coach," says Don, a 26-year-old former football player at Lehigh. "Any fatigue, any weakness, any sign that being hit actually hurt and he was like 'Waah! [fake crying] Widdle Donny got a boo boo. Should we kiss it guys?' He'd completely humiliate us for showing anything but complete toughness. I'm sure he thought he was building up our strength and ability to play, but it wore me out trying to pretend all the time, to suck it up and just take it."

The response was consistent: Guys hear the voices of the men in their lives—fathers, coaches, brothers, grandfathers, uncles, priests—to inform their ideas of masculinity.

This is no longer surprising to me. One of the more startling things I found when I researched the history of the idea of masculinity in America for a previous book was that men subscribe to these ideals not because they want to impress women, let alone any inner drive or desire to test themselves against some abstract standards. They do it because they want to be positively evaluated by other men. American men want to be a "man among men," an Arnold Schwarzenegger-like "man's man," not a Fabio-like "ladies' man." Masculinity is largely a "homosocial" experience: performed for, and judged by, other men.

15   Noted playwright David Mamet explains why women don't even enter the mix. "Women have, in men's minds, such a low place on the social ladder of this country that it's useless to define yourself in terms of a woman. What men need is men's approval." While women often become a kind of currency by which men negotiate their status with other men, women are for possessing, not for emulating.

The Gender Police

Other guys constantly watch how well we perform. Our peers are a kind of "gender police," always waiting for us to screw up so they can give us a ticket for crossing the well-drawn boundaries of manhood. As young men, we become relentless cowboys, riding the fences, checking the boundary line between masculinity and femininity, making sure that nothing slips over. The possibilities of being unmasked are everywhere. Even the most seemingly insignificant misstep can pose a threat or activate that haunting terror that we will be found out.

On the day the students in my class "Sociology of Masculinity" were scheduled to discuss homophobia, one student provided an honest and revealing anecdote. Noting that it was a beautiful day, the first day of spring after a particularly brutal Northeast winter, he decided to wear shorts to class. "I had this really nice pair of new Madras shorts," he recounted. "But then I thought to myself, these shorts have lavender and pink in them. Today's class topic is homophobia. Maybe today is not the best day to wear these shorts." Nods all around.

Our efforts to maintain a manly front cover everything we do. What we wear. How we talk. How we walk. What we eat (like the recent flap over "manwiches"—those artery-clogging massive burgers, dripping with extras). Every mannerism, every movement contains a coded gender language. What happens if you refuse or resist? What happens if you step outside the definition of masculinity? Consider the words that would be used to describe you. In workshops it generally takes less than a minute to get a list of about twenty terms that are at the tip of everyone's tongues: wimp, faggot, dork, pussy, loser, wuss, nerd, queer, homo, girl, gay, skirt, Mama's boy, pussy-whipped. This list is so effortlessly generated, so consistent, that it composes a national well from which to draw epithets and put-downs.

Ask any teenager in America what is the most common put-down in middle school or high school? The answer: "That's so gay." It's said about anything and everything—their clothes, their books, the music or TV shows they like, the sports figures they admire. "That's so gay" has become a free-floating put-down, meaning bad, dumb, stupid, wrong. It's the generic bad thing.

20   Listen to one of America's most observant analysts of masculinity, Eminem. Asked in an MTV interview in 2001 why he constantly used "faggot" in every one of his raps to put down other guys, Eminem told the interviewer, Kurt Loder,

The lowest degrading thing you can say to a man when you're battling him is to call him a faggot and try to take away his manhood. Call him a sissy, call him a punk. "Faggot" to me doesn't necessarily mean gay people. "Faggot" to me just means taking away your manhood.

But does it mean homosexuality? Does it really suggest that you suspect the object of the epithet might actually be attracted to another guy? Think, for example, of how you would answer this question: If you see a man walking down the street, or meet him at a party, how do you "know" if he is homosexual? (Assume that he is not wearing a T-shirt with a big pink triangle on it, and that he's not already holding hands with another man.)

When I ask this question in classes or workshops, respondents invariably provide a standard list of stereotypically effeminate behaviors. He walks a certain way, talks a certain way, acts a certain way. He's well dressed, sensitive, and emotionally expressive. He has certain tastes in art and music—indeed, he has *any* taste in art and music! Men tend to focus on the physical attributes, women on the emotional. Women say they "suspect" a man might be gay if he's interested in what she's talking about, knows something about what she's talking about, or is sensitive and a good listener. One recently said, "I suspect he might be gay if he's looking at my eyes, and not down my blouse." Another said she suspects he might be gay if he shows no sexual interest in her, if he doesn't immediately come on to her.

Once I've established what makes a guy "suspect," I ask the men in the room if any of them would want to be thought of as gay. Rarely does a hand go up—despite the fact that this list of attributes is actually far preferable to the restrictive one that stands in the "Be a Man" box. So, what do straight men do to make sure that no one gets the wrong idea about them?

25   Everything that is perceived as gay goes into what we might call the Negative Playbook of Guyland. Avoid everything in it and you'll be all right. Just make sure that you walk, talk, and act in a different way from the gay stereotype; dress terribly; show no taste in art or music; show no emotions at all. Never listen to a thing a woman is saying, but express immediate and unquenchable sexual interest. Presto, you're a real man, back in the "Be a Man" box. Homophobia— the fear that people might *misperceive* you as gay—is the animating fear of American guys' masculinity. It's what lies underneath the crazy risk-taking behaviors practiced by boys of all ages, what drives the fear that other guys will see you as weak, unmanly, frightened. The single cardinal rule of manhood, the one from which all the other characteristics—wealth, power, status, strength, physicality—are derived is to offer constant proof that you are not gay.

Homophobia is even deeper than this. It's the fear *of* other men—that other men will perceive you as a failure, as a fraud. It's a fear that others will see you as weak, unmanly, frightened. This is how John Steinbeck put it in his novel *Of Mice and Men:*

> "Funny thing," [Curley's wife] said. "If I catch any one man, and he's alone, I get along fine with him. But just let two of the guys get together an' you won't talk. Jus' nothin' but mad." She dropped her fingers and put her hands on her hips. "You're all scared of each other, that's what. Ever'one of you's scared the rest is goin' to get something on you."

In that sense, homosexuality becomes a kind of shorthand for "unmanliness"—and the homophobia that defines and animates the daily conversations of Guyland is at least as much about masculinity as it is about sexuality.

But what would happen to a young man if he were to refuse such limiting parameters on who he is and how he's permitted to act? "It's not like I want to stay in that box," says Jeff, a first-year Cornell student at my workshop. "But as soon as you step outside it, even for a second, all the other guys are like, 'What are you, dude, a fag?' It's not very safe out there on your own. I suppose as I get older, I'll get more secure, and feel like I couldn't care less what other guys say. But now, in my fraternity, on this campus, man, I'd lose everything."

30   The consistency of responses is as arresting as the list is disturbing: "I would lose my friends." "Get beat up." "I'd be ostracized." "Lose my self-esteem." Some say they'd take drugs or drink. Become withdrawn, sullen, a loner, depressed. "Kill myself," says one guy. "Kill them," responds another. Everyone laughs, nervously. Some say they'd get mad. And some say they'd get even. "I dunno," replied Mike, a sophomore at Portland State University. "I'd probably pull a Columbine. I'd show them that they couldn't get away with calling me that shit."

Guys know that they risk everything—their friendships, their sense of self, maybe even their lives—if they fail to conform. Since the stakes are so enormous, young men take huge chances to prove their manhood, exposing themselves to health risks, workplace hazards, and stressrelated illnesses. Here's a revealing factoid. Men ages 19 to 29 are three times less likely to wear seat belts than women the same age. Before they turn nineteen though, young men are actually more likely to wear seat belts. It's as if they suddenly get the idea that as long as they're driving the car, they're completely in control, and therefore safe. Ninety percent of all driving offenses, excluding parking violations, are committed by men, and 93 percent of road ragers are male. Safety is emasculating! So they drink too much, drive too fast, and play chicken in a multitude of dangerous venues.

The comments above provide a telling riposte to all those theories of biology that claim that this definition of masculinity is "hard-wired," the result of millennia of evolutionary adaptation or the behavioral response to waves of aggression-producing testosterone, and therefore inevitable. What these theories fail to account for is the way that masculinity is coerced and policed relentlessly by other guys. If it were biological, it would be as natural as breathing or blinking. In truth, the Guy Code fits as comfortably as a straightjacket.

Boys' Psychological Development: Where the Guy Code Begins

Masculinity is a constant test—always up for grabs, always needing to be proved. And the testing starts early. Recently, I was speaking with a young black mother, a social worker, who was concerned about a conversation she had had with her husband a few nights earlier. It seems that her husband had taken their son to the barber, which, she explained to me, is a central social institution in the African-American community. As the barber prepared the boy's hair for treatment, using, apparently some heat and some painful burning chemicals, the boy began to cry. The barber turned to the boy's father and pronounced, "This boy is a wimp!" He went on, "This boy has been spending too much time with his mama! Man, you need to put your foot down. You have got to get this boy away from his mother!"

35   That evening the father came home, visibly shaken by the episode, and announced to his wife that from that moment on the boy would not be spending as much time with her, but instead would do more sports and other activities with him, "to make sure he doesn't become a sissy."

After telling me this story, the mother asked what I thought she should do. "Gee," I said, "I understand the pressures that dads feel to 'toughen up' their sons. But how old is your boy, anyway?"

"Three and a half," she said.

I tried to remind her, of course, that crying is the natural human response to pain, and that her son was behaving appropriately. But her story reminded me of how early this pressure starts to affect an emotionally impervious manly stoicism.

Ever since Freud, we've believed that the key to boys' development is
separation, that the boy must switch his identification from mother to father
in order to "become" a man. He achieves his masculinity by repudiation,
dissociation, and then identification. It is a perilous path, but a necessary one,
even though there is nothing inevitable about it—and nothing biological either.
Throw in an overdominant mother, or an absent father, and we start worrying
that the boy will not succeed in his masculine quest.

40   Boys learn that their connection to mother will emasculate them, turn them
into Mama's Boys. And so they learn to act *as if* they have made that leap by
pushing away from their mothers. Along the way they suppress all the feelings
they associate with the maternal—compassion, nurturance, vulnerability,
dependency. This suppression and repudiation is the origin of the Boy Code. It's
what turns those happy, energetic, playful, and emotionally expressive 5-year-
olds into sullen, withdrawn, and despondent 9-year-olds. In the recent spate of
bestselling books about boys' development, psychologists like William Pollack,
James Garbarino, Michael Thompson, Dan Kindlon, and others, argue that from
an early age boys are taught to refrain from crying, to suppress their emotions,
never to display vulnerability. As a result, boys feel effeminate not only if they
express their emotions, but even if they *feel* them. In their bestseller, *Raising
Cain,* Kindlon and Thompson describe a "culture of cruelty" in which peers
force other boys to deny their emotional needs and disguise their feelings. It's no
wonder that so many boys end up feeling emotionally isolated.

These books about boys map the inner despair that comes from such
emotional numbness and fear of vulnerability. Pollack calls it the "mask of
masculinity," the fake front of impervious, unemotional independence, a
swaggering posture that boys believe will help them to present a stoic front.
"Ruffled in a manly pose," the great Irish poet William Butler Yeats put it in his
poem "Coole Park" (1929), "For all his timid heart."

The ruffling starts often by age 4 or 5, when he enters kindergarten, and it gets
a second jolt when he hits adolescence. Think of the messages boys get: Stand
on your own two feet! Don't cry! Don't be a sissy! As one boy in Pollack's book
summarizes it: "Shut up and take it, or you'll be sorry." When I asked my 9-year-
old son, Zachary, what he thought of when I said "be a man" he said that one
of his friends said something about "taking it like a man. So," he explained, "I
think it means acting tougher than you actually are."

Recently a colleague told me about a problem he was having. It seems his 7-year-old son, James, was being bullied by another boy on his way home from school. His wife, the boy's mother, strategized with her son about how to handle such situations in the future. She suggested he find an alternate route home, tell a teacher, or perhaps even tell the boy's parents. And she offered the standard "use your words, not your fists" conflict-reducer. "How can I get my wife to stop treating James like a baby?" my colleague asked. "How will he ever learn to stand up for himself if she turns him into a wimp?"

The Boy Code leaves boys disconnected from a wide range of emotions and prohibited from sharing those feelings with others. As they grow older, they feel disconnected from adults, as well, unable to experience the guidance towards maturity that adults can bring. When they turn to anger and violence it is because these, they believe, perhaps rightly, are the only acceptable forms of emotional expression allowed them. Just as the Boy Code shuts boys down, the Guy Code reinforces those messages, suppressing what was left of boyhood exuberance and turning it into sullen indifference.

45   No wonder boys are more prone to depression, suicidal behavior, and various other forms of out-of-control or out-of-touch behaviors than girls are. No wonder boys drop out of school and are diagnosed as emotionally disturbed four times more often as girls, get into fights twice as often, and are six times more likely than girls to be diagnosed with Attention Deficit and Hyperactivity Disorder (ADHD).

The Pressure to Conform

I often ask my students to imagine two American men—one, 75 years old, black, and gay, who lives in downtown Chicago, and the other, a 19-year-old white heterosexual farm boy living 100 miles south of Chicago. How might their ideas about masculinity differ? And what ideas about masculinity might they have in common, ideas that transcend class, race, age, and sexual or regional differences?

While the Guy Code isn't everywhere exactly the same, and while there are some variations by class or race or age or sexuality, the pressure to conform is so powerful a centripetal force that it minimizes differences, pushing guys into a homogenous, ill-fitting uniform. The sociologist Erving Goffman once described the dominant image of masculinity like this:

In an important sense there is only one complete unblushing male in America: a young, married, white, urban, northern, heterosexual, Protestant, father, of college education, fully employed, of good complexion, weight, and height, and a recent record in sports ... Any male who fails to qualify in any one of these ways is likely to view himself—during moments at least—as unworthy, incomplete, and inferior.

This dynamic is critical. Every single man will, at some point in his life, "fail to qualify." That is, every single one of us will feel, at least at moments, "unworthy, incomplete, and inferior." It is from those feelings of inadequacy and inferiority that we often act recklessly—taking foolish risks, engaging in violence—all as an attempt to repair, restore, or reclaim our place in the sacred box of manhood.

50   It's equally true that guys express the Guy Code differently at different times of their lives. Even at different times of day! Even if he believes that to be a man is to always be in charge, to be aggressive and powerful, he is unlikely to express that around his coaches or teachers, let alone his parents. There are times when even the most manly of men must accept authority, obey orders, and shut up and listen.

This is especially true in Guyland, because this intermediate moment, poised between adolescence and adulthood, enables young men to be somewhat strategic in their expression of masculinity. They can be men when it suits them, when they want to be taken seriously by the world around them, and they can also be boys when it suits them, when they don't want to be held to account as adults for their actions, but simply want to get away with it.

Violence as Restoration

The Guy Code, and the Boy Code before it, demands a lot—that boys and young men shut down emotionally, that they suppress compassion, and inflate ambition. And it extracts compliance with coercion and fear. But it also promises so much as well. Part of what makes the Guy Code so seductive are the rewards guys think will be theirs if they only walk the line. If they embrace the Code, they will finally be in charge and feel powerful. And so, having dutifully subscribed, young men often feel cheated—and pissed off—when the rewards associated with power are not immediately forthcoming.

Violence is how they express all that disappointment. Rage is the way to displace the feelings of humiliation, to restore the entitlement. "The emotion of shame is the primary or ultimate cause of all violence," writes psychiatrist James Gilligan. "The purpose of violence is to diminish the intensity of shame and replace it as far as possible with its opposite, pride, thus preventing the individual from being overwhelmed by the feeling of shame." "It's better to be mad than sad," writes psychologist James Garbarino.

Virtually every male in America understands something about violence. We know how it works, we know how to use it, and we know that if we are perceived as weak or unmanly, it will be used against us. Each of us cuts his own deal with it.

55   It's as American as apple pie. Resorting to violence to restore one's honor from perceived humiliations has been around ever since one caveman chided another on the size of his club, but few modern societies have made violence such a cultural and psychological foundation. Cultural historian Richard Slotkin's history of the American frontier claims that our understanding of violence is regenerative: It enables us to grow. The great anthropologist Margaret Mead once commented that what made American violence stand out was our nearly obsessive need to legitimate the use of violence; ours is an aggression, she wrote, "which can never be shown except when the other fellow starts it" and which is "so unsure of itself that it had to be proved." Americans like to think that we don't start wars, we just finish them.

And what's true on the battlefield is also true on the playground. Watch two boys squaring off sometime. "You wanna start something?" one yells. "No, but if you start it, I'll finish it!" shouts the other. Adolescent male violence is so restorative that it's even been prescribed by generations of dads to enable their boys to stand up for themselves. And they've had plenty of support from experts, like J. Alfred Puffer, author of *The Boy and His Gang,* a child-rearing manual from the early twentieth century which offered this counsel:

> There are times when every boy must defend his own rights if he is not to become a coward and lose the road to independence and true manhood … The strong willed boy needs no inspiration to combat, but often a good deal of guidance and restraint. If he fights more than, let us say, a half dozen times a week—except, of course, during his first week at a new school—he is probably over-quarrelsome and needs to curb. The sensitive, retiring boy, on the other hand, needs encouragement to stand his ground and fight.

In this bestseller, boys were encouraged to fight once a day, except during the first week at a new school, when it was presumed they would fight more often!

The contemporary Guy Code also descends from older notions of honor—a man had to be ready to fight to prove himself in the eyes of others. In the early nineteenth century, Southern whites called it "honor"; by the turn of the century it was called "reputation." Later in the century, "having a chip on your shoulder"—walking around mad, ready to rumble—were installed as fighting words in the American South, as a generation of boys were desperate to prove their manhood after the humiliating defeat in the Civil War. By the 1950s, blacks in the northern ghettos spoke of "respect," which has now been transformed again into not showing "disrespect," or "dissing." It's the same code, the same daring. And today that postbellum "chip on your shoulder" has morphed into what one gang member calls the "accidental bump," when you're walking down the street, "with your chest out, bumping into people and hoping they'll give you a bad time so you can pounce on them and beat 'em into the goddamn concrete."

60   Violence, or the threat of violence, is a main element of the Guy Code: Its use, legitimacy, and effectiveness are all well understood by most adolescent guys. They use violence when necessary to test and prove their manhood, and when others don't measure up, they make them pay.

The Three Cultures of Guyland

Practically every week we can read about a horrible hazing incident on campus, or an alcohol-related driving accident following a high-school prom, or allegations of a date rape at a party the previous weekend. Bullying is ubiquitous in middle schools and high schools across America, and not infrequently a case of bullying is so outrageous it becomes newsworthy. Rape on campus occurs with such alarming frequency that most colleges now incorporate sexual awareness training into their freshman orientation practices (apparently students not only must learn how to find their way around campus and how to use a library, but they must also learn how not to rape their classmates).

Every single emergency room in every single hospital adjoining or near a college campus stocks extra supplies on Thursday nights—rape kits for the sexual assault victims, IV fluids for those who are dehydrated from alcohol-induced vomiting, blood for drunk driving accidents. On many campuses, at least one party gets "out of hand" each week, and someone is seriously injured: A group of guys stage a "train" or a "ledge party," or someone gets so sick from drinking that they need to be hospitalized. And that's just the more "routine" weekend events. Newspaper and magazine stories, alarmist television exposés, and campus crusaders typically focus on the extreme cases—the fatal drunk driving accidents, the murder-by-hazing.

Though it may not be possible to read these headlines without a shudder of horror, most adults among us, particularly those of us with sons and daughters who live in Guyland, are nonetheless often able to convince ourselves that these stories are not about *our* kids. We might even think the media is a bit hysterical. Our sons aren't rapists. They don't tie cinderblocks to each other's penises and then throw those blocks off the roof, for crying out loud. They don't drink and drive, or get in fistfights, or paint swastikas on each other's passed-out drunken bodies. They're good kids. We believe these stories are anomalies, that the perpetrators are deviants, bad apples who otherwise don't represent the majority of guys. We look to psychology to explain these rare occurrences: bad parenting, most likely, or the cumulative negative effects of media consumption. We treat these as individual cases, not as a social and cultural phenomenon that impacts all guys, including the ones we know and love.

And, as I've argued, for the most part that's true. Most guys *are* good guys, but that doesn't lessen the reality of the violence that surrounds them, or the ways that they, and we, collaborate by turning a blind eye. If we really want to help guide our sons to manhood, it's imperative that we, as a society, look at their world with eyes wide open. We must be willing to ask the hard questions. How do such events happen? And what do such extreme cases tell us about the dynamics of Guyland, the operations of the Guy Code in action?

65   Guyland rests on three distinct cultural dynamics: a culture of entitlement, a culture of silence, and a culture of protection. Taken together, these cultures do more than make these more extreme cases the actions of a small group of predatory thugs. They suggest the ways in which we, too, are implicated. Why? Because if we really want to help these guys, then we must know the world they live in.

The Culture of Entitlement

Many young men today have a shockingly strong sense of male superiority and a diminished capacity for empathy. They believe that the capacity for empathy and compassion has to be suppressed, early on, in the name of achieving masculinity. That this is true despite the progress of the women's movement, parents who are psychologically aware and moral, stunning opportunities for men and women, is disappointing at best. But there is no way around it:

Most young men who engage in acts of violence—or who watch them and do nothing, or who joke about them with their friends—fully subscribe to traditional ideologies about masculinity. The problem isn't psychological; these guys aren't deviants. If anything, they are overconforming to the hyperbolic expressions of masculinity that still inform American culture.

This culture of entitlement is the reward for subscribing to the Guy Code. As boys they may have felt powerless as they struggled heroically to live up to impossible conventions of masculinity. As William Pollack argues, "it's still a man's world, but it's not a boys' world." But *someday it would be*. Someday, if I play my cards right, if I follow all the rules, the world will be mine. Having worked so hard and sacrificed so much to become a man—it'll be my turn. Payback. I'm entitled.

It's facile to argue about whether or not young men "have" power: Some do, some don't. Some are powerful in some settings, but not in others. Besides, power isn't a possession, it's a relationship. It's about the ability to do what you want in the world. Few *people* feel that sort of power even as adults: Most of us "have to" work, we are weighed down by family and workplace obligations. But even when they feel powerless, unlike women, men feel *entitled* to power.

This sense of entitlement is crucial for understanding Guyland—and the lives of young men as they pass into adulthood. Here is another example. Not long ago, I appeared on a television talk show opposite three "angry white males" who felt they had been the victims of workplace discrimination. They were in their late twenties and early thirties— just on the other side of the Guyland divide. The show's title, no doubt to entice a large potential audience was "A Black Woman Stole My Job." Each of the men described how he was passed over for jobs or promotions for which all believed themselves qualified. Then it was my turn to respond. I said I had one question about one word in the title of the show. I asked them about the word "my." Where did they get the idea it was "their" job? Why wasn't the show called "A Black Woman Got *a* Job," or "A Black Woman Got *the* Job"? These men felt the job was "theirs" because they felt entitled to it, and when some "other" person—black, female—got the job, that person was really taking what was "rightfully" theirs.

70   Another example of entitlement appeared in an Anna Quindlen column in the *New York Times*. "It seems like if you're a white male you don't have a chance," commented a young man who attended a college where 5 percent of his classmates were black. By way of explanation, Quindlen commented

What the kid really meant is that he no longer has the edge, that the rules of a system that may have served his father will have changed. It is one of those good-old-days constructs to believe it was a system based purely on merit, but we know that's not true. It is a system that once favored him, and others like him. Now sometimes—just sometimes—it favors someone different.

Young men feel like Esau, that sad character in the Bible who sold his birthright for a bowl of lentils and never felt whole again. From that moment, everything belonged to Jacob, and we never hear of Esau again. And, like Esau, young men often feel that they've been tricked out of it, in Esau's case by a pair of hairy arms offered to his blind father, and in the case of guys today, by equally blind fathers who have failed to pass down to them what was "rightfully" supposed to be theirs.

The Culture of Silence

If thwarted entitlement is the underlying cause of so much of the violence in Guyland, and if violence is so intimately woven into the fabric of the Guy Code as to be one of its core elements, how come no one says anything about it?

Because they're afraid. They're afraid of being outcast, marginalized, shunned. Or they're afraid that the violence just might be turned against them if they voice their opposition too vehemently. So they learn to keep their mouths shut, even when what they're seeing goes against everything they know to be good. The Guy Code imposes a "code of silence on boys, requiring them to suffer without speaking of it and to be silent witnesses to acts of cruelty to others," write Dan Kindlon and Michael Thompson. Boys and men learn to be silent in the face of other men's violence. Silence is one of the ways boys *become* men.

75 They learn not to say anything when guys make sexist comments to girls. They learn not to say anything when guys taunt or tease another guy, or start fights, or bully or torment a classmate or a friend. They scurry silently if they're walking down the street and some guys at a construction site—or, for that matter, in business suits—start harassing a woman. They learn not to tell anyone about the homoerotic sadism that is practiced on new kids when they join a high-school or college athletic team, or the school band, or a fraternity. Or when they hear that a bunch of guys gang raped a classmate. They tell no parents, no teachers, no administrators. They don't tell the police. And they certainly don't confront the perpetrators.

A friend recently wrote to me about his experience leading a workshop for high-school kids in the frozen Yukon Territories of Canada. From the stories of their teachers, it was clear that the school had a tough and aggressive boy culture. He was surprised, then, when the boys opened up, and spoke with candor and honesty. During a break, though, he heard them talking about the fighting that went on each week at their school. A circle would form around a fight as it began. And the boys would cheer with glee.

He was taken aback. Suddenly these same boys, who minutes earlier had been earnest and caring, were now gleefully recounting blow-by-blow descriptions of the fights. Apparently without effort, they had shifted into masculine performance mode, each trying to outdo the other with shows of verbal bravado.

He interrupted them. "Wait a minute," he said. "I've spent the past day and a half with you guys, hearing you talk about your lives. I know you don't like that fighting. I know you don't like having to prove you're a real man. So how come you're going on about how great these fights are? Why do you stand in that circle and cheer the others on?"

The group went deadly silent. No one met his eyes. No one smirked or glanced that conspiratorial look that young people often share when an adult is challenging them. Finally, one boy looked up.

80   "So why do you cheer the fights?" my friend asked.

"Because if you don't, they'll turn on you. Because if you don't, you'll be the next one inside the ring."

If they're quiet, they believe, if they hide in the mass, if they disappear, maybe the bullies will ignore them, pick on someone else.

The silence is not limited to boys. Girls, too, know about the Guy Code, know how weaker guys are targeted, bullied, battered, and they keep quiet also. "We know that it's wrong," Ellen, a sophomore at the University of Illinois told me. "But we know that if we go along with it, the cool guys will like us. No big deal. It isn't like they're hitting *us,* is it?"

That silence, though, is what gives the perpetrators and the victims the idea that everyone supports the Guy Code. It's what gives everyone a mark of shame. And it's what keeps it going—even when so many guys are aching to change it, or eliminate it altogether. The first rule of the Guy Code is that you can express no doubts, no fears, no vulnerabilities. No questions even. As they might say in Las Vegas: What happens in Guyland stays in Guyland.

The Culture of Protection

85 By upholding the culture of silence, guys implicitly support the criminals in their midst who take that silence as tacit approval. And not only does that silence support them, it also protects them. It ensures that there will be no whistleblowers and, as we'll see, that there will be no witnesses when, and if, the victims themselves come forward. Nobody knows anything, nobody saw anything, nobody remembers anything.

Yet it's one thing for the guys themselves to protect one another— as we've seen, there's a tremendous amount at stake for them, and the pressure is high to conform—it's another thing entirely when the entire community that surrounds these guys also protects them. When the parents, teachers, girlfriends, school administrators, and city officials make the decision to look the other way, to dismiss these acts of violence as "poor judgment" or "things getting a little out of hand." I call this protective bubble of community support that surrounds Guyland the *culture of protection*. Communities rally around "their" guys, protecting the criminals and demeaning their victims. This shields the participants from taking full responsibility for their actions and often provides a cushion of support between those who feel entitled and the rest of the world.

It's natural for parents to want to protect their children. Parents work hard to keep their children safe—we immunize them, try to get them into the best schools, and intercede on their behalf if they are victimized or bullied. But sometimes this natural instinct to protect children may also infantalize them, may keep them from accepting responsibility for their actions, or confronting the negative consequences of their mistakes. And sometimes, parents' efforts to protect and defend their young adults may actually enable them to transgress again, or even to escalate the severity of their actions to the point where they are trying to get away with something truly criminal.

Not only do parents' responses characterize this culture of protection, but the entire community's response may shield them as well. From teachers, coaches, and school administrators who look the other way, as long as it didn't happen on school property, to the community determined to maintain the illusion that theirs is an ideal community in which to live and raise children, it's often neighbors and friends who exacerbate the problem by siding with the perpetrators against the victims.

The culture of silence and the culture of protection sustain many of guys' other excessive behaviors—from Justin Volpe and his police friends who sodomized Abner Louima, to the military brass who looked the other way when cadets at the Air Force Academy were routinely sexually assaulting female cadets, to the codes of silence on campus following any number of hazing deaths. And those who do stand up and challenge the culture of male entitlement—the whistleblowers—are often so vilified, ostracized from their communities, and threatened with retaliation that they might as well join the Witness Protection Program. Parents who stick up for their victimized kids can find themselves shunned by their neighbors and former friends; administrators who try and discipline perpetrators often face a wall of opposition and lawsuits—especially if the perpetrators happen to be athletes on winning teams.

"Our Guys"

90 A startling—and extreme—example of how these three cultures play out in Guyland is the infamous sexual assault in Glen Ridge, New Jersey, in 1989. It is well documented in the bestselling book *Our Guys* by Bernard Lefkowitz and also in a made-for-TV movie. I use this example, and others like it, not because the crime itself is typical—thankfully it is not—but because the cultural dynamics that enable the most extreme and egregious offenses in Guyland are equally present even in the more everyday aspects of guys' lives. We need to take a close look at the kind of culture that allows this to happen even once. Sociologists often point to extreme examples of phenomena, as if to say: If we can see such processes at work even here, then surely we can see them at work in more quotidian events. And, indeed, the response—by the criminals, their peers, and the larger community—was typical of the social dynamics that sustain and support Guyland as a whole.

In the spring of 1989, thirteen high-status athletes at Glen Ridge High School lured a 17-year-old "slightly retarded" girl into one of the guys' basement. Chairs had been arranged, theater style, around a sofa in the middle of the room. Most of the boys arranged themselves on the chairs, while a few led the girl to the sofa and got her to perform oral sex on one of the highest-status boys.

As the event began to unfold, one sophomore noticed "puzzlement and confusion" in the girl's eyes, and turned to his friend and said, "Let's get out of here." Another senior baseball player, age 17, said he started to "feel queasy" and thought to himself, "I don't belong here." He and another baseball player got up to leave. On the way out, he said to another guy, "It's wrong. C'mon with me." But the other guy stayed. In all, six of the young men left the scene, while seven others—six seniors and one junior—remained in the basement. All of them were 17 or 18 years old.

As the girl was forced to continue giving oral sex to the boy, the other boys laughed, yelled encouragement to their friends, and derisively shouted, "You whore!" One guy got a baseball bat, which he forced into her vagina. As he did this (and followed with a broom handle), the girl heard one boy say, "Stop. You're hurting her." But another voice chimed in, "Do it more."

Later, the girl remembered that the boys were all laughing, while she was crying. When they finished, they warned her not to tell anyone and she left the house. The event concluded with an athletic ritual of togetherness as the boys stood in a circle, clasping "one hand on top of the other," Lefkowtiz writes, "all their hands together, like a basketball team on the sidelines at the end of a time-out."

95 In the eyes of their friends, their parents, and their community, these guys were not pathological deviants. They were all high-status athletes, well respected in their schools and in their communities. They were not crazed psychotics, they were regular guys. Our guys.

So, too, were the football players at Wellington C. Mepham High School, a well-funded, well-heeled high school in a relatively affluent Long Island neighborhood, who participated in another extreme example. When students returned from vacation in the fall of 2004, they were confronted by rumors of a terrifying hazing incident that had taken place during the summer. While away at a training camp in Pennsylvania in August, three varsity members of Mepham's football team sexually abused three young teammates in a hazing ritual. According to the police report, the boys were sodomized with pine cones, broom handles, and golf balls, all of which had been coated with Mineral Ice, a Ben-Gay–like cream that produces intense menthol-induced coolness, and is typically used to treat sore muscles. When applied to moist or broken skin, or used internally, it causes severe pain. Thirteen other players watched, but did nothing.

Once again, the perpetrators were respected members of the community—good boys, Boy Scouts, pillars of the tight-knit community. Just regular guys.

When I've described the sexual assaults in Glen Ridge to young men around the country, they instantly and steadfastly agree: those guys who actually did it are thugs, and their behavior is indefensible. "C'mon, man," said one, "they should be charged with criminal assault and go to jail. QED." And they show equal contempt for the guys who stayed, watched, and did nothing. "What is up with that?" another said. "It's just wrong."

When we consider the guys who left, many of the guys I've spoken with assure me that they too would have left at the first sign of the assault. Self-congratulation comes easily and quickly. "No way am I staying there," one guy said. "At the first sign of trouble, I'm gone," said another. Other guys readily agree. All seem to identify with the guys who left, who refused to participate. And they're all feeling pretty good about it until a female student invariably asks, "Yeah, but did they call the police? Did they tell anybody?"

100   No. No one called the police. No one told a teacher or an administrator. No one told their parents. No one told *anybody*.

And the next day, *everyone* at Glen Ridge High School knew what had happened. Everyone knew, that is, that a bunch of guys had "had sex with" that particular girl and other guys had watched. And she let them! And that next day not one student told their parents, their teachers, their administrators. Not one student—male or female—called the police to report the assault.

In fact, it wasn't until two weeks later that the girl herself finally told her parents what had happened to her, and why she was crying all the time, unable to sleep and eat, and why she was so bruised and sore "down there."

In the Mepham case, the assault was perpetrated by three guys while thirteen other players watched. They did not intervene to stop this cruel and horrific assault on their teammates. They did not tell the coaches, their parents, school administrators, or the police. They did nothing. "Of course, we heard about it instantly," one Mepham graduate told me. "Everybody did. Man, it was like the only thing everyone was talking about the next day. 'Hey, did you hear what went down at the football camp?'"

It's those *other* guys who illustrate the second cultural dynamic of Guyland—the *culture of silence*. And not only did none of the bystanders in Glen Ridge or Mepham intervene, but none told a parent or a teacher, or reported the assault to the police. As the case played out in Glen Ridge for six whole years the guys consistently refused to "turn" on their friends and provide incriminating evidence.

105   The motto of Guyland is "Bros Before Hos." One remains steadfastly loyal to your guy friends, your bros, and one never even considers siding with women, the hos, against a brother. It is the guys to whom your primary allegiance must always be offered, and for many that may even extend to abetting a crime. Anything less is a betrayal of Guyland.

No one is immune to the culture of silence. Every single kid is culpable. If you still don't think this has anything to do with you, ask yourself what you would have done. If you think this has nothing to do with your son, ask him what he would do if he heard about such a thing. Then ask him when was the last time he actually *did* hear about such a thing.

The culture of silence is the culture of complicity. The bystanders may think that they withdraw their support—by turning away, leaving the scene, or just standing stoically by—but their silence reinforces the behaviors anyway. It's as strong an unwritten code as the police department's famed "blue wall of silence," or the Mafia's infamous rule of "omerta," or the secret rituals of the Masons. Breaking the silence is treason, worse, perhaps, than the activities themselves.

The relationship between perpetrators and bystanders is crucial in Guyland. Peer loyalty shields the perpetrators, and helps us explain the question of numbers. Despite the fact that the overwhelming majority of guys do not sexually assault their teammates, gang rape college women at fraternity parties, or indulge in acts of unspeakable cruelty, they also do nothing to stop it.

Most bystanders are relatively decent guys. But they are anything but "innocent." The bystander comforts himself with the illusion "this isn't about me. I've never bullied anyone." This is similar to the reaction of white people when confronted with discussions of racism or sexism on campus. "It's not about me! My family didn't own slaves." Or "I never raped anyone. These discussions about sexual violence are not about me."

110   It *is* about them. The perpetrators could not do what they do without the amoral avoidance and silence of the bystanders. In a way, the violence is done *for* them—and so it is most definitely *about* them.

When the story about the Mepham football hazing broke, and the national media descended on sleepy Bellmore, Long Island, the community reacted as one—it defended the players and the coaches who denied any responsibility. Parents of the boys who had been abused were threatened with death if they pressed charges. "It's simple," read one letter to a victim's parents. "Keep your mouth shut and nothing will happen to your family." Campus rallies were held for the team, both the coaches and the players.

When the school administration took the drastic (and courageous) step of canceling the entire football season, Mepham students felt that *they* had been victimized by an overzealous superintendent. "I don't see why we should all be penalized for the actions of a few football players," commented one girl.

Not everyone participates in this culture of protection, of course. Recall the case of Spur Posse a few years ago. The Southern California clique of young men kept tallies of the girls they had had sex with (many of the girls, some as young as 11, had been coerced). When the boys were exposed as sexual predators and rapists, their fathers seemed almost proud. "That's my boy!" said one. "If these girls are going to give it away, my boy is going to take it," said another. The mothers, however, were surprised, even shocked. They wanted to talk to their sons, find out how such a thing was possible. So the culture of protection is not uniform; there are gender gaps—and these gaps between mothers and fathers will form a crucial part of our discussion of what we, as a society, can do to make Guyland a more hospitable place.

The Guy Code keeps young men from venturing beyond the borders of Guyland. The good guys are silenced and the predators and bullies are encouraged. What we need, of course, is exactly the reverse—to empower the silent guys to disable the predators, to facilitate young men's entry into an adulthood propelled by both energy and ethics, and animated by both courage and compassion.

CRSOCRSOCRSO

115   Now that we have a sense of the philosophical principles that underlie Guyland, we need to see the way the Guy Code operates in the lives of young men in America today. The next few chapters will explore the spaces they call home much as an anthropologist might explore a different culture—examining its terrain, its economy, its rites and rituals, its belief systems and cultural practices, and the behaviors and attitudes that support and sustain it.

Credit ——————————————————————————————————
Ch. 3. "Bros Before Hos: The Guy Code" pp. 44–69 from *Guyland: The Perilous World Where Boys Become Men* by Michael Kimmel. Copyright © 2008 by Michael Kimmel. Reprinted by permission of HarperCollins Publishers.

Girl

JAMAICA KINCAID

Wash the white clothes on Monday and put them on the stone heap; wash the
color clothes on Tuesday and put them on the clothesline to dry; don't walk
barehead in the hot sun; cook pumpkin fritters in very hot sweet oil; soak your
little cloths right after you take them off; when buying cotton to make yourself
a nice blouse, be sure that it doesn't have gum on it, because that way it won't
hold up well after a wash; soak salt fish overnight before you cook it; is it true
that you sing benna in Sunday school?; always eat your food in such a way
that it won't turn someone else's stomach; on Sundays try to walk like a lady
and not like the slut you are so bent on becoming; don't sing benna in Sunday
school; you mustn't speak to wharf-rat boys, not even to give directions; don't
eat fruits on the street—flies will follow you; *but I don't sing benna on Sundays
at all and never in Sunday school;* this is how to sew on a button; this is how to
make a button-hole for the button you have just sewed on; this is how to hem
a dress when you see the hem coming down and so to prevent yourself from
looking like the slut I know you are so bent on becoming; this is how you iron
your father's khaki shirt so that it doesn't have a crease; this is how you iron
your father's khaki pants so that they don't have a crease; this is how you grow
okra—far from the house, because okra tree harbors red ants; when you are
growing dasheen, make sure it gets plenty of water or else it makes your throat
itch when you are eating it; this is how you sweep a corner; this is how you
sweep a whole house; this is how you sweep a yard; this is how you smile to
someone you don't like too much; this is how you smile to someone you don't
like at all; this is how you smile to someone you like completely; this is how
you set a table for tea; this is how you set a table for dinner; this is how you set
a table for dinner with an important guest; this is how you set a table for lunch;
this is how you set a table for breakfast; this is how to behave in the presence
of men who don't know you very well, and this way they won't recognize
immediately the slut I have warned you against becoming; be sure to wash
every day, even if it is with your own spit; don't squat down to play marbles—
you are not a boy, you know; don't pick people's flowers—you might catch
something; don't throw stones at blackbirds, because it might not be a blackbird
at all; this is how to make a bread pudding; this is how to make doukona; this is
how to make pepper pot; this is how to make a good medicine for a cold; this is
how to make a good medicine to throw away a child before it even becomes a
child; this is how to catch a fish; this is how to throw back a fish you don't like,

and that way something bad won't fall on you; this is how to bully a man; this is how a man bullies you; this is how to love a man; and if this doesn't work there are other ways, and if they don't work don't feel too bad about giving up; this is how to spit up in the air if you feel like it, and this is how to move quick so that it doesn't fall on you; this is how to make ends meet; always squeeze bread to make sure it's fresh; *but what if the baker won't let me feel the bread?;* you mean to say that after all you are really going to be the kind of woman who the baker won't let near the bread?

Credit ——
Reprinted with the permission from Jamaica Kincaid/*The New Yorker;* © by Conde Nast.

Learning to Read

MALCOLM X

It was because of my letters that I happened to stumble upon starting to acquire some kind of a homemade education.

I became increasingly frustrated at not being able to express what I wanted to convey in letters that I wrote, especially those to Mr. Elijah Muhammad. In the street, I had been the most articulate hustler out there—I had commanded attention when I said something. But now, trying to write simple English, I not only wasn't articulate, I wasn't even functional. How would I sound writing in slang, the way I would *say* it, something such as, "Look, daddy, let me pull your coat about a cat, Elijah Muhammad—"

Many who today hear me somewhere in person, or on television, or those who read something I've said, will think I went to school far beyond the eighth grade. This impression is due entirely to my prison studies.

It had really begun back in the Charlestown Prison, when Bimbi first made me feel envy of his stock of knowledge. Bimbi had always taken charge of any conversations he was in, and I had tried to emulate him. But every book I picked up had few sentences which didn't contain anywhere from one to nearly all of the words that might as well have been in Chinese. When I just skipped those words, of course, I really ended up with little idea of what the book said. So I had come to the Norfolk Prison Colony still going through only book-reading motions. Pretty soon, I would have quit even these motions, unless I had received the motivation that I did.

5   I saw that the best thing I could do was get hold of a dictionary—to study, to learn some words. I was lucky enough to reason also that I should try to improve my penmanship. It was sad. I couldn't even write in a straight line. It was both ideas together that moved me to request a dictionary along with some tablets and pencils from the Norfolk Prison Colony school.

I spent two days just riffling uncertainly through the dictionary's pages. I'd never realized so many words existed! I didn't know *which* words I needed to learn. Finally, just to start some kind of action, I began copying.

In my slow, painstaking, ragged handwriting, I copied into my tablet everything printed on that first page, down to the punctuation marks.

I believe it took me a day. Then, aloud, I read back, to myself, everything I'd written on the tablet. Over and over, aloud, to myself, I read my own handwriting.

I woke up the next morning, thinking about those words—immensely proud to realize that not only had I written so much at one time, but I'd written words that I never knew were in the world. Moreover, with a little effort, I also could remember what many of these words meant. I reviewed the words whose meanings I didn't remember. Funny thing, from the dictionary first page right now, that "aardvark" springs to my mind. The dictionary had a picture of it, a longtailed, long-eared, burrowing African mammal, which lives off termites caught by sticking out its tongue as an anteater does for ants.

10   I was so fascinated that I went on—I copied the dictionary's next page. And the same experience came when I studied that. With every succeeding page, I also learned of people and places and events from history. Actually the dictionary is like a miniature encyclopedia. Finally the dictionary's A section had filled a whole tablet—and I went on into the B's. That was the way I started copying what eventually became the entire dictionary. It went a lot faster after so much practice helped me to pick up handwriting speed. Between what I wrote in my tablet, and writing letters, during the rest of my time in prison I would guess I wrote a million words.

I suppose it was inevitable that as my word-base broadened, I could for the first time pick up a book and read and now begin to understand what the book was saying. Anyone who has read a great deal can imagine the new world that opened. Let me tell you something: from then until I left that prison, in every free moment I had, if I was not reading in the library, I was reading on my bunk. You couldn't have gotten me out of books with a wedge. Between Mr. Muhammad's teachings, my correspondence, my visitors, … and my reading of books, months passed without my even thinking about being imprisoned. In fact, up to then, I never had been so truly free in my life.

The Norfolk Prison Colony's library was in the school building. A variety of classes was taught there by instructors who came from such places as Harvard and Boston universities. The weekly debates between inmate teams were also held in the school building. You would be astonished to know how worked up convict debaters and audiences would get over subjects like "Should Babies Be Fed Milk?"

Available on the prison library's shelves were books on just about every general subject. Much of the big private collection that Parkhurst[1] had willed to the prison was still in crates and boxes in the back of the library—thousands of old books. Some of them looked ancient: covers faded, oldtime parchment-looking binding. Parkhurst … seemed to have been principally interested in history and religion. He had the money and the special interest to have a lot of books that you wouldn't have in a general circulation. Any college library would have been lucky to get that collection.

As you can imagine, especially in a prison where there was heavy emphasis on rehabilitation, an inmate was smiled upon if he demonstrated an unusually intense interest in books. There was a sizable number of well-read inmates, especially the popular debaters. Some were said by many to be practically walking encyclopedias. They were almost celebrities. No university would ask any student to devour literature as I did when this new world opened to me, of being able to read and *understand.*

15   I read more in my room than in the library itself. An inmate who was known to read a lot could check out more than the permitted maximum number of books. I preferred reading in the total isolation of my own room.

When I had progressed to really serious reading, every night at about ten P.M. I would be outraged with the "lights out." It always seemed to catch me right in the middle of something engrossing.

Fortunately, right outside my door was a corridor light that cast a glow into my room. The glow was enough to read by, once my eyes adjusted to it. So when "lights out" came, I would sit on the floor where I could continue reading in that glow.

At one-hour intervals at night guards paced past every room. Each time I heard the approaching footsteps, I jumped into bed and feigned sleep. And as soon as the guard passed, I got back out of bed onto the floor area of that light-glow, where I would read for another fifty-eight minutes until the guard approached again. That went on until three or four every morning. Three or four hours of sleep a night was enough for me. Often in the years in the streets I had slept less than that.

The teachings of Mr. Muhammad stressed how history had been "whitened"— when white men had written history books, the black man simply had been left out. Mr. Muhammad couldn't have said anything that would have struck me much harder. I had never forgotten how when my class, me and all of those whites, had studied seventh-grade United States history back in Mason, the history of the Negro had been covered in one paragraph, and the teacher had gotten a big laugh with his joke, "'Negroes' feet are so big that when they walk, they leave a hole in the ground."

20   This is one reason why Mr. Muhammad's teachings spread so swiftly all over the United States, among *all* Negroes, whether or not they became followers of Mr. Muhammad. The teachings ring true—to every Negro. You can hardly

show me a black adult in America—or a white one, for that matter—who knows from the history books anything like the truth about the black man's role. In my own case, once I heard of the "glorious history of the black man," I took special pains to hunt in the library for books that would inform me on details about black history.

I can remember accurately the very first set of books that really impressed me. I have since bought that set of books and I have it at home for my children to read as they grow up. It's called *Wonders of the World*. It's full of pictures of archeological finds, statues that depict, usually, non-European people.

I found books like Will Durant's *Story of Civilization*. I read H. G. Wells' *Outline of History*. *Souls of Black Folk* by W. E. B. Du Bois gave me a glimpse into the black people's history before they came to this country. Carter G. Woodson's *Negro History* opened my eyes about black empires before the black slave was brought to the United States, and the early Negro struggles for freedom.

J. A. Rogers' three volumes of *Sex and Race* told about race-mixing before Christ's time; and Aesop being a black man who told fables; about Egypt's Pharaohs; about the great Coptic Christian Empire;[2] about Ethiopia, the earth's oldest continuous black civilization, as China is the oldest continuous civilization.

Mr. Muhammad's teaching about how the white man had been created led me to *Findings in Genetics,* by Gregor Mendel. (The dictionary's G section was where I had learned what "genetics" meant.) I really studied this book by the Austrian monk. Reading it over and over, especially certain sections, helped me to understand that if you started with a black man, a white man could be produced; but starting with a white man, you never could produce a black man—because the white chromosome is recessive. And since no one disputes that there was but one Original Man, the conclusion is clear.

25   During the last year or so, in the *New York Times,* Arnold Toynbee used the word "bleached" in describing the white man. His words were: "White (i.e., bleached) human beings of North European origin …" Toynbee also referred to the European geographic area as only a peninsula of Asia. He said there was no such thing as Europe. And if you look at the globe, you will see for yourself that America is only an extension of Asia. (But at the same time Toynbee is among those who have helped to bleach history. He has written that Africa was the only continent that produced no history. He won't write that again. Every day now, the truth is coming to light.)

I never will forget how shocked I was when I began reading about slavery's total horror. It made such an impact upon me that it later became one of my favorite subjects when I became a minister of Mr. Muhammad's. The world's most monstrous crime, the sin and the blood on the white man's hands, are almost impossible to believe. Books like the one by Frederick Olmsted opened my eyes to the horrors suffered when the slave was landed in the United States. The European woman, Fanny Kemble, who had married a Southern white slaveowner, described how human beings were degraded. Of course I read *Uncle Tom's Cabin*. In fact, I believe that's the only novel I have ever read since I started serious reading.

Parkhurst's collection also contained some bound pamphlets of the Abolitionist Anti-Slavery Society of New England. I read descriptions of atrocities, saw those illustrations of black slave women tied up and flogged with whips; of black mothers watching their babies being dragged off, never to be seen by their mothers again; of dogs after slaves, and of the fugitive slave catchers, evil white men with whips and clubs and chains and guns. I read about the slave preacher Nat Turner, who put the fear of God into the white slave master. Nat Turner wasn't going around preaching pie-in-the-sky and "non-violent" freedom for the black man. There in Virginia one night in 1831, Nat and seven other slaves started out at his master's home and through the night they went from one plantation "big house" to the next, killing, until by the next morning 57 white people were dead and Nat had about 70 slaves following him. White people, terrified for their lives, fled from their homes, locked themselves up in public buildings, hid in the woods, and some even left the state. A small army of soldiers took two months to catch and hang Nat Turner. Somewhere I have read where Nat Turner's example is said to have inspired John Brown to invade Virginia and attack Harpers Ferry nearly thirty years later, with thirteen white men and five Negroes.

I read Herodotus, "the father of History," or, rather, I read about him. And I read the histories of various nations, which opened my eyes gradually, then wider and wider, to how the whole world's white men had indeed acted like devils, pillaging and raping and bleeding and draining the whole world's non-white people. I remember, for instance, books such as Will Durant's *The Story of Oriental Civilization,* and Mahatma Gandhi's accounts of the struggle to drive the British out of India.

Book after book showed me how the white man had brought upon the world's black, brown, red, and yellow peoples every variety of the suffering of exploitation. I saw how since the sixteenth century, the so-called "Christian trader" white man began to ply the seas in his lust for Asian and African empires, and plunder, and power. I read, I saw, how the white man never has gone among the non-white peoples bearing the Cross in the true manner and spirit of Christ's teachings—meek, humble, and Christlike.

30   I perceived, as I read, how the collective white man had been actually nothing but a piratical opportunist who used Faustian machinations[3] to make his own Christianity his initial wedge in criminal conquests. First, always "religiously," he branded "heathen" and "pagan" labels upon ancient non-white cultures and civilizations. The stage thus set, he then turned upon his non-white victims his weapons of war.

I read how, entering India—half a *billion* deeply religious brown people—the British white man, by 1759, through promises, trickery, and manipulations, controlled much of India through Great Britain's East India Company. The parasitical British administration kept tentacling out to half of the sub-continent. In 1857, some of the desperate people of India finally mutinied—and, excepting the African slave trade, nowhere has history recorded any more unnecessary bestial and ruthless human carnage than the British suppression of the non-white Indian people.

Over 115 million African blacks—close to the 1930's population of the United States—were murdered or enslaved during the slave trade. And I read how when the slave market was glutted, the cannibalistic white powers of Europe next carved up, as their colonies, the richest areas of the black continent. And Europe's chancelleries for the next century played a chess game of naked exploitation and power from Cape Horn to Cairo.

Ten guards and the warden couldn't have torn me out of those books. Not even Elijah Muhammad could have been more eloquent than those books were in providing indisputable proof that the collective white man had acted like a devil in virtually every contact he had with the world's collective non-white man. I listen today to the radio, and watch television, and read the headlines about the collective white man's fear and tension concerning China. When the white man professes ignorance about why the Chinese hate him so, my mind can't help flashing back to what I read, there in prison, about how the blood forebears of this same white man raped China at a time when China was trusting and helpless. Those original white "Christian traders" sent into China millions of pounds of opium. By 1839, so many of the Chinese were addicts that China's desperate government destroyed twenty thousand chests of opium. The first Opium war[4] was promptly declared by the white man. Imagine! Declaring *war* upon someone who objects to being narcotized! The Chinese were severely beaten, with Chinese-invented gunpowder.

The Treaty of Nanking made China pay the British white man for the destroyed opium; forced open China's major ports to British trade; forced China to abandon Hong Kong; fixed China's import tariffs so low that cheap British articles soon flooded in, maiming China's industrial development.

35   After a second Opium War, the Tientsin Treaties legalized the ravaging opium trade, legalized a British-French-American control of China's customs. China tried delaying that Treaty's ratification; Peking was looted and burned.

"Kill the foreign white devils!" was the 1901 Chinese war cry in the Boxer Rebellion.[5] Losing again, this time the Chinese were driven from Peking's choicest areas. The vicious, arrogant white man put up the famous signs, "Chinese and dogs not allowed."

Red China after World War II closed its doors to the Western white world. Massive Chinese agricultural, scientific, and industrial efforts are described in a book that *Life* magazine recently published. Some observers inside Red China have reported that the world never has known such a hate-white campaign as is now going on in this non-white country where, present birth-rates continuing, in fifty more years Chinese will be half the earth's population. And it seems that some Chinese chickens will soon come home to roost, with China's recent successful nuclear tests.

Let us face reality. We can see in the United Nations a new world order being shaped, along color lines—an alliance among the non-white nations. America's U.N. Ambassador Adlai Stevenson complained not long ago that in the United Nations "a skin game" was being played. He was right. He was facing reality. A "skin game" is being played. But Ambassador Stevenson sounded like Jesse James accusing the marshal of carrying a gun. Because who in the world's history ever has played a worse "skin game" than the white man?

Mr. Muhammad, to whom I was writing daily, had no idea of what a new world had opened up to me through my efforts to document his teachings in books.

40   When I discovered philosophy, I tried to touch all the landmarks of philosophical development. Gradually, I read most of the old philosophers, Occidental and Oriental. The Oriental philosophers were the ones I came to prefer; finally, my impression was that most Occidental philosophy had largely been borrowed from the Oriental thinkers. Socrates, for instance, traveled in Egypt. Some sources even say that Socrates was initiated into some of the Egyptian mysteries. Obviously Socrates got some of his wisdom among the East's wise men.

I have often reflected upon the new vistas that reading opened to me. I knew right there in prison that reading had changed forever the course of my life.

As I see it today, the ability to read awoke inside me some long dormant craving to be mentally alive. I certainly wasn't seeking any degree, the way a college confers a status symbol upon its students. My homemade education gave me, with every additional book that I read, a little bit more sensitivity to the deafness, dumbness, and blindness that was afflicting the black race in America. Not long ago, an English writer telephoned me from London, asking questions. One was, "What's your alma mater?" I told him, "Books." You will never catch me with a free fifteen minutes in which I'm not studying something I feel might be able to help the black man.

Yesterday I spoke in London, and both ways on the plane across the Atlantic I was studying a document about how the United Nations proposes to insure the human rights of the oppressed minorities of the world. The American black man is the world's most shameful case of minority oppression. What makes the black man think of himself as only an internal United States issue is just a catch-phrase, two words, "civil rights." How is the black man going to get "civil rights" before first he wins his *human* rights? If the American black man will start thinking about his *human* rights, and then start thinking of himself as part of one of the world's great peoples, he will see he has a case for the United Nations.

I can't think of a better case! Four hundred years of black blood and sweat invested here in America, and the white man still has the black man begging for what every immigrant fresh off the ship can take for granted the minute he walks down the gangplank.

But I'm digressing. I told the Englishman that my alma mater was books, a good library. Every time I catch a plane, I have with me a book that I want to read—and that's a lot of books these days. If I weren't out here every day battling the white man, I could spend the rest of my life reading, just satisfying my curiosity—because you can hardly mention anything I'm not curious about. I don't think anybody ever got more out of going to prison than I did. In fact, prison enabled me to study far more intensively than I would have if my life had gone differently and I had attended some college. I imagine that one of the biggest troubles with colleges is there are too many distractions, too much panty-raiding, fraternities, and boola-boola and all of that. Where else but in a prison could I have attacked my ignorance by being able to study intensely sometimes as much as fifteen hours a day?

Credit

Reading Games:
Strategies for Reading Scholarly Sources

KAREN ROSENBERG

If at First You Fall Asleep ...

During my first year in college, I feared many things: calculus, cafeteria food, the stained, sweet smelling mattress in the basement of my dorm.* But I did not fear reading. I didn't really think about reading at all, that automatic making of meaning from symbols in books, newspapers, on cereal boxes. And, indeed, some of my coziest memories of that bewildering first year involved reading. I adopted an overstuffed red chair in the library that enveloped me like the lap of a department store Santa. I curled up many evenings during that first, brilliant autumn with my English homework: Toni Morrison's *The Bluest Eye,* Gloria Naylor's *Mama Day*, Sandra Cisneros' *The House on Mango Street.* I'd read a gorgeous passage, snuggle deeper into my chair, and glance out to the sunset and fall leaves outside of the library window. This felt deeply, unmistakably collegiate.

But English was a requirement—I planned to major in political science. I took an intro course my first semester and brought my readings to that same chair. I curled up, opened a book on the Chinese Revolution, started reading, and fell asleep. I woke up a little drooly, surprised at the harsh fluorescent light, the sudden pitch outside. Not to be deterred, I bit my lip and started over. I'd hold on for a paragraph or two, and then suddenly I'd be thinking about my classmate Joel's elbows, the casual way he'd put them on the desk when our professor lectured, sometimes resting his chin in his hands. He was a long limbed runner and smelled scrubbed—a mixture of laundry detergent and shampoo. He had black hair and startling blue eyes. Did I find him sexy?

Crap! How many paragraphs had my eyes grazed over while I was thinking about Joel's stupid elbows? By the end of that first semester, I abandoned ideas of majoring in political science. I vacillated between intense irritation with my assigned readings and a sneaking suspicion that perhaps the problem was me—I was too dumb to read academic texts. Whichever it was—a problem with the readings or with me—I carefully chose my classes so that I could read novels, poetry, and plays for credit. But even in my English classes, I discovered, I had to read dense scholarly articles. By my Junior year, I trained myself to spend days from dawn until dusk hunkered over a carrel in the library's basement armed with a dictionary and a rainbow of highlighters. Enjoying my reading seemed hopelessly naïve—an indulgence best reserved for beach blankets and bathtubs. A combination of obstinacy, butt-numbingly hard chairs, and caffeine helped me survive my scholarly reading assignments. But it wasn't fun.

Seven years later I entered graduate school. I was also working and living on my own, cooking for myself instead of eating off cafeteria trays. In short, I had a life. My days were not the blank canvas they had been when I was an undergraduate and could sequester myself in the dungeon of the library basement. And so, I finally learned how to read smarter, not harder. Perhaps the strangest part of my reading transformation was that I came to *like* reading those dense scholarly articles; I came to crave the process of sucking the marrow from the texts. If you can relate to this, if you also love wrestling with academic journal articles, take joy in arguing with authors in the margins of the page, I am not writing for you.

5   However, if your reading assignments confound you, if they send you into slumber, or you avoid them, or they seem to take you *way* too long, then pay attention. Based on my experience as a frustrated student and now as a teacher of reading strategies, I have some insights to share with you designed to make the reading process more productive, more interesting, and more enjoyable.

Joining the Conversation[1]

Even though it may seem like a solitary, isolated activity, when you read a scholarly work, you are participating in a conversation. Academic writers do not make up their arguments off the top of their heads (or solely from creative inspiration). Rather, they look at how others have approached similar issues and problems. Your job—and one for which you'll get plenty of help from your professors and your peers—is to locate the writer and yourself in this larger conversation. Reading academic texts is a deeply social activity; talking with your professors and peers about texts can not only help you understand your readings better, but it can push your thinking and clarify your own stances on issues that really matter to you.

In your college courses, you may have come across the term "rhetorical reading."[2] Rhetoric in this context refers to how texts work to persuade readers—a bit different from the common connotation of empty, misleading, or puffed up speech. Rhetorical reading refers to a set of practices designed to help us understand how texts work and to engage more deeply and fully in a conversation that extends beyond the boundaries of any particular reading. Rhetorical reading practices ask us to think deliberately about the role and relationship between the writer, reader, and text.

When thinking about the writer, we are particularly interested in clues about the writer's motivation and agenda. If we know something about what the writer cares about and is trying to accomplish, it can help orient us to the reading and understand some of the choices the writer makes in his or her work.

As readers, our role is quite active. We pay attention to our own motivation and agenda for each reading. On one level, our motivation may be as simple as wanting to do well in a class, and our agenda may involve wanting to understand as much as necessary in order to complete our assignments. In order to meet these goals, we need to go deeper, asking, "Why is my professor asking me to read this piece?" You may find clues in your course syllabus, comments your professor makes in class, or comments from your classmates. If you aren't sure why you are being asked to read something, ask! Most professors will be more than happy to discuss in general terms what "work" they want a reading to do—for example, to introduce you to a set of debates, to provide information on a specific topic, or to challenge conventional thinking on an issue.

10   Finally, there is the text—the thing that the writer wrote and that you are reading. In addition to figuring out *what* the text says, rhetorical reading strategies ask us to focus on *how* the text delivers its message. In this way of thinking about texts, there is not one right and perfect meaning for the diligent reader to uncover; rather, interpretations of the reading will differ depending on the questions and contexts readers bring to the text.

Strategies for Rhetorical Reading

Here are some ways to approach your reading that better equip you for the larger conversation. First, consider the **audience.** When the writer sat down to write your assigned reading, to whom was he or she implicitly talking? Textbooks, for the most part, have students like you in mind. They may be boring, but you've probably learned what to do with them: pay attention to the goals of the chapter, check out the summary at the end, ignore the text in the boxes because it's usually more of a "fun fact" than something that will be on the test, and so on. Magazines in the checkout line at the supermarket also have you in mind: you can't help but notice headlines about who is cheating or fat or anorexic or suicidal. Writers of scholarly sources, on the other hand, likely don't think much about you at all when they sit down to write. Often, academics write primarily for other academics. But just because it's people with PhDs writing for other people with PhDs doesn't mean that you should throw in the towel. There's a formula for these types of texts, just like there's a formula for all the *Cosmo* articles that beckon with titles that involve the words "hot," "sex tips," "your man," and "naughty" in different configurations.

It's just that the formula is a little more complicated.

The formula also changes depending on the flavor of study (physics, management, sociology, English, etc.) and the venue. However, if you determine that the audience for your reading is other academics, recognize that you are in foreign territory. You won't understand all of the chatter you hear on street corners, you may not be able to read the menus in the restaurants, but, with a little practice, you will be able to find and understand the major road signs, go in the right direction, and find your way.

How can you figure out the primary audience? First, look at the publication venue. (Here, to some extent, you can judge a book by its cover). If the reading comes from an academic journal, then chances are good that the primary audience is other academics. Clues that a journal is academic (as opposed to popular, like *Time* or *Newsweek*) include a citation format that refers to a volume number and an issue number, and often this information appears at the top or bottom of every page. Sometimes you can tell if a reading comes from an academic journal based on the title—e.g., do the *Journal for Research in Mathematics Education* or *Qualitative Research in Psychology* sound like they are written for a popular audience? What if you're still not sure? Ask your reference librarians, classmates, your instructor, or friends and family who have more experience with these types of readings than you do.

15   There are two implications that you should be aware of if you are not the primary audience for a text. First, the author will assume prior knowledge that you likely don't have. You can expect sentences like "as Durkheim has so famously argued ..." or "much ink has been spilled on the implications of the modernization hypothesis" where you have no idea who Durkheim is or what the modernization hypothesis says. That's OK. It might even be OK to not look these things up at all and still get what you need from the reading (but you won't know that yet). In the first reading of an article, it's smart to hold off on looking too many things up. Just be prepared to face a wall of references that don't mean a whole lot to you.

Second, if you're not the primary audience, don't be surprised if you find that the writing isn't appealing to you. Whereas a novelist or a magazine writer works hard to draw us in as readers, many academic authors don't use strategies to keep us hooked. In fact, many of these strategies (use of sensory language, suspense, etc.) would never get published in academic venues. By the same token, you'll use very different strategies to read these scholarly texts.

You may be wondering, if you're not the intended audience for the text, why do you have to read it in the first place? This is an excellent question, and one that you need to answer before you do your reading. As I mentioned earlier in the discussion of the role of the reader, you may need to do a little sleuthing to figure this out. In addition to the suggestions I provided earlier, look to your course notes and syllabus for answers. Often professors will tell you why they assign specific readings. Pay attention—they will likely offer insights on the context of the reading and the most important points. If after all of this, you still have no idea why you're supposed to read six articles on the history of Newtonian physics, then ask your professor. Use the answers to help you focus on the really important aspects of the texts and to gloss over the parts that are less relevant to your coursework. If you remain confused, continue to ask for clarification. Ask questions in class (your classmates will be grateful). Go to office hours. Most faculty love the opportunity to talk about readings that they have chosen with care.

Once you have an idea who the intended audience is for the article and why you are assigned to read it, don't sit down and read the article from start to finish, like a good mystery. Get a lay of the land before you go too deep. One way to do this is to study the architecture of the article. Here are some key components to look for:

The title. As obvious as it sounds, pay attention to the title because it can convey a lot of information that can help you figure out how to read the rest of the article more efficiently. Let's say that I know my reading will be about the Russian Revolution. Let's say I even know that it will be about the role of music in the Russian Revolution. Let's say the title is "'Like the beating of my heart': A discourse analysis of Muscovite musicians' letters during the Russian Revolution." This tells me not only the subject matter of the article (something about letters Russian musicians wrote during the Revolution) but it also tells me something about the methodology, or the way that the author approaches the subject matter. I might not know exactly what discourse analysis is, but I can guess that you can do it to letters and that I should pay particular attention to it when the author mentions it in the article. On the other hand, if the title of the article were "Garbage cans and metal pipes: Bolshevik music and the politics of proletariat propaganda" I would know to look out for very different words and concepts. Note, also, that the convention within some academic disciplines to have a pretty long title separated by a colon usually follows a predictable pattern. The text to the left of the colon serves as a teaser, or as something to grab a reader's attention (remember that the author is likely not trying to grab your attention, so you may not find these teasers particularly effective—though it is probably packed with phrases that would entice someone who already studies the topic). The information to the right of the colon typically is a more straightforward explanation of what the article is about.

20   **The abstract.** Not all of your readings will come with abstracts, but when they do, pay close attention. An abstract is like an executive summary. Usually one paragraph at the beginning of an article, the abstract serves to encapsulate the main points of the article. It's generally a pretty specialized summary that seeks to answer specific questions. These include: the main problem or question, the approach (how did the author(s) do the work they write about in the article?), the shiny new thing that this article does (more on this later, but to be published in an academic journal you often need to argue that you are doing something that has not been done before), and why people who are already invested in this field should care (in other words, you should be able to figure out why

another academic should find the article important). The abstract often appears in database searches, and helps scholars decide if they want to seek out the full article.

That's a whole lot to accomplish in one paragraph.

As a result, authors often use specialized jargon to convey complex ideas in few words, make assumptions of prior knowledge, and don't worry much about general readability. Abstracts, thus, are generally dense, and it's not uncommon to read through an abstract and not have a clue about what you just read. This is a good place to re-read, highlight, underline, look up what you don't know. You still may not have a firm grasp on everything in the abstract, but treat the key terms in the abstract like parts of a map when you see them in the main text, leading you to treasure: understanding the main argument.

The introduction. The introduction serves some of the same functions as the abstract, but there is a lot more breathing room here. When I started reading academic texts, I'd breeze through the introduction to get to the "meat" of the text. This was exactly the wrong thing to do. I can't remember how many times I'd find myself in the middle of some dense reading, perhaps understanding the content of a particular paragraph, but completely unable to connect that paragraph with the overall structure of the article. I'd jump from the lily pad of one paragraph to the next, continually fearful that I'd slip off and lose myself in a sea of total confusion (and I often did slip).

If the author is doing her/his job well, the introduction will not only summarize the whole piece, present the main idea, and tell us why we should care, but it will also often offer a road map for the rest of the article. Sometimes, the introduction will be called "introduction," which makes things easy. Sometimes, it's not. Generally, treat the first section of an article as the introduction, regardless if it's explicitly called that or not.

25   There are times where your reading will have the introduction chopped off. This makes your work harder. The two most common instances of introduction-less readings are assigned excerpts of articles and lone book chapters. In the first case, you only have a portion of an article so you cannot take advantage of many of the context clues the writer set out for readers. You will need to rely more heavily on the context of your course in general and your assignment in particular to find your bearings here. If the reading is high stakes (e.g., if you have to write a paper or take an exam on it), you may want to ask your

professor how you can get the whole article. In the second case, your professor assigns a chapter or two from the middle of an academic book. The chapter will hopefully contain some introductory material (and generally will include much more than the middle of a journal article), but you will likely be missing some context clues that the author included in the introduction to the whole book. If you have trouble finding your footing here, and it's important that you grasp the meaning and significance of the chapter, seek out the book itself and skim the introductory chapter to ground you in the larger questions that the author is addressing. Oddly, even though you'll be doing more reading, it may save you time because you can read your assigned chapter(s) more efficiently.

Roadmaps included in the introduction are often surprisingly straightforward. They often are as simple as "in the first section, we examine … in the second section we argue …" etc. Search for these maps. Underline them. Highlight them. Go back to them when you find your comprehension slipping.

Section headings. A section heading serves as a title for a particular part of an article. Read all of these to get a sense of the trajectory of the text before delving into the content in each section (with the exception of the introduction and the conclusion which you should read in detail). Get a passing familiarity with the meanings of the words in the section headings—they are likely important to understanding the main argument of the text.

Conclusion. When writing papers, you've likely heard the cliché "in the introduction, write what you will say, then say it, then write what you just said." With this formula, it would seem logical to gloss over the conclusion, because, essentially, you've already read it already. However, this is not the case. Instead, pay close attention to the conclusion. It can help you make sure you understood the introduction. Sometimes a slight re-phrasing can help you understand the author's arguments in an important, new way. In addition, the conclusion is often where authors indicate the limitations of their work, the unanswered questions, the horizons left unexplored. And this is often the land of exam and essay questions … asking you to extend the author's analysis beyond its own shores.

At this point, you have pored over the title, the introduction, the section headings, and the conclusion. You haven't really read the body of the article yet. Your next step is to see if you can answer the question: what is the **main argument or idea** in this text?

30   Figuring out the main argument is *the* key to reading the text effectively
and efficiently. Once you can identify the main argument, you can determine
how much energy to spend on various parts of the reading. For example, if I
am drowning in details about the temperance movement in the United States
in the 19th Century, I need to know the main argument of the text to know
if I need to slow down or if a swift skim will do. If the main argument is that
women's organizing has taken different forms in different times, it will probably
be enough for me to understand that women organized against the sale and
consumption of alcohol. That might involve me looking up "temperance"
and getting the gist of women's organizing. However, if the main argument
were that scholars have misunderstood the role of upper class white women
in temperance organizing in Boston from 1840–1865, then I would probably
need to slow down and pay closer attention.

Unless the reading is billed as a review or a synthesis, the only way that
an academic text can even get published is if it claims to argue something
new or different. However, unlike laundry detergent or soft drinks, academic
articles don't advertise what makes them new and different in block letters
inside cartoon bubbles. In fact, finding the main argument can sometimes be
tricky. Mostly, though, it's just a matter of knowing where to look. The abstract
and the introduction are the best places to look first. With complicated texts,
do this work with your classmates, visit your campus writing center (many of
them help with reading assignments), or drag a friend into it.

Once you understand the different parts of the text and the writer's main
argument, use this information to see how and where you can enter the
conversation. In addition, keep your own agenda as a reader in mind as
you do this work.

Putting It All Together

Collectively, these suggestions and guidelines will help you read and understand
academic texts. They ask you to bring a great deal of awareness and preparation
to your reading—for example, figuring out who the primary audience is for the
text and, if you are not that audience, why your professor is asking you to read
it anyway. Then, instead of passively reading the text from start to finish, my
suggestions encourage you to pull the reading into its constituent parts—the
abstract, the introduction, the section headings, conclusion, etc.—and read
them unevenly and out of order to look for the holy grail of the main argument.
Once you have the main argument you can make wise decisions about which
parts of the text you need to pore over and which you can blithely skim. The
final key to reading smarter, not harder is to make it social. When you have

questions, ask. Start conversations with your professors about the reading. Ask your classmates to work with you to find the main arguments. Offer a hand to your peers who are drowning in dense details. Academics write to join scholarly conversations. Your professors assign you their texts so that you can join them too.

Works Cited

Norgaard, Rolf. *Composing Knowledge: Readings for College Writers*. Boston: Bedford/ St. Martin's, 2007. Print.

Rounsaville, Angela, Rachel Goldberg, Keith Feldman, Cathryn Cabral, and Anis Bawarshi, eds. *Situating Inquiry: An Introduction to Reading, Research, and Writing at the University of Washington*. Boston: Bedford/St. Martin's, 2008. Print.

Credit

Rosenberg, Karen. "Reading Games: Strategies for Reading Scholarly Sources." *Writing Spaces: Readings on Writing, Vol. 2*. Eds. Charles Lowe and Pavel Zemiliansky. Anderson, SC: Parlor Press, 2011. 210–220. Used with author's permission.

The Case

TIM SEIBLES

White people don't know they're white.

Newspaper. Coffee. Gosh-whataday!

Not everyone doesn't admire them. In fact,
a lot of people like their *time-for-the-news* TV voices.

It's not that they're not beautiful. Just check out a beach.
Oh, they're beautiful all right.

Sometimes though, if you're not white
and a lot of other people are—
but they don't know it:

Well, it can make you feel like you need to be somewhere
way far away.

And if you go to the supermarket and look
at the magazine racks you might start getting
that "uh-oh" feeling.

Most of the time you just laugh, that's all—you just
have to laugh and probably shake lots of hands.

Once a woman I worked with said
*I never even **think** of you as black.*

She was being un- pre- ju- diced.

You shouldn't get angry about stuff though.

I know some brothers, they see a white face
and their whole bodies sneer—

even if everything was going perfect that day, even
if the white face never did anything,
never said nothin'.

And then, of course, there are the Nazi-like skinheads
and the other etceteras

who wannabe all about whiteness—hating the gooks,
the spics, and all the geronimos et cetera.

Oh, they're white enough all right.

Credit

Tim Seibles, "The Case" from Hammerlock. Copyright © 1999 by Tim Seibles. Reprinted with the permission of The Permissions Company, Inc., on behalf of the Cleveland State University Poetry Center.

Queer Characters in Comic Strips

EDWARD H. SEWELL, JR.

"Gay and lesbian readers," Matthew Pustz says, "have felt that their experience has ... been marginalized by the [comics] industry, prompting the production of titles such as *Gay Comix, Dykes to Watch Out For,* and *Hothead Paisan, Homicidal Lesbian Terrorist* that might better speak to this audience" (Pustz, 1999, p. 101).

This chapter explores the role of queer[1] characters in comic strips found in both dominant mainstream newspapers and in alternative queer publications or on the Internet.[2] After a discussion of opposing points of view within critical/queer theory and the foundational arguments they suggest for our critique, a few examples of comic strips with queer characters from both mainstream dominant culture newspapers and from alternative queer sources are examined in light of a queer theory perspective.

Within the critical theory community, there is a less-than-friendly debate about what ideological approach can provide the best framework for reading, understanding, and interpreting queer texts (see for example Abelove, 1995; Dilley, 1999; Fuss, 1991; Gamson, 1995, 2000; Honeychurch, 1996; Jagose, 1996; Seidman, 1993, 1996; Slagle, 1995).

Seidman provides a simple explanation of the implications of a queer theory perspective:

5   Queer theory is suggesting that the study of homosexuality should not be a study of a minority—the making of the lesbian/gay/bisexual subject—but a study of those knowledges and social practices that organize "society" as a whole by sexualizing—heterosexualizing or homosexualizing—bodies, desires, acts, identities, social relationships, knowledges, culture, and social institutions. (Seidman, 1996, pp. 12–13)

Some critical scholars argue that the queer, while marginal in the dominant culture, can be tolerated in, if not openly accepted into, that culture. Many queer theory scholars argue, however, that toleration and marginalization are not acceptable goals or even options for queers. Abelove, based on the experiences self-identified queer students have shared in class, clearly presents the queer sense of "place" when he says:

... they [students who call themselves queer] do not typically experience their own subjectivity as marginal, even at those moments when they feel more oppressed by homophobic and heterosexist discourses and institutions.

> Marginalization isn't their preferred trope. It doesn't seem to them to be cogent as a narrative device for organizing the telling of their own lives or, for that matter, of their history. What these queers prefer to say and believe or try to believe instead is that they are both present and at the center. (Abelove, 1995, p. 48)

The popular "gay" slogan of the 1970s, "We are everywhere," contrasts with the 1990s slogan of Queer Nation, "We are here. We are queer. Get used to it."

"The queer movement," Slagle points out, "is unique in that it avoids essentialism on two separate levels. First, while liberationists have argued for years that gay men, lesbians, and bisexuals are essentially no different from heterosexuals, the new activists argue that queers are different but that marginalization is not justified on the basis of these differences. Second, queer activists avoid essentializing strategies within the movement itself." (Slagle, 1995, p. 87)

10   One important aspect of queer theory is the performative function of being queer. Halperin argues that performative functions of sexual identity are more related to a location of identity than abstract identity:

> [T]o come out is precisely to expose oneself to a different set of dangers and constraints, to make oneself into a convenient screen onto which straight people can project all the fantasies they routinely entertain about gay people … coming out puts into play a different set of political relations and alters the dynamics of personal and political struggle. *Coming out is an act of freedom, not in the sense of liberation but in the sense of resistance* [emphasis in the original]. (Halperin, 1995, p. 30)

While coming out is an event with major personal implications, being queer is primarily a performative function defining how the queer acts once s/he has decided to live their queerness in a straight world. This performative function is the most common focus of media treatments of the queer community as demonstrated by how queer guests are portrayed on television talk shows (Gamson, 1998) hosted by presumably straight hosts for dominant heterosexual audiences where only the extreme queer caricature is presented as normative.

The rift between assimilation into the dominant heterosexual culture and separation from it also is evident in the treatments of queer characters in mainstream newspaper comic strips and those run in alternative queer publications and on the Internet. Queer characters in mainstream comic strips are well integrated into heterosexual society in that they look and act "straight" before coming out as queer, and they look and act in a manner appropriate to the dominant heterosexual culture after coming out. They can quickly blend back into their pre-coming out comfortable context in which they may be "gay" and marginal, but still are quite acceptable to those with whom they must interact on a daily basis. There is no homophobic-induced harassment or violence, no offensive remarks about them being a "faggot," and no gay-bashing. They come out and fade back in rather quickly with no lasting consequences.

Lawrence Grossberg (1993, 1996) argues that cultural studies needs to move from essentialist models based on identity differences without separation to models based on articulation, singularity, and otherness. The logic of difference leads to negativity while the logic of otherness leads to positivity. Marginality is replaced by a sense of effectively belonging in which "agency involves relations of participation and access, the possibilities of moving into particular sites of activity and power, and of belonging to them in such a way as to be able to enact their powers" (Grossberg, 1996, p. 99). Thus, in terms of comic strips, rather than simply being different and marginal in a dominant social context, the queer character should be presented in a context that permits a sense of being unique and "other" from the dominant heterosexual culture. Queers need their own "space" in which they can acknowledge their own values, be authentic, and be powerful as individuals and not be simply seen as people with a variant "lifestyle" or "agenda."

15   Queer characters have not been completely absent in mainstream comic strips. Indeed, several early comic strips appearing in major newspapers made oblique references to queer characters. Milt Caniff's *Terry and the Pirates* introduced a gay male character (Papa Pyzon) in 1936 and a lesbian character (Sanjak) in 1939 (Applegate, 1994). In an interview for *The Comics Journal,* issue no. 108, Caniff said of Papa Pyzon: "People just thought he was a sissy. The idea of any kind of sexual deviation didn't even enter into peoples' minds in those days." Likewise, he said of Sanjak that "in those days the word 'lesbian' simply wouldn't have been understood by half your audience, and the other half would have resented it" (cited in Applegate, 1994). Mark Burstein suggested in *The Fort Mudge Post,* issue no. 32 (March 1993) that Howland Owl and Churchy LeFemme, two characters in Walt Kelly's *Pogo* comic strip, may have been gay lovers. According to Applegate (1994) "[Burstein's] suggestion based on sight gags and lines taken out of context, generated outraged protests and the conclusion that Kelly may have been engaging in whimsy, but that he certainly didn't seriously intend for readers to infer that Churchy and Howland were gay."

Given these oblique or coded references to queer characters in the comic strips before the 1970s, it was not until February 11, 1976, that Garry Trudeau in the *Doonesbury* comic strip introduced the first openly gay male character

(Trudeau, 1978, n.p.). Andy Lippincott was a regular character living successfully in a tolerant but heterosexual world. He was dating Joanie Caucus and there was even the assumption that they might get married. Then, one day, Andy announces that he is gay (Figure 11.1).

Figure 11.1. Andy Lippincott comes out. From Trudeau, G. B. (1976, February 9–10). Doonesbury. DOONESBURY © G. B. Trudeau. Reprinted with permission of UNIVERSAL PRESS SYNDICATE. All rights reserved.

There is nothing to visually distinguish Andy from any other character in the strip. Indeed, when Joanie hints to a mutual friend that the relationship between she and Andy is not going to go anywhere, the friend assumes she is the queer party in the relationship.

There is no argument, no recrimination, no strong negative reaction to Andy's "coming out" of the closet. There are no homophobic remarks, no gay-bashing. What Trudeau did by introducing a gay character was admirable. It took a great deal of courage and went against all the accepted standards of the comic strips page. Andy's sexual orientation, however, basically disappears from the strip for 7 years until September 1982 when Lacey Davenport, an older female character who had been a regular in the comic strip, is running for political office in San Francisco. At a meeting of the Bay Area Gay Alliance, Andy reappears as one of the leaders in the organization. There still is nothing about his character to identify him as queer other than the context—a queer meeting—in which the reader encounters him.

While Lacey tries to understand her new gay constituency, she lacks basic knowledge about some key characteristics of what it means to be queer as illustrated in a conversation with two of the men:

20   "But have you really tried, I mean, REALLY tried, dating girls your own age?" Lacey asks.

"It doesn't quite work that way, ma'am," one of the men answers.

"I must say, dears, this little chat has been most enlightening. I had no idea the gay community was facing so many problems. As you can imagine, this is all new ground for me. We never had any gays among our family and friends. Well, actually, that's not true. Dick's Uncle Orville came out of the closet last year. He's a federal judge in Chicago."

"That's great! What made him do it?" interrupts one of the men.

"High interest rates," Lacey says, "His butler tried to blackmail him, and he couldn't afford it."

Trudeau, though heterosexual, demonstrates some clear insights into the queer community as he focuses our attention on stereotypes common within the dominant culture that represent the standard cultural caricature of queers.

Lacey wins the election and some time passes until March 27, 1989, when Trudeau introduces into the strip a discussion of AIDS. Once again, Lacey Davenport is the vehicle for discussing the queer community in relationship to what was at the time being described as a national epidemic, and once again common misconceptions and humor work in tandem to make a positive point. While the queer community suffers devastating losses, the dominant culture represented by Lacey finds it difficult to even say the word AIDS when speaking to a queer gathering.

The next time Andy is mentioned in the strip is on June 2, 1990, after he has died of AIDS. The world-view of the dominant culture and the queer community in this episode are not congruent, as a conversation between Joanie and a young queer at the funeral aptly demonstrates. Joanie has just delivered a eulogy for Andy, and as she sits down, an exchange with a young man seated behind her ensues:

"Excuse me? That was a lovely eulogy!"

"Oh ... thank you," Joanie responds.

"Would you mind if I asked you a personal question?" the young man asks, "Are you a transvestite?"

"No, I'm a mother of two," she answers.

"A mother of two?" he says, "Wow … Andy sure knew some interesting people!"

25   Between 1976 and 1990, *Doonesbury* included 27 panels related to queer characters and issues. During this same time period, no other mainline newspaper comic strip talked about queers or AIDS.[3]

Trudeau "outed" a second queer character in September 1993. Mark Slackmeyer, a disc jockey, has a dream in which Andy, or his ghost, appears and plants the idea in Mark's mind that he might be gay. Mark, of course, denies the possibility at first, thinks about it, and finally goes to his friend Mike Doonesbury to talk about it:

"I'm scared, Mike," Mark confesses, "Being gay in this culture is too damn hard. I'd rather continue to be a sexual agnostic."

"What's going on out there?" J.J. [Mike's wife], calls from another room.

"It's Mark, J.J.—He thinks he might be gay," responds Mike.

"Of course he's gay. I've known that for years."

J.J., who has "lots of gay friends," offers to introduce them to Mark who says, "I don't think so, J.J., I'm not quite there yet … " J.J., though in the dominant heterosexual culture, appears to be very familiar with the queer community and actually thinks she can help Mark become a part of this marginal subculture in which she, though an outsider, feels quite comfortable.

In December 1993, Mark tells his father he is gay; in January 1994, he outs himself on National Public Radio; and in May 1994, he comes out to his mother. While there are some initial negative responses and questions, in each episode Mark is accepted and quickly assimilated back into heterosexual culture. Mark, along with his partner and co-disc jockey Chase, continues to regularly introduce gay topics into *Doonesbury* through their radio show. Commenting on congressional and presidential actions related to gay marriage, for example, Mark says:

30   … and Clinton's failure to veto the anti-gay marriage bill was a new low in election-year gutlessness! What were Clinton and Congress thinking? That their official censure would cause gays to rethink their sexual orientation? Does the family-values crowd believe in the value of commitment or don't they? Here's the irony, gang—come the election, conservatives should be prepared to accept full credit for promoting unstable, irresponsible gay relationships! (Trudeau, 1998, p. 77)

During an on-air interview with presidential candidate George W. Bush, Mark asks, "Why not unburden yourself right now so you won't be tempted to lie later?" Bush replies, "Yeah, right, why don't *you*?" Mark accepts the challenge: "Okay, I ducked the draft, smoked pot, and I'm gay. Your turn." "Um ..." says Bush, "Gotta run" (Trudeau, 1999, p. 64).

Each time Trudeau introduced a queer theme in *Doonesbury,* some newspapers chose not to run the comic strip, some dropped it altogether, and some moved it from the comics page to the editorial page. Both characters who came out as gay had been regular characters in the strip before Trudeau "outed" them. They had established significant roles within the context of the heterosexual culture in which they lived and worked before coming out. After revealing their sexual orientation, followed by a brief time of adjustment without any strongly negative attitudes, behavior, or lasting effect from the homosexual culture, they returned to their previously established role in the dominant culture status quo.

Readers of newspaper comics learned over the years to expect socially controversial topics in *Doonesbury,* which was not the "typical" family-oriented comic strip. When Lawrence, a regular character in Lynn Johnston's *For Better or For Worse,* came out as gay in 1993, there was a quick public response, both negative and positive (Lawlor, et al., 1994). The syndicate management warned newspaper editors about the potentially controversial content that was going to be presented so they could plan their course of action.

On March 26, 1993, Lawrence, while having a typical casual teenage conversation with his best friend Michael about a new puppy that Lawrence's mother loves dearly, says:

35   "I can't get over how much my mom loves that dog, man,"

"Yeah," responds Michael, "Know what she told my mom? She said the puppy would keep her happy 'til you had children!"

"What?" asks Lawrence with a surprised look. "Then that puppy better live a long time, Mike, because I'm probably never gonna *have* children."

"Hey, how do you know?" asks Michael.

"... 'cause I'm probably never going to get married. Ever," replies Lawrence.

"I don't get what you're saying, man! If you, you know—fall in love?"

"I have fallen in love," says Lawrence," ... but it's not with a girl."

The physical expressions on each boy's face and their body reactions clearly suggest apprehension about the topic's unexpected turn and development. The conversation continues and Lawrence comes out to Michael (see the conversation in Figure 11.2).

Figure 11.2. Lawrence comes out. From Johnston, L. (1993, March 26–27). *For Better or for Worse*. FOR BETTER OR FOR WORSE © UFS. Reprinted by permission. All rights reserved.

Michael is angry with Lawrence, but with time and thought, he decides to remain friends with him. He even convinces Lawrence to tell his mom he is gay. The conversation between Lawrence and his mom goes like this:

"This isn't going to be easy," Lawrence begins.

"Don't worry, honey," Mom says, "Whatever it is, we'll handle it together— calmly and sensibly."

"I'm gay," Lawrence says with an apprehensive look.

"Don't be RIDICULOUS!" his mom exclaims, "I don't believe you!"

"It's the truth, mom," Lawrence says.

"It's a phase," Mom says, "You'll pass through it!"

"It isn't a phase, mom!" Lawrence says, "I've always been gay! It's the way I AM!!"

"It's my fault," Mom says, "I was too protective! I should have pushed you harder."

Lawrence's father throws him out of the house and his mom calls Michael's mom in panic about her missing son. A search is undertaken and Lawrence is found. In the end Lawrence is accepted and assimilated back into the dominant culture of his family and friends.

40   According to reports in *Editor & Publisher* (Astor, 1993a, 1993b), at least 18 newspapers cancelled *For Better or For Worse,* while about 50 ran an alternate comic strip in place of the controversial episode. Newspapers and trade magazines ran major articles on the controversy, and many newspapers received volumes of letters to the editor on both sides of the issue (Kramer, 1993; Neal, 1993).

Since his initial "coming out" experience, Lawrence continues to appear from time to time in the strip. In one sequence he took his boyfriend, Ben, to the prom. In August 1997, Johnston again angered some readers and newspaper editors when she ran an episode in which Ben, now Lawrence's partner, considers moving to Paris to study piano, and Lawrence has to decide whether to go with him. Each time Lawrence appeared in an episode, some newspapers canceled the strip or replaced it with reruns of earlier episodes (Murray, 1997; Friess, 1997).

Lynn Johnston recalls the event and her reaction:

> Lawrence has been Michael Patterson's close friend and neighbor for many years. He has always been "the kid next door." For the longest time, he appeared consistently with Michael and his friends—but a few years ago, I began to find it harder and harder to bring Lawrence into the picture. Somehow, his life had taken a different turn and I couldn't quite understand why he wasn't still part of the gang. I began to concentrate on him, see his room, his things, his life.

> I know all these people so well. I know where their houses are, what their furniture's like, where they work. I know their voices and their mannerisms, their thoughts are open to me … and yet, I couldn't connect with Lawrence.

> After "being" with him for some time, I realized that the reason he was having so much trouble communicating with Michael and his friends was because Lawrence, now in his late teens, was different. Lawrence was gay. (Johnston, 1994, p. 106)

As was the case with Trudeau, it is clear that Johnston knows something about the queer community, but she is not a part of it. She writes: "It [Lawrence's story] was written for my friend Michael Vade-Boncoeur, a comedy writer, performer, and childhood friend for whom my son [Michael] and the character in the strip were named. It was written under the guidance of my husband's brother, Ralph Johnston … who, when he came out, gave me the honor of trusting me first" (Johnston, 1999, p. 75).

45   Although many readers protested the inclusion of a gay character in *For Better or For Worse,* the endings are always happy. Lawrence is not beaten up. After the initial negative reaction from his dad, he is accepted back into the family. There are no offensive names directed toward Lawrence, and as Johnston says of Lawrence, " … he works at Lakeside Landscaping, where he excels in design. He is faithful to his partner, Ben, who is presently studying composition in Paris. He keeps in touch with the Patterson's, who are almost his family, and even though he says he's different … he really hasn't changed at all" (Johnston, 1999, p. 76).

Many in the queer community cannot understand or accept that the process of "coming out" in a heterosexual culture can happen with such calmness and peaceful acceptance. Only a person who is part of the dominant cultural point of view, some queer theorists would argue, could create a world where coming out as queer could have a "fairy tale" ending.

These examples clearly illustrate the acceptable narrative script for queer characters when the comic strip creator is, as far as readers know, heterosexual. Assimilation is normal and easy, being different clearly has its limits, and everyone "lives happily ever after." The world portrayed in the mainstream comic strip does not correlate well with the experiences of people who, in their real lives in the dominant culture, "come out" and identify themselves as queer.

In the 1960s, in response to an ad in the *New York Times* that read "Gay cartoonist wanted," Al Shapiro created *Harry Chess, The Man from A.U.N.T.I.E.* under the pen name A. Jay. This was the first gay comic strip, and it played on the James Bond/*Man from U.N.C.L.E.* theme that was current at the time (Triptow, 1989; Streitmatter, 1995b, pp. 98, 104). Other strips from the 1960s and 1970s included Joe Johnson's *Miss Thing,* Trina Robbins' *Sandy Comes Out,* Roberta Gregory's *Dynamite Damsels,* Howard Cruse's *Barefootz,* and Alison Bechdel's *The Crush.*[5]

Robert Triptow (1989) says of the audiences for these early comic strips: "There are a lot of similarities between comics fandom and the gay subculture. The average comics reader, usually a teenage 'fanboy,' is acquainted with the oppression of conformist society—as is the average gay person. Gay life is often looked down upon as (at best) trivial and self-indulgent …" (p. 4). Gerard Donelan describes his experience as a queer cartoonist:

50   Hasn't everyone at one time had the urge to cut out a cartoon because "That's me!"? That's what I wanted to do with my cartoons for the gay community. I wanted to do what Joe Johnston's *Miss Thing* in the early days of The Advocate had done for me when I was first coming out. I wanted some fairy to see one of my cartoons, say, "That's me!" and realize that there are others who do what "I" do, feel as "I" feel. I wanted to help show other gay people that "we" have a validity, a sense of humor and a sense of community. (Donelan, 1987, preface, n.p.)

Some queer newspapers in major urban centers include comic strips in their weekly editions. The *Washington (DC) Blade,* for example, runs comic strips each week including Alison Bechdel's *Dykes to Watch Out For,* Eric Orner's *The Unfabulous Social Life of Ethan Green,* John Anderson's *Honestly Ethel,* Glen Hanson and Allan Neuwirth's *Chelsea Boys,* Paige Braddock's *Jane's World,* and Noreen Stevens' *Chosen Family.* It can be argued, however, that these newspapers more and more represent a "niche" publication rather than an "alternative" one (Streitmatter 1995a, 1995b; Fejes & Lennon, 2000). Fred Fejes and Ron Lennon conclude: "The developing lesbian/gay niche media have acquired the legitimacy and the authority to define and speak for the community. Yet in doing so they run the risk again of marginalizing, and making invisible groups who have already suffered and been stigmatized because of their sexual and cultural differences" (Fejes & Lennon, 2000, p. 40).

Alison Bechdel, probably the most widely known queer cartoonist, talks about the effect of a niche market attitude in terms of editorial standards and changes: "[A] comic strip is pretty much editorial proof. Newspapers can't delete, add, or rearrange anything I do. I'm in complete control." She quickly corrects herself, however: "Actually, I lied when I said newspapers can't change anything I do. The *Washington Blade* doesn't permit swearing or reference to certain body parts in their newspaper, so I provide them with a self-bowdlerized alternative when one of my strips contains naughty words" (Bechdel, 1998, p 185). Books based on her strip are available in mainstream bookstores and thus are readily available to a much wider non-queer audience as would be expected of a "niche" publication.

Universal Press Syndicate even approached Bechdel at a meeting of the National Lesbian and Gay Journalists Association conference about syndicating her strip, but the terms were unacceptable (Fitzgerald, 1994). One change that would have been required before syndication, according to Lee Salem of Universal Press, was that "the title would have to go [to appeal] to a mainstream audience." Other stipulations Salem said in included that the strip could not be too political, and that of the four or six characters, only two could be lesbians and they would have to be nonpartisan (cited in Fitzgerald, 1994, p. 14). "I'm not interested in writing for a mainstream audience," Bechdel said: "I'm really happy. I can draw naked people. I can write about politics. I mean, papers are still suspending episodes of *Doonesbury*. I'm not interested in making those kind of compromises" (cited in Fitzgerald, 1994, p. 14). What would a queer comic strip in a mainstream newspaper look like? "I imagine it would be like a lot of the African-American strips," said Bechdel, "like *Jump Start,* which is a nice strip but all the characters are kind of assimilated. The strip would be about straight and gay people living together, maybe. Well, I don't know, but it just wouldn't have any controversy" (cited in Fitzgerald, 1994, p. 15).

Our focus is on comic strips that move beyond the niche market and are directed toward a specifically identified queer audience. Queer comic strips that do not fit into the "niche" category are printed by small alternative presses or are self-published. They are available only at queer bookstores[4] or on the Internet.

55 The first example is from *XY Magazine,* which is targeted at a young queer population and runs a comic strip as a regular feature. In 1997, the comic strip by Abby Denson, *Tough Love,* featured a high school sophomore, Brian, who talces a martial arts class taught by a "cute" guy named Chris. Brian dreams of taking Chris to the prom, but he doesn't know if Chris is gay. Julie, a straight friend, has been pressuring Brian to take her to the prom until he tells her he is gay. They remain friends since she is "okay" with his sexual orientation. At school, Brian encounters Chris, half-naked, in the locker room. Brian blushes, and Chris invites him over to watch Kung Fu movies. In the course of conversation, Brian discovers that Chris did have a Chinese boyfriend, but when Li's parents discovered he was queer, they sent him back to China "to make him straight." Brian and Chris go to bed together.

Back at school, word has gotten out about Brian's sexual orientation. Some "jocks" discover that Brian is queer, find him alone in the gym and begin to bully him (Figure 11.3). As the encounter continues, the language gets more explicit when one of the jocks says, "He probably went through our lockers for underwear and shit, what a pervert!" They are interrupted when Chris arrives and uses his martial arts skills to rescue Brian. They spend the night together. Chris asks Brian if he's out to his parents, and when Brian says no, Chris asks, "Brian, are you going to tell her [Brian's mother] you're gay?" "Yes ... not now ... eventually," Brian replies, "I want to, but I'm afraid .... Chris, I know you're right. But I need some time. Please be patient with me on this."

Figure 11.3. Brian is bullied by "jocks." From Denson, A. (1997, July). *Tough Love,* 6(8), p. 45. © 1997 Abby Denson, *XY Magazine.* Reprinted by permission. All rights reserved.

It is clear that the story is written for teenagers who are dealing with their own sexuality and sexual orientation. It addresses basic experiences in the language typical of teenagers, especially those who have been labeled as gay, queer, or fag. There is little question about whether this is a "family" cartoon appropriate for a mainstream newspaper comic strips page. The only "straight" male characters are homophobic bullies who enjoy bashing queers. The experience it narrates is clearly different from that portrayed in either *Doonesbury* or *For Better or For Worse.*

Club Survival 101 by Joe Phillips, another comic strip from *XY Magazine,* ran in 1999. The main character is a college guy, Camron (Cam to his friends), who, is somewhat "out" but who has not made the transition from straight to queer culture. The strip follows him as he goes to the gay club for the first time, where his friend, Trevor, sees him:

> "My God! I can't believe you actually made it! Your first time in a gay club! I'm so proud!"

> "Whatever ... I don't see what the big deal is," Cam says, "Trevor, tell me why everybody is hugging each other like they're goin' off to war."

> "Oh relax," Trevor says, "Um ... Cam? Who told you to dress like a confused straight boy? I take my eyes off you for two minutes and you leave the house lookin' like beach trade."

60   The dialogue is filled with queer jargon that at times may be quite difficult for non-queer readers to understand completely. Trevor introduces the idea that there is something about the way a person dresses that identifies him or her as queer, at least in a queer environment. A stranger comes up behind Cam, puts his hand on Cam's shoulder, and says: "Oh no she didn't! Yer wearin' A+F after sundown! What in gay hell is wrong with you, Mary? This ain't no rave!" The stranger leads Cam into a back room where a complete transformation takes place. Including a change in the style of his clothes, Cam, now restyled and recreated into an appropriately queer image that fits into the queer club scene, returns to the dance floor. Trevor sees the transformation and says: "Oh, there you ... who the hell are you now, the queer formerly known as trade?" (Figure 11.4). They watch the male dancers and mingle with the young gay crowd.

The story continues as the young college guy transitions from straight to queer culture. He meets a wide range of characters and behaves in a manner appropriate to the gay club scene. All the characters in the strip are queer. The role of clothing as a defining characteristic in the queer culture that distinguishes it from the dominant culture is emphasized when at the bottom of the last page of the strip is the notice: "Character clothing and merchandise can be found at http://www.xgear.com."

Figure 11.4. Cam is transformed. From Phillips, J. (1999, March). *Club Survival 101,* 1(17), p. 42. © 1999 Joe Phillips, *XY Magazine*. Reprinted by permission. All rights reserved.

Kyle's Bed & Breakfast by Greg Fox is an on-line comic strip[5] about a queer man who owns a bed and breakfast. Its focus is the lives and experiences of several men who live there or who are friends of the owner. Each character in the strip is modeled after "typical" queer personality types. Kyle, the owner of the B&B, is a 30-something single man. Brad Steele, a 19-year-old minor league baseball player who is still "in the closet" when in the "straight" world, is just beginning to come to terms with being queer. He lives at the B&B and works as a handyman in exchange for his rent. Richard Rubin is a 24-year-old part-time club deejay, gossip, and fashion disaster. Richard means well but lacks basic social skills. Lance Powers, a 28-year-old African-American advertising executive, has just been relocated from LA to New York. Eduardo Vasquez is an 18-year-old high school senior whose parents threw him out when he came out to them. A Hispanic, he is portrayed as young and foolish. There is one female character who makes cameo appearances, but the story centers almost entirely on male characters who clearly represent some diversity within the queer community.

One of the early episodes revolves around a new baseball player, Jeff Olsen, who has been traded to the minor league baseball team on which Brad plays. One of the men on the team says to Brad, "Well … he's supposed to be an awesome catcher, but, um … he's a little 'light in the cleats'." "Huh?" Brad interjects. The teammate continues:, "He's a *FAG*. Least that's what the rumor is. He's been bounced around between five teams this season. Good catchers don't get bounced around that much … unless there's a *reason*."

When Brad and Jeff encounter one another in the locker room, Brad makes it clear that he does not want to be associated with anyone who may even be suspected of being a queer (Figure 11.5). Jeff is harassed by the men on the team and is quickly traded to a new team, but before leaving, he and Brad have a confrontation. Kyle and Jeff are talking when Brad comes into the room and the conversation escalates into an argument centered on what it means for a man to remain in the closet rather than being honest about his sexual orientation (Figure 11.6).

65   The action in *Kyle's Bed & Breakfast* does not take place within the dominant heterosexual culture. It does not present a majority of straight characters. The endings are not always happy. The characters use a jargon and language that step well outside the boundaries of the dominant culture. There is little question that this comic strip is created by a queer artist/writer, about queer characters, and for a queer audience.

Figure 11.5. Brad learns Jeff is queer. From Fox, G. (1999). *Kyle's Bed and Breakfast,* 1(5). © 1999 Greg Fox. Reprinted by permission of the publisher. All rights reserved.

Figure 11.6. Brad and Jeff argue. From Fox, G. (1999). *Kyle's Bed and Breakfast,* 1(6). © 1999 Greg Fox. Reprinted by permission of the publisher. All rights reserved.

Conclusion

Heterosexual cartoonists may introduce queer characters into their comic strips, they may be sympathetic in their treatment, and they may even encounter negative reactions from readers and newspaper editors about their openness and empathy. They live, however, in the dominant heterosexual culture and are an integral part of it in their socialization and thinking. The queer character does not have any clear distinguishing characteristics to differentiate him (so far all the queer characters in mainstream comic strips have been men) from the dominant culture. He is different in a non-obvious, non-threatening way so he can be easily and thoroughly assimilated. He seems to look like everyone else, talk like everyone else, think like everyone else, and behave like all the other heterosexual characters.

Queer cartoonists, on the other hand, tend to include only queer characters or perhaps a small set of heterosexual characters who provide the necessary protagonist needed to create a good narrative. The focus is not on assimilation into a dominant culture, but rather on the creation of a thoroughly queer culture that often is in opposition, if not direct conflict, with the dominant heterosexual culture. Queer individuals often look different, certainly think and act different, and generally feel "out of place" or they have the need to hide their queerness when working within the "straight" world environment. Characters who cannot or will not face up to being queer, such as Brad in *Kyle's Bed & Breakfast,* have internal battles as well as external confrontations about their unwillingness to explore and possibly further own up to their sexual orientation or queerness.

The Internet provides a welcoming environment for queer comic strips. Smaller audiences can access a strip with a clearly defined focus without consideration of issues such as cost of publication, distribution, or editorial oversight—all issues that tend to thwart, if not kill, diversity on the comics pages of dominant culture newspapers.

Will an authentically queer comic strip, by an openly queer cartoonist, appear on the comics pages of your local newspaper? Perhaps the time will come. It happened with African-American and Hispanic comic strips. Queer characters must be allowed to live in a queer world doing queer things with the dominant culture playing a marginalized role. The Queer Nation slogan might be rephrased for queer comic strips as "We're here. We're queer. Give us our queer space!"

Works Cited

Abelove, H. (1995). The queering of lesbian/gay history. *Radical History Review, 62,* 44–57.

Applegate, D. (1994, Fall). Coming out in the comic strips. *Hogan's Alley,* 1, pp. 75–78.

Astor, D. (1993a, April 3). Comic with gay character is dropped by some newspapers. *Editor & Publisher,* p. 32.

Astor, D. (1993b, April 10). More papers cancel controversial comic. *Editor & Publisher,* pp. 34–35.

Bechdel, A. (1998). *The indelible Alison Bechqel: Confessions, comix, and miscellaneous dykes to watch out for.* Ithaca, NY: Firebrand Books.

Dilley, P. (1999). Queer theory: Under construction. *Qualitative Studies in Education, 12,* 457–472.

Donelan, G. P. (1987). *Drawing on the gay experience.* Los Angeles, CA: Liberation Publications.

Fejes, F., & Lennon, R. (2000). Defining the lesbian/gay community? Market research and the lesbian/gay press. *Journal of Homosexuality, 39,* 25–42.

Fitzgerald, M. (1994, October 15). The biggest closet in newspapering. *Editor & Publisher,* pp. 14–15.

Friess (1997, Fall). Syndicate warns papers about gay-themed comic strip. *Alternatives* [newsletter of the National Lesbian & Gay Journalists Assoctiation].

Fuss, D. (1991). Inside/out. In D. Fuss (Ed.), *Inside/out: Lesbian theories, gay theories* (pp. 1–12). New York: Routledge.

Gamson, J. (1995). Must identity movements self-destruct? A queer dilemma. *Social Problems, 42,* 390–407.

Gamson, J. (1998). *Freaks talk back: Tabloid talk shows and sexual nonconformity.* Chicago, IL: University of Chicago Press.

Gamson, J. (2000). Sexualities, queer theory, and qualitative research. In N. K. Denzin & Y. S. Lincoln (Eds.), *Handbook of qualitative research,* second edition (pp. 347–365). Thousand Oaks, CA: Sage.

Grossberg, L. (1993). Cultural studies and new worlds. In C. McCarthy & W. Crichlow (Eds.), *Race, identity and representation* (pp. 89–105). New York: Routledge.

Grossberg, L. (1996). Identity and cultural studies: Is that all there is? In S. Hall & P. duGay (Eds.), *Questions of cultural identity* (pp. 87–107). Thousand Oaks, CA: Sage.

Halperin, D. (1995). *Saint Foucault: Toward a gay hagiography.* New York: Oxford University Press.

Honeychurch, K. G. (1996). Researching dissident subjectivities: Queering the grounds of theory and practice, *Harvard Educational Review, 66,* 339–355.

Jagose, A. (1996). *Queer theory: An introduction.* New York: New York University Press.

Johnston, L. (1994). *It's the thought that counts ....* Kansas City, MO: Andrews & McMeel.

Johnston, L. (1999). *The lives behind the lines.* Kansas City, MO: Andrews & McMeel.

Kramer, S. D. (I 993, April 13). 'Coming out.' *The Washington Post,* B5.

Lawlor, S. D., Sparkes, A., & Wood, J. (1994, July). *When Lawrence came out: Taking the funnies seriously.* Paper presented at the International Communication Association. Sydney, Australia.

Murray, J. (1997, August 25). Cartoon carries message of tolerance. *The Gazette* (Montreal), B3.

Neal, J. (1993, April 23). Family-oriented comic strip character says he's gay. *Comics Buyer's Guide.*

Pustz, M. J. (1999). *Comic book culture: Fanboys and true believers.* Jackson, MS: University Press of Mississippi.

Rotella, G. (2000, August 15). The word that failed. *The Advocate,* p. 112.

Sabin, R. (1996). *Comics, comix & graphic novels.* London: Phaidon.

Seidman, S. (1993). Identity and politics in a "postmodern" gay culture: Some historical and conceptual notes. In M. Warner (Ed.), *Fear of a queer planet: Queer politics and social theory* (pp. 105–142). Minneapolis, MN: University of Minnesota Press.

Seidman, S. (1996). Introduction. In S. Seidman (Ed.), *Queer theory/sociology* (pp. 1–29). Cambridge, MA: Blackweli.

Slagle, A. (1995). In defense of Queer Nation: From identity politics to a politics of difference. *Western Journal of Communication, 59,* 85–102.

Streitmatter, R. (1995a). Creating a venue for the "Love that dare not speak its name": Origins of the gay and lesbian press. *Journalism and Mass Communication Quarterly, 72,* 436–447.

Streitmatter, R. (1995b). *Unspeakable: The rise of the gay and lesbian press in America.* Boston: Faber and Faber.

Triptow, R. (1989). *Gay comics*. New York: New American Library.

Trudeau, G. B. (1978). *Doonesbury's greatest hits*. NY: Henry Holt.

Trudeau, G. B. (1998). *The bundled Doonesbury: A pre-millennial anthology*. Kansas City, MO: Andrews & McMeel.

Trudeau, G. B. (1999). *Buck wild Doonesbury*. Kansas City, MO: Andrews & McMeel.

Credit

Republished with permission of Peter Lang Inc., International Academic Publishers, from In Comics and Ideology, eds. McAllister et al., pp. 251–274, 2001; Permission conveyed through Copyright Clearance Center, Inc.

"God Don't Never Change":
Black English from a Black Perspective

GENEVA SMITHERMAN

Ain nothin in a long time lit up the English teaching profession like the current hassle over Black English. One finds beaucoup socio-linguistic research studies and language projects for the "disadvantaged" on the scene in nearly every sizable Black community in the country.[1] And educators from K through grad. school bees debating whether: 1) Blacks should learn and use only standard white English (hereafter referred to as WE); 2) Blacks should command both dialects, i.e., be bidialectal (hereafter BD); 3) Blacks should be allowed (??????????) to use standard Black English (hereafter BE or BI, for Black Idiom, a more accurate term). The appropriate choice having everything to do with American political reality, which is usually ignored, and nothing to do with the educational process, which is usually claimed. I say without qualification that we cannot talk about BI apart from Black Culture and the Black Experience. Nor can we specify educational goals for Blacks apart from considerations about the structure of white American society.

Both Black and white critics of American society have dealt extensively with the rather schizophrenic nature of the American politico-social sensibility, caused by the clash of the emphasis on class flexibility and individualism with the concomitant stress on class conformity and group status. It is interesting to note the way this class consciousness neurosis is reflected in the area of language.

A quick look at the tradition of schoolroom grammars and the undergirding ideology of early English grammarians reveals that the current "national mania for correctness" has been around a long time. You see, from the Jump, the English language itself, didn't command no respect, for Latin was the lingo of the elite. (Outside thought: if WE wasn't given no propers, you know BI wouldn't be given any.) What those grammarians did was to take note of the actual usage of English only for the purpose of denouncing and reforming that usage. Clearly these grammarians was comin from a position that English could and must be subjected to a process of regularizing, based on a Latin/Classical model On the British side, there was Bishop Robert Lowth (Short Introduction to English Grammar, 1763), who conceptualized his grammar in terms of giving "order and permanence" to the "unruly, barbarous" tongue of the AngloSaxons:

"The English language, as it is spoken by the politest part of the nation, and as it stands in the writings of our most approved authors, often offends against every part of Grammar." The continuity of this line of thinking in the American sensibility is best exemplified by Lindley Murray *(English Grammar,* 1795). Now Murray was really a deep dude cause, see, his book, was not gon simply introduce the proper method of English usage among the young, but inculcate in them all the morals and virtues commensurate with correct English. Dig it, now, here what he say:

> The author of the following work [referring to himself, like they always did, in the ridiculous third person] wishes to promote the cause of virtue as well as of learning; and with this view, he has been studious, through the whole of the work, not only to avoid every example and illustration, which might have an improper effect on the minds of youth, but also to introduce on many occasions such as have a moral and religious tendency.

By the Twentieth Century, the individual norm had been replaced by a group norm. According to Charles C. Fries *(American English Grammar,* 1940), the job of the public schools was to teach

> the type of English used by the socially acceptable of most of our communities [since] in the matter of the English language, it is clear that any one who cannot use the language habits in which the major affairs of the country are conducted, the language habits of the socially acceptable of most of our communities, would have a serious handicap.

Obviously this didn't make things no better for the common folk. It was just substituting one linguistic authority for another—the individual Latinate standards of a Lowth or Murray for the group Anglican standards of middle America. Both authorities and norms is based on race and class position and is simply attempts to make the "outsiders" talk like the "insiders." This superimposition of a dialect norm has little to do with language power, linguistic versatility, or variety of expression and everything to do with making what one grammarian labeled the "depraved language of common people" *(The Art of Speaking,* 1668), and by extension, the common people themselves, conform to white, middle-class society. Thus nowadays, "nonstandard" dialect is that which "deviates" from the collective language of the majority culture. For example, it is now all right to use the contracted form (which offended the idiosyncratic sensibilities of those early grammarians like crazy), so it is acceptable to say *It's that way* for *It is that way.* Similarly, we can, without causing too much consternation, use the objective case after copula, as *It is me* for *It is I.* The point is that both examples represent forms regularly used by middle-class and white Americans. But dig now, in no way, do the new language pacesetters accept *It bees that way* (a popular BI statement; an expression of Black existentialist reflection and thought; used by Nina Simone as the title of a hit recording). See, an idiomatic phrase like this comes from a "lower-class" dialect (and a people) that is given no respect.

On the one hand, then, the denigration of BI is but a manifestation of white America's class anxiety. After all, as Baldwin says, in a country where everybody has status, it is possible that nobody has status. So Americans, lacking a fixed place in the society, don't know where they be in terms of social and personal identity. For this reason, it has been useful to have nigguhs around, so at least they always knows where the *bottom* bees. On the other hand, then, the pejorative attitude toward BI is a manifestation of white America's racism (undergirded by or coupled with class elitism). I shall cite three examples reflecting racism in the area of linguistics.

5   Toward the end of the last century, Ambrose Gonzales collected stories from the Gullah (or, as we called it down in Tennessee, "Geechee") region of the Carolina Coast and published these in *Black Border*. Speaking about the language of the Gullah Black folk, Gonzales contended:

> The [Gullah] words are, of course, not African, for the African brought over or retained only a few words of his jungle-tongue, and even these few are by no means authenticated as part of the original scant baggage of the negro slaves … Slovenly and careless of speech, these Gullahs seized upon the peasant English used by some of the early settlers and by the white servants of the wealthier colonists, wrapped their clumsy tongues about it as well as they could, and, enriched with certain expressive African words, it issued through their flat noses and thick lips as so workable a form of speech that it was gradually adopted by the other slaves and became in time the accepted Negro speech of the lower districts of South Carolina and Georgia. With characteristic laziness, these Gullah Negroes took short cuts to the ears of their auditors, using as few words as possible, sometimes making one gender serve for three, one tense for several, and totally disregarding singular and plural numbers.

(Outside thought: such absurd nonsense was validly challenged by Black historian-turned-linguist Lorenzo Dow Turner in his *Africanisms in the Gullah Dialect*, 1949.)

In 1924, in an article titled "The English of the Negro," and again in 1925, in his *English Language in America*, George Philip Krapp discussed Black speech patterns throughout the South. (Outside thought: his discussion is appropriately titled by his last name.) In reconstructing the evolution of this dialect, Krapp argued that there were "no African elements … in the English of negroes [sic]";

rather this dialect reflected "archaic survivals" of English which had lingered because the "negro, being socially backward, has held onto many habits which the white world has left behind." Finally, Krapp dismissed Black speech by concluding that "negro English … is merely a debased dialect of English, learned by the negroes from the whites."

Well, even though Gonzales and Krapp were writing in what my fifteen-year-old son terms the "olden days," ain't nothin changed. In a recent record, *The Dialect of Black Americans,* distributed for educational purposes by Western Electric, we are told of Joseph, a recent Black high school graduate, who was refused a job because "his speech carries no respect. In fact it generates negative attitudes, and the middle-class Black must be careful of the language he uses—or which language he uses." Sound familiar? Sure, just another variation on the linguistic purist/class anxiety theme of Lowth, Murray, and Fries; and the linguistic ethnocentricism and rampant racism of Gonzales and Krapp. (Outside thought: still at 1763 and it's 1973.)

In conceptualizing linguistic performance models for Black students, our contemporary objectives must be informed by such historical socio-political realities as I have touched upon here. They must also be informed by accurate, comprehensive descriptions of BI. Both kinds of information are so highly interrelated as to be virtually inseparable. Let me proceed, then, to discuss this latter point in some detail.

Most linguists and educators currently belaboring the "problem" of what has come to be popularly termed "Black English" have conceptualized the dialect in very narrow, constricting, and ultimately meaningless terms. Depending on the "scholarship" consulted or the rap sessions overheard in teachers' lounges, one finds 8–10 patterns of usage labeled BE. For example: zero -s morpheme in sentences such as *He work all the time, Those scientist inventing many thing, My mother name Mary;* copula deletion as in *He a hippie* (also in the preceding example); multiple negation as *Can't nobody do nothin in his room;* and, of course, that famous and oft-quoted use of be as finite verb, as in *They be slow all the time.* And so on and so on. The point is that such a list contains only a very small ultimately unimportant set of *surface* grammatical features. One searches in vain for any discussion of surface vs. deep structure significance in the so-called "scholarly" literature on BI. I'm talkin bout deep structure in the Chomskian sense of the term. What, after all, is the underlying semantic differentiation between *He work all the time* and *He works all the time?* Or even between *My mother's name is Mary* and *My mother name Mary?* But this is logical. because if BI were really deep structurally different from WE, then there would be a situation of mutual unintelligibility. Oh, yeah, white folks understand BI speakers, it ain't a question of communication. Whites might not like what they hear, but they bees hearin and comprehendin every bit of it. Just as white speakers from one region of the country understand whites from another region. As a matter of fact, though I doubt if many white folks would admit it, they have far greater difficulty with British English than with BI. Yet British English commands great prestige in this country. (Outside thought: since America was once a British colony, this is what Frantz Fanon might call the "colonized mentality.")

10 This "much ado about nothing" is what led to the accusation by a Brother, at a recent Black professional meeting, that the research on BI was bogus scholarship, pseudo-intellectual attempts to create a field of knowledge or a discipline out of nothing. He was not misled, as, unfortunately, many English teachers are, by the overcomplexification, linguistic jargon, and statistical paraphernalia—i.e., scholarly trappings that make some of the articles on BI almost unreadable, and the linguists themselves nearly unintelligible. (Dig it, "zero -s morpheme" is just another way of saying that the kid left off an "s.") The dire consequence of this whole business to the English teaching profession can be illustrated by the case of a Black freshman at Wayne State, who submitted the following:

> [TEACHER'S, ASSIGNMENT: Take a position on the war in Viet Nam and present arguments to defend your position.]

> I think the war in Viet Nam bad. Because we don't have no business over there. My brother friend been in the war, and he say it's hard and mean. I do not like war because it's bad. And so I don't think we have no business there. The reason the war in China is bad is that American boys is dying over there.

The paper was returned to the student with only *one* comment: "Correct your grammar and resubmit." What sheer and utter nonsense!

Now, my advice to teachers is to overlook these matters of sheer mechanical "correctness" and get on with the educational business at hand. Don't let students get away with sloppy, irresponsible writing just because it happen to conform to a surface notion of correctness. Yeah, that's right, there is such a thang as sloppy "correct" writing—writing, for instance, where every statement is generalized comment without any specific, supporting details; or where the same modification structures or sentence patterns are used with tedious repetition; or where the student uses one simple kernel structure after another instead of combining and condensing. While *zero -s* and *-ed morphemes* may be easier "issues" for the already overworked English profs to deal with, I would warn such teachers not to abdicate their *real* responsibility: that of involving students in the totality and complexity of the communication process. And I would denounce as futile and time-wasting the attempts to move Black students from, for example, "He tired" to "He is tired" or from "They sold they house" to "They sold their house." Not only are such ventures misuses of important educational time, they are perhaps, albeit subtly, racist because such goals involve only lateral moves and Black folks need (upward) vertical moves. That what we mean when we sing with Curtis Mayfield "We movin on up," *Up,* not sideways.

None of this has been to assert that there is not a distinctive verbal style that characterizes contemporary Black American speech. But it is to reiterate a point I've made many times heretofore: it's *style, not language per se,* in which the uniqueness of Black expression lies. This style must be located in the situational context, in the Black Cultural Universe. And anybody who *knows* anythang about BI knows that that's where it's at. (Outside thought: emphasis on *knows,* cause like my daddy the preacher say, everybody talking bout Heaven ain't goin there.) I'm talking bout the Black Lexicon, and bout the rhetorical devices and unique patterns of communication found in what Richard Wright called the "Forms of Things Unknown." Such stylistic/language forms are an indigenous part of the Black historical past and are rooted in the Black Cultural sensibility. They achieve a dynamism of meaning which emanates from a shared sense of oppression, and they represent, perhaps, the continuity of our African sensibility in the New World. Although older Black writers used these forms only sporadically in they works (even Richard Wright himself), the new Black writers, the poets especially, are hip to the significance of these patterns from our Oral Tradition and have appropriated them with maximum power and poetic effect. I shall cite a few illuminating examples.

Don Lee effectively uses items from the Black Lexicon when he describes Malcolm X as being from "a long line of super-cools/doo-rag lovers/ revolutionary "pimps."[2] He employs Capping, Signification, and Black Rhythmic Pattern in his poem denouncing the self-styled Black revolutionary, who is all talk and no action—dig on the title alone: "But he was cool or: he even stopped for green lights."[3] Black prison poet Etheridge Knight does a poetic variation of the Toast in his poem about the Black prisoner Hard Rock, a super-bad dude, about whom there is a "jewel of a myth that Hard Rock had once bit/A screw on the thumb and poisoned him with syphilitic spit."[4] Maya Angelou plays the Dozens on both Blacks and whites in her companion poems "The Thirteens."[5] The ritualistic barbershop scene in John Oliver Killens' novel *Cotillion*[6] is shot through with a secular version of the Call-Response Pattern. And Richard Wright's own "Fire and Cloud,"[7] a short story about a militant Black minister, contains one of the most effective prose renditions of the sacred manifestation of this basic pattern.

Why is it that these substantive features of BI are never included in the descriptive monographs of "Black English"? Why is it that only the superfluous features of usage are extrapolated and dealt with in "language programs for the disadvantaged"? And isn't it interesting that these Superficial features of BI are easily translatable into WE? Whereas ain't no way in the world you can transform the "Forms of Things Unknown." Methinks there is some insidious design afoot to cut off Black students from they cultural roots, from, according to Frantz Fanon, "those they left behind," to create a new class of super-niggers, nouveau-white Blacks, who will rap in the oppressor's dialect, totally obliterating any knowledge or use of BI—a form of language firmly imbedded in the African-American past. Because, you see, the plain and simple fact is that language does not exist in a vacuum but in the socio-cultural reality. And with this broad view of BI, a view informed by cognizance of our historical past and political present, *even* those surface features take on a different meaning. As Baraka says:

> I heard an old Negro street singer last week. Reverend Pearly Brown, singing, "God don't never change!" This is a precise thing he is singing. He does not mean "God does not ever change!" He means "God don't never change!" The difference … is in the final human reference … the form of passage through the world. A man who is rich and famous who sings, "God don't never change," is confirming his hegemony and good fortune … or merely calling the bank. A blind hopeless black American is saying something very different. …

Being told to "speak proper," meaning that you become fluent with the jargon of power, is also a part of not "speaking proper." That is the culture which desperately understands that it does not "speak proper," or is not fluent with the terms of social strength, also understands somewhere that its desire to gain such fluency is done at a terrifying risk. The bourgeois Negro accepts such risk as profit. But does *close-ter* (in the context of "jes a close-ter, walk wi-thee") mean the same thing as *closer*? Close-ter, in the term of its user is, believe me, exact. It means a quality of existence, of actual physical disposition perhaps in its manifestation as a *tone* and *rhythm* by which people live, most often in response to common modes of thought best enforced by some factor of environmental emotion that is exact and specific. Even the picture it summons is different, and certainly the "Thee" that is used to connect the implied "Me" with, is different. The God of the damned cannot know the God of the damner, that is, cannot know he is God. As no Blues person can really believe emotionally in Pascal's God, or Wittgenstein's question, "Can the concept of God exist in a perfectly logical language?" Answer: "God don't never change."[8]

Credit

Smitherman, Geneva. "'God Don't Never Change': Black English from a Black Perspective." *College English* 34.6. (1973): 828–833. Originally published 1973 by the National Council of Teachers of English.

Praisesong for a Mountain

BIANCA LYNNE SPRIGGS

O, mountain,
I am your daughter.

Once, before I knew you,
I mistook you
for a low-hanging thunderhead.

Or thought maybe
you were a blue whale
that had lost its way,
blinded by the sun.

O, mountain,
    linger—
be my whole horizon.

Let me never open
my eyes and see a thing
but your hoary grace.

You are the missing
rib of the Earth.

You are the climax
of a god's birth.

You are the mausoleum
of burnt-out stars.

O, mountain,
I wish one day
to be buried
in your third eye.

Lend me something
of yourself:
your posture,
your grip,
your innermost
jewel-toned seam,
so that I too, may endure.

Credit
Permission granted from author Bianca Lynne Spriggs.

Annoying Ways People Use Sources

KYLE D. STEDMAN

How Slow Driving Is Like Sloppy Writing

I hate slow drivers.* When I'm driving in the fast lane, maintaining the speed limit exactly, and I find myself behind someone who thinks the fast lane is for people who drive ten miles per hour *below* the speed limit, I get an annoyed feeling in my chest like hot water filling a heavy bucket. I wave my arms around and yell, "What …? But, hey … oh come *on!*" There are at least two explanations for why some slow drivers fail to move out of the way:

1. They don't know that the generally accepted practice of highway driving in the U.S. is to move to the right if an upcoming car wants to pass. Or,

2. They know the guidelines but don't care.

But here's the thing: writers can forget that their readers are sometimes just as annoyed at writing that fails to follow conventions as drivers are when stuck behind a car that fails to move over. In other words, there's something similar between these two people: the knowledgeable driver who thinks, "I thought all drivers *knew* that the left lane is for the fastest cars," and the reader who thinks, "I thought all writers *knew* that outside sources should be introduced, punctuated, and cited according to a set of standards."

One day, you may discover that something you've written has just been read by a reader who, unfortunately, was annoyed at some of the ways you integrated sources. She was reading along and then suddenly exclaimed, "What …? But, hey … oh come on!" If you're lucky, this reader will try to imagine why you typed things the way you did, giving you the benefit of the doubt. But sometimes you'll be slotted into positions that might not really be accurate. When this frustrated reader walks away from your work, trying to figure out, say, why you used so many quotations, or why you kept starting and ending paragraphs with them, she may come to the same conclusions I do about slow drivers:

1. You don't know the generally accepted practices of using sources (especially in academic writing) in the U.S. Or,

2. You know the guidelines but don't care.

And it will be a lot harder for readers to take you seriously if they think you're ignorant or rude.

This judgment, of course, will often be unfair. These readers might completely ignore the merits of your insightful, stylistically beautiful, or revolutionarily important language—just as my anger at another driver makes me fail to admire his custom paint job. But readers and writers don't always see eye to eye on the same text. In fact, some things I write about in this essay will only bother your pickiest readers (some teachers, some editors, some snobby friends), while many other readers might zoom past how you use sources without blinking. But in my experience, I find that teachers do a disservice when we fail to alert students to the kind of things that some readers might be annoyed at—however illogical these things sometimes seem. People are often unreasonably picky, and writers have to deal with that—which they do by trying to anticipate and preemptively fix whatever might annoy a broad range of readers. Plus, the more effectively you anticipate that pickiness, the more likely it is that readers will interpret your quotations and paraphrases in the way you want them to—critically or acceptingly, depending on your writing context.

It helps me to remember that the conventions of writing have a fundamentally *rhetorical* nature. That is, I follow different conventions depending on the purpose and audience of my writing, because I know that I'll come across differently to different people depending on how well I follow the conventions expected in any particular writing space. In a blog, I cite a source by hyperlinking; in an academic essay, I use a parenthetical citation that refers to a list of references at the end of the essay. One of the fundamental ideas of rhetoric is that speakers/writers/composers shape what they say/write/create based on what they want it to do, where they're publishing it, and what they know about their audience/readers. And those decisions include nitty-gritty things like introducing quotations and citing paraphrases clearly: not everyone in the entire world approaches these things the same way, but when I strategically learn the expectations of my U.S. academic audience, what

I really want to say comes across smoothly, without little annoying blips in my readers' experience. Notice that I'm not saying that there's a particular *right* or *wrong* way to use conventions in my writing—if the modern U.S. academic system had evolved from a primarily African or Asian or Latin American cultural consciousness instead of a European one, conventions for writing would probably be very different. That's why they're *conventions* and not *rules*.

The Annoyances

5 Because I'm not here to tell you *rules*, *decrees*, or *laws*, it makes sense to call my classifications *annoyances*. In the examples that follow, I wrote all of the annoying examples myself, but all the examples I use of good writing come from actual student papers in first year composition classes at my university; I have their permission to quote them.

Armadillo Roadkill

Everyone in the car hears it: buh-BUMP. The driver insists to the passengers, "But that armadillo—I didn't see it! It just came out of nowhere!"

> *Armadillo Roadkill: dropping in a quotation without introducing it first*

Sadly, a poorly introduced quotation can lead readers to a similar exclamation: "It just came out of nowhere!" And though readers probably won't experience the same level of grief and regret when surprised by a quotation as opposed to an armadillo, I submit that there's a kinship between the experiences: both involve a normal, pleasant activity (driving; reading) stopped suddenly short by an unexpected barrier (a sudden armadillo; a sudden quotation).

Here's an example of what I'm talking about:

> We should all be prepared with a backup plan if a zombie invasion occurs. "Unlike its human counterparts, an army of zombies is completely independent of support" (Brooks 155). Preparations should be made in the following areas …

Did you notice how the quotation is dropped in without any kind of warning? (Buh-BUMP.)

The Fix: The easiest way to effectively massage in quotations is by purposefully returning to each one in your draft to see if you set the stage for your readers—often, by signaling that a quote is about to come, stating who the quote came from, and showing how your readers should interpret it. In the above example, that could be done by introducing the quotation with something like this (new text bolded):

> We should all be prepared with a backup plan if a zombie invasion occurs. **Max Brooks suggests a number of ways to prepare for zombies' particular traits, though he underestimates the ability of humans to survive in harsh environments. For example, he writes,** "Unlike its human counterparts, an army of zombies is completely independent of support" (155). **His shortsightedness could have a number of consequences ...**

In this version, I know a quotation is coming ("For example"), I know it's going to be written by Max Brooks, and I know I'm being asked to read the quote rather skeptically ("he underestimates"). The sentence with the quotation itself also now begins with a "tag" that eases us into it ("he writes").

10   Here's an actual example from Alexsandra. Notice the way she builds up to the quotation and then explains it:

> In the first two paragraphs, the author takes a defensive position when explaining the perception that the public has about scientists by saying that "there is anxiety that scientists lack both wisdom and social responsibility and are so motivated by ambition ..." and "scientists are repeatedly referred to as 'playing God'" (Wolpert 345). With this last sentence especially, his tone seems to demonstrate how he uses the ethos appeal to initially set a tone of someone that is tired of being misunderstood.

Alexsandra prepares us for the quotation, quotes, and then analyzes it. I love it. This isn't a hard and fast rule—I've seen it broken by the best of writers, I admit—but it's a wise standard to hold yourself to unless you have a reason not to.

Dating Spider-Man

An annoyance that's closely connected to Armadillo Roadkill is the tendency writers sometimes have of starting or ending paragraphs with quotations. This

Dating Spider-Man: starting or ending a paragraph with a quotation

isn't technically *wrong*, and there are situations when the effect of surprise is what you're going for. But often, a paragraph-beginning or paragraph-closing quotation feels rushed, unexplained, disjointed.

It's like dating Spider-Man. You're walking along with him and he says something remarkably interesting—but then he tilts his head, hearing something far away, and suddenly shoots a web onto the nearest building and *zooms* away through the air. As if you had just read an interesting quotation dangling at the end of a paragraph, you wanted to hear more of his opinion, but it's too late—he's already moved on. Later, he suddenly jumps off a balcony and is by your side again, and he starts talking about something you don't understand. You're confused because he just dropped in and expected you to understand the context of what was on his mind at that moment, much like when readers step into a paragraph that begins with a quotation. Here's an example:

> *[End of a preceding paragraph:]* ... Therefore, the evidence clearly suggests that we should be exceptionally careful about deciding when and where to rest.

> "When taking a nap, always rest your elbow on your desk and keep your arm perpendicular to your desktop" (Piven and Borgenicht 98). After all, consider the following scenario ...

There's a perfectly good reason why this feels odd—which should feel familiar after reading about the Armadillo Roadkill annoyance above. When you got to the quotation in the second paragraph, you didn't know what you were supposed to think about it; there was no guidance.

The Fix is the same: in the majority of situations, readers appreciate being guided to and led away from a quotation by the writer doing the quoting. Readers get a sense of pleasure from the safe flow of hearing how to read an upcoming quotation, reading it, and then being told one way to interpret it. Prepare, quote, analyze.

I mentioned above that there can be situations where starting a paragraph with a quotation can have a strong effect. Personally, I usually enjoy this most at the beginning of essays or the beginning of sections—like in this example from the very beginning of Jennifer's essay:

> "Nothing is ever simple: Racism and nobility can exist in the same man, hate and love in the same woman, fear and loyalty, compromise and idealism, all the yin-yang dichotomies that make the human species so utterly confounding, yet so utterly fascinating" (Hunter). The hypocrisy and complexity that Stephen Hunter from the *Washington Post* describes is the basis of the movie *Crash* (2004).

Instantly, her quotation hooks me. It doesn't feel thoughtless, like it would feel if I continued to be whisked to quotations without preparation throughout the essay. But please don't overdo it; any quotation that opens an essay or section ought to be integrally related to your topic (as is Jennifer's), not just a cheap gimmick.

Uncle Barry and His Encyclopedia of Useless Information

15 You probably know someone like this: a person (for me, my Uncle Barry) who constantly tries to impress me with how much he knows about just about everything. I might casually bring up something in the news ("Wow, these health care debates are getting really heated, aren't they?") and then find myself barraged by all of Uncle Barry's ideas on government-sponsored health care—which *then* drifts into a story about how his cousin Maxine died in an underfunded hospice center, which had a parking lot that he could have designed better, which reminds him of how good he is at fixing things, just like the garage door at my parents' house, which probably only needs a little … You get the idea. I might even think to myself, "Wait, I want to know more about that topic, but you're zooming on before you contextualize your information at all."

Uncle Barry and his Encyclopedia of Useless Information: using too many quotations in a row

This is something like reading an essay that relies too much on quotations. Readers get the feeling that they're moving from one quotation to the next without ever quite getting to hear the *real* point of what the author wants to say, never getting any time to form an opinion about the claims. In fact, this often makes it sound as if the author has almost no authority at all. You may have been annoyed by paragraphs like this before:

> Addressing this issue, David M. Potter comments, "Whether Seward meant this literally or not, it was in fact a singularly accurate forecast for territorial Kansas" (199). Of course, Potter's view is contested, even though he claims, "Soon, the Missourians began to perceive the advantages of operating without publicity" (200). Interestingly, "The election was bound to be irregular in any case" (201).

Wait—huh? This author feels like Uncle Barry to me: grabbing right and left for topics (or quotes) in an effort to sound authoritative.

The Fix is to return to each quotation and decide why it's there and then massage it in accordingly. If you just want to use a quote to cite a *fact*, then consider paraphrasing or summarizing the source material (which I find is usually harder than it sounds but is usually worth it for the smoothness my paragraph gains). But if you quoted because you want to draw attention to the source's particular phrasing, or if you want to respond to something you agree with or disagree with in the source, then consider taking the time to surround *each* quotation with guidance to your readers about what you want them to think about that quote.

In the following passage, I think Jessica demonstrates a balance between source and analysis well. Notice that she only uses a single quotation, even though she surely could have chosen more. But instead, Jessica relies on her instincts and remains the primary voice of authority in the passage:

> Robin Toner's article, "Feminist Pitch by a Democrat named Obama," was written a week after the video became public and is partially a response to it. She writes, "The Obama campaign is, in some ways, subtly marketing its candidate as a post-feminist man, a generation beyond the gender conflicts of the boomers." Subtly is the key word. Obama is a passive character throughout the video, never directly addressing the camera. Rather, he is shown indirectly through speeches, intimate conversations with supporters and candid interaction with family. This creates a sense of intimacy, which in turn creates a feeling of trust.

Toner's response to the Obama video is like a diving board that Jessica bounces off of before she gets to the really interesting stuff: the pool (her own observations). A bunch of diving boards lined up without a pool (tons of quotes with no analysis) wouldn't please anyone—except maybe Uncle Barry.

Am I in the Right Movie?

When reading drafts of my writing, this is a common experience: I start to read a sentence that seems interesting and normal, with everything going just the way I expect it to. But then the unexpected happens: a quotation blurts itself into the sentence in a way that

Am I in the Right Movie? failing to integrate a quotation into the grammar of the preceding sentence

doesn't fit with the grammar that built up to quotation. It feels like sitting in a movie theater, everything going as expected, when suddenly the opening credits start for a movie I didn't plan to see. Here are two examples of what I'm talking about. Read them out loud, and you'll see how suddenly wrong they feel.

1. Therefore, the author warns that a zombie's vision "are no different than those of a normal human" (Brooks 6).

2. Sheila Anne Barry advises that "Have you ever wondered what it's like to walk on a tightrope—many feet up in the air?" (50)

In the first example, the quoter's build-up to the quotation uses a singular subject—*a zombie's vision*—which, when paired with the quotation, is annoyingly matched with the plural verb *are*. It would be much less jolting to write, "a zombie's vision *is*," which makes the subject and verb agree. In the second example, the quoter builds up to the quotation with a third-person, declarative independent clause: *Sheila Anne Barry advises*. But then the quotation switches into second person—*you*—and unexpectedly asks a question—completely different from the expectation that was built up by the first part of the sentence.

20   **The Fix** is usually easy: you read your essay out loud to someone else, and if you stumble as you enter a quotation, there's probably something you can adjust in your lead-in sentence to make the two fit together well. Maybe you'll need to choose a different subject to make it fit with the quote's verb (*reader* instead of *readers; each* instead of *all*), or maybe you'll have to scrap what you first wrote and start over. On occasion you'll even feel the need to transparently modify the quotation by adding an [s] to one of its verbs, always being certain to use square brackets to show that you adjusted something in the quotation. Maybe you'll even find a way to quote a shorter part of the quotation and squeeze it into the context of a sentence that is mostly your own, a trick that can have a positive effect on readers, who like smooth water slides more than they like bumpy slip-and-slides. Jennifer does this well in the following sentence, for example:

> In *Crash*, no character was allowed to "escape his own hypocrisy" (Muller), and the film itself emphasized that the reason there is so much racial tension among strangers is because of the personal issues one cannot deal with alone.

She saw a phrase that she liked in Muller's article, so she found a way to work it in smoothly, without the need for a major break in her thought. Let's put ourselves in Jennifer's shoes for a moment: it's possible that she started drafting this sentence using the plural subject *characters*, writing "In *Crash*, no characters were allowed ..." But then, imagine she looked back at the quote from Muller and saw that it said "escape *his* own hypocrisy," which was a clue that she had to change the first part of her sentence to match the singular construction of the quote.

I Can't Find the Stupid Link

You've been in this situation: you're on a website that seems like it might be interesting and you want to learn more about it. But the home page doesn't tell you much, so you look for an "About Us" or "More Information" or "FAQ" link. But no matter where you search—Top of page? Bottom? Left menu?—you can't find the stupid link. This is usually the fault of web designers, who don't always take the time to test their sites as much as they should with actual users.

> *I Can't Find the Stupid Link: no connection between the first letter of a parenthetical citation and the first letter of a works cited entry*

The communication failure here is simple: you're used to finding certain kinds of basic information in the places people usually put it. If it's not there, you're annoyed.

Similarly, a reader might see a citation and have a quick internal question about it: *What journal was this published in? When was it published? Is this an article I could find online to skim myself? This author has a sexy last name—I wonder what his first name is?* Just like when you look for a link to more information, this reader has a simple, quick question that he or she expects to answer easily. And the most basic way for readers to answer those questions (when they're reading a work written in APA or MLA style) is (1) to look at the information in the citation, and (2) skim the references or works cited section alphabetically, looking for the first letter in the citation. There's an assumption that the first letter of a citation will be the letter to look for in the list of works cited.

25   In short, the following may annoy readers who want to quickly learn more about the citation:

> *[Essay Text:]* A respected guide on the subject suggests, "If possible, always take the high ground and hold it" (*The Zombie Survival Guide* 135).

> [Works Cited Page:] Brooks, Max. *The Zombie Survival Guide: Complete Protection from the Living Dead*. New York: Three Rivers, 2003. Print.

The reader may wonder when *The Zombie Survival Guide* was published and flip back to the works cited page, but the parenthetical citation sends her straight to the *Z*'s in the works cited list (because initial *A*'s and *The*'s are ignored when alphabetizing). However, the complete works cited entry is actually with the *B*'s (where it belongs).

The Fix is to make sure that the first word of the works cited entry is the word you use in your in-text citation, every time. If the works cited entry starts with Brooks, use (Brooks) in the essay text.

Citations not including last names may seem to complicate this advice, but they all follow the same basic concept. For instance, you might have:

- **A citation that only lists a title**. For instance, your citation might read ("Gray Wolf General Information"). In this case, the assumption is that the citation can be found under the *G* section of the works cited page. Leah cites her paraphrase of a source with no author in the following way, indicating that I should head to the *G*'s if I want to learn more about her source:

  Alaska is the only refuge that is left for the wolves in the United States, and once that is gone, they will more than likely become extinct in this country ("Gray Wolf General Information").

- **A citation that only lists a page number.** Maybe the citation simply says (25). That implies that somewhere in the surrounding text, the essay writer must have made it stupendously clear what name or title to look up in the works cited list. This happens a lot, since it's common to introduce a quotation by naming the person it came from, in which case it would be repetitive to name that author again in the citation.

- **A quotation without a citation at all.** This happens when you cite a work that is both A) from a web page that doesn't number the pages or paragraphs and B) is named in the text surrounding the quotation. Readers will assume that the author is named nearby. Stephanie wisely leaves off any citation in the example below, where it's already clear that I should head to the O's on the works cited page to find information about this source, a web page written by Opotow:

> To further this point, Opotow notes, "Don't imagine you'll be unscathed by the methods you use. The end may justify the means … But there's a price to pay, and the price does tend to be oneself."

I Swear I Did Some Research!

Let's look in depth at this potentially annoying passage from a hypothetical student paper:

> It's possible that a multidisciplinary approach to understanding the universe will open new doors of understanding. If theories from sociology, communication, and philosophy joined with physics, the possibilities would be boundless. This would inspire new research, much like in the 1970s when scientists changed their focus from grand-scale theories of the universe to the small concerns of quantum physics (Hawking 51).

I Swear I Did Some Research: dropping in a citation without making it clear what information came from that source

In at least two ways, this is stellar material. First, the author is actually voicing a point of view; she sounds knowledgeable, strong. Second, and more to the point of this chapter, the author includes a citation, showing that she knows that ethical citation standards ask authors to cite paraphrases and summaries—not just quotations.

30   But on the other hand, which of these three sentences, exactly, came from Hawking's book? Did *Hawking* claim that physics experts should join up with folks in other academic disciplines, or is that the student writer? In other words, at which point does the author's point of view meld into material taken specifically from Hawking?

I recognize that there often aren't clean answers to a question like that. What we read and what we know sometimes meld together so unnoticeably that we don't know which ideas and pieces of information are "ours" and which aren't. Discussing "patchwriting," a term used to describe writing that blends words and phrases from sources with words and phrases we came up with ourselves, scholar Rebecca Moore Howard writes, "When I believe I am not patchwriting,

I am simply doing it so expertly that the seams are no longer visible—or I am doing it so unwittingly that I cannot cite my sources" (91). In other words, *all* the moves we make when writing came from somewhere else at some point, whether we realize it or not. Yikes. But remember our main purpose here: to not look annoying when using sources. And most of your instructors aren't going to say, "I understand that I couldn't tell the difference between your ideas and your source's because we quite naturally patchwrite all the time. That's fine with me. Party on!" They're much more likely to imagine that you plopped in a few extra citations as a way of defensively saying, "I swear I did some research! See? Here's a citation right here! Doesn't that prove I worked really hard?"

The Fix: Write the sentences preceding the citation with specific words and phrases that will tell readers what information came from where. Like this (bolded words are new):

> It's possible that a multidisciplinary approach to understanding the universe will open new doors of understanding. **I believe that** if theories from sociology, communication, and philosophy joined with physics, the possibilities would be boundless. This would inspire new research, much like **the changes Stephen Hawking describes happening** in the 1970s when scientists changed their focus from grand-scale theories of the universe to the small concerns of quantum physics (51).

Perhaps these additions could still use some stylistic editing for wordiness and flow, but the source-related job is done: readers know exactly which claims the essay writer is making and which ones Hawking made in his book. The last sentence and only the last sentence summarizes the ideas Hawking describes on page 51 of his book.

One warning: you'll find that scholars in some disciplines (especially in the sciences and social sciences) use citations in the way I just warned you to avoid. You might see sentences like this one, from page 64 of Glenn Gordon Smith, Ana T. Torres-Ayala, and Allen J. Heindel's article in the *Journal of Distance Education*:

> Some researchers have suggested "curriculum" as a key element in the design of web-based courses (Berge, 1998; Driscoll, 1998; Meyen, Tangen, & Lian, 1999; Wiens & Gunter, 1998).

Whoa—that's a lot of citations. Remember how the writer of my earlier example cited Stephen Hawking because she summarized his ideas? Well, a number of essays describing the results of experiments, like this one, use citations with a different purpose, citing previous studies whose general conclusions support the study described in this new paper, like building blocks. It's like saying to your potentially skeptical readers, "Look, you might be wondering if I'm a quack. But I can prove I'm not! See, all these other people published in similar areas! Are you going to pick fights with all of *them* too?" You might have noticed as well that these citations are in APA format, reflecting the standards of the social sciences journal this passage was published in. Well, in this kind of context APA's requirement to cite the year of a study makes a lot of sense too—after all, the older a study, the less likely it is to still be relevant.

Conclusion: Use Your Turn Signals

35 You may have guessed the biggest weakness in an essay like this: what's annoying varies from person to person, with some readers happily skimming past awkward introductions to quotations without a blink, while others see a paragraph-opening quotation as something to complain about on Facebook. All I've given you here—all I *can* give you unless I actually get to know you and your various writing contexts—are the basics that will apply in a number of academic writing contexts. Think of these as signals to your readers about your intentions, much as wise drivers rely on their turn signals to communicate their intentions to other drivers. In some cases when driving, signaling is an almost artistic decision, relying on the gut reaction of the driver to interpret what is best in times when the law doesn't mandate use one way or the other. I hope your writing is full of similar signals. Now if I could only convince the guy driving in front of me to use *his* blinker ….

Works Cited

Barry, Sheila Anne. *Tricks & Pranks to Fool Your Friends*. New York: Sterling, 1984. Print.

Brooks, Max. *The Zombie Survival Guide: Complete Protection from the Living Dead*. New York: Three Rivers, 2003. Print.

"Gray Wolf General Information." *Environmental Conservation Online System*. U.S. Fish and Wildlife Service, 15 Oct. 2008. Web. 23 Oct. 2008.

Hawking, Stephen. *A Brief History of Time: From the Big Bang to Black Holes*. New York: Bantam, 1988. Print.

Howard, Rebecca Moore. "The New Abolitionism Comes to Plagiarism." *Perspectives on Plagiarism and Intellectual Property in a Postmodern World*. Ed. Lisa Buranen and Alice M. Roy. Albany: SUNY P, 1999. 87–95. Print.

Hunter, Stephen. "'Crash': The Collision Of Human Contradictions." *The Washington Post*. The Washington Post Company, 6 May 2005. Web. 21 Feb. 2008.

Muller, Bill. "Crash: LA Tale Confronts, Then Shatters, Stereotypes." *The Arizona Republic*. AZCentral.com, 6 May 2005. Web. 21 Feb. 2008.

Opotow, Susan. "Moral Exclusion and Torture: The Ticking Bomb Scenario and the Slippery Ethical Slope." *Peace and Conflict Studies* 13.4 (2007): 457–61. PsycINFO. Web. 27 Sept. 2008.

Piven, Joshua, and David Borgenicht. *The Worst-Case Scenario Survival Handbook: Work*. San Francisco: Chronicle, 2003. Print.

Potter, David M. *The Impending Crisis: 1848–1861*. Ed. Don E. Fehrenbacher. New York: Harper & Row, 1976. Print.

Smith, Glenn Gordon, Ana T. Torres-Ayala, and Allen J. Heindel. "Disciplinary Differences in E-learning Instructional Design: The Case of Mathematics." *Journal of Distance Education* 22.3 (2008): 63–88. Web. 10 Sept. 2009.

Toner, Robin. "Feminist Pitch by a Democrat Named Obama." *The New York Times*. The New York Times Company, 2 Dec. 2007. Web. 22 Oct. 2008.

Wolpert, Lewis. "Is Cell Science Dangerous?" *Journal of Medical Ethics* 33.6 (2007): 345–48. Academic Search Premier. Web. 28 Jan. 2009.

Credit

Stedman, Kyle D. "Annoying Ways People Use Sources" *Writing Spacess: Readings on Writing, Vol. 2*. Eds. Charles Lowe and Pavel Zemiliansky. Anderson, SC: Parlor Press, 2011. 242–256. Available online at http://writingspaces.org/sites/default/files/stedman--annoying-ways.pdf.

A Family Affair: Competing Sponsors of Literacy in Appalachian Students' Lives

SARA WEBB-SUNDERHAUS

My aunt teaches me how to do school.

—Katie May

He wants to blame me going back to school for his problems, which it is not.

—Pamela, discussing her husband's drug addiction

Sponsors [...] set the terms for access to literacy and wield powerful incentives for compliance and loyalty.

—Deborah Brandt, Literacy in American Lives

Growing up as an Urban Appalachian[1] in Cincinnati, Ohio, I became painfully aware of the stories that some people tell about Appalachians: stories of hillbillies, rednecks, and white trash; stories of incest and other deviant sexual practices; stories of laziness, ignorance, and hatred. When I entered graduate school, I became aware of other kinds of stories about Appalachians. While there were stories of illiteracy and relentless poverty, there were also stories that idealized Appalachian families and that venerated the "pure" Anglo-Saxon whiteness of the Appalachian people. But I didn't recognize the Appalachian people I knew and loved, or myself, in any of these stories. These stories demonized and romanticized Appalachians; as folklorist Patrick B. Mullen writes, "[T]he Anglo Appalachian is a complex construction containing both romantic and rational scientific elements; hidden beneath a romantic view is a pathological one" (129). The multifaceted stories I learned from my family about Appalachia and its people—the stories I learned down on the tobacco farms of Lewis County, Kentucky—usually were not being told in my fields of study. It was my awareness of these other stories of Appalachia that inspired my research, which examines the interplay of literacy and identity among Appalachians enrolled in college composition courses.

Deborah Brandt's *Literacy in American Lives* posits that literacy is not only an individual development, but also an economic one, since "literacy looms as one of the great engines of profit and competitive advantage in the twentieth century" (18). The individual and the economic are intertwined, Brandt argues, and she frames her analysis by examining what she calls "sponsors of literacy."

According to Brandt, sponsors are "any agents, local or distant, concrete or abstract, who enable, support, teach, and model, as well as recruit, regulate, suppress, or withhold, literacy—and gain advantage by it in some way" (19). These sponsors are conduits for the larger economic forces of literacy, as Brandt writes that they are "the means by which these forces present themselves to—and through—individual learners" (19). While interviewing the participants in the case studies that make up her book, Brandt found that sponsors were often individuals: "older relatives, teachers, religious leaders, supervisors, military officers, librarians, friends, editors, influential authors" (19). However, as Brandt notes, sponsors can include commercial entities, such as companies who award prizes in a jingle-writing contest and restaurants who offer gift certificates to children who read a designated number of books, as well as institutions, such as the African-American church.

I have found Brandt's concept of sponsorship useful in describing the literacy beliefs of students enrolled in an English Composition course at Riverton University and State University-Sciotoville, two open-admission universities in Central Appalachia.[2] When I began my project, I was particularly interested in the role of educational institutions in shaping literacy beliefs and the students' performance of identity, particularly their Appalachian identity. My research with these students led me to conclude that literacy beliefs and practices were part and parcel of the students' performance of identity, representing an important stage on which their Appalachian-ness—or non-Appalachian-ness, in some cases—was portrayed. Institutional beliefs about, and rewards for, certain types of literacy help foster or sponsor certain beliefs and performances from the students. Yet schools are not the only, or even necessarily the most influential, sponsors of literacy in American lives. Brandt writes that "sponsors of literacy are more prolific, diffused, and heterogeneous" (197) than in the past, when schools played a prominent role in literacy education; she later adds, "Schools are no longer the major disseminators of literacy" (198). Thus, the question that surfaced during my research was, if educational institutions are a key sponsor of these students' literacies, how do other sponsors impact the students' performance of identity, and more specifically Appalachian-ness, with regard to literacy? Who are the "prolific, diffused, and heterogeneous" sponsors in these students' lives?

This article will focus on one group of sponsors, namely immediate and extended family members, and the complexity of their sponsorship. Sponsorship is a messy process, one that cannot be neatly delineated. The same could be said of some Appalachian families as well. Appalachian Studies scholars often write of a romanticized Appalachian family that serves as a comforting fortress for its members; for example, Loyal Jones writes, "Mountain people usually feel an obligation to family members and are more truly themselves when within the family circle" (75). Other scholars write of conflicts between the culture of family and the culture of school, with family culture being more acceptable to Appalachians, according to Michael Maloney: "[T]here's a deep conflict between the values in school and the values at home [...] Appalachians expect relationships to be personal; they aren't comfortable with functional relationships" (34). Yet for the students in my study, the Appalachian family did not function only in the comforting, supportive ways typically described by scholars. While many individual family members were encouraging sponsors of their students' literacies, some of these same individuals also worked to inhibit the students' emerging literacy beliefs and practices. Seemingly contradictory messages about literacy could come from the same person, such that the same person could be both a sponsor and an inhibitor—or perhaps more accurately, a sponsor of a competing meaning of literacy—in a student's life. And it was through, and upon, these inhibitors of literacy that the larger social forces described by Brandt were often enacted. In other words, far from being a fortress from the outside world, the families of my participants created a space in which these social forces fostered particular kinds of sponsorship.

The Study

5   During the summer of 2004, I conducted an ethnographic case study of two English Composition classes and the students enrolled in them. The data I gathered came from multiple sources including participant-observations, transcripts of individual classes, a brief demographic survey, formal interviews, and, in the case of one class, an extended survey based on my interview script. I attended each class twice a week, making audio recordings of class sessions and taking notes so that I could paint a rich portrait full of "thick detail" for each course. I also made audio recordings of the five interviews I conducted with each of my case study participants, as well as the interviews with the instructors and other students. I asked each student to complete a brief demographic survey, and from those surveys I selected two to three students from each course to be my case study participants. My selections were based on students' willingness and availability to participate as well as their representativeness

of their respective classes. While two students from each course became case study participants who were interviewed weekly for the duration of each five-week course, many other students participated in my research, thanks to their contributions in class and their participation in short, occasional interviews inside and outside of class. Particular student voices you will hear in this article include those of Mike, Michelle, and Pamela, all of whom were students at Riverton University; and Katie May and Julie, students at State University-Sciotoville.

Tables 1 and 2 provide demographic information about the two classes and universities that were the focus of the project:

Table 1: Riverton

	Campus	Class
Enrollment	1,800 students	14 students
Male-Female Enrollment	40% M, 60% F	14% M, 86% F
Average Age of Students	33	23.8
Race of Students	93% white (all U.S. campuses)	86% white, 7% African-Amer., 7% Asian-Amer.
Commuting Students	All	All
First Generation College	"Most"	64%
Born and Raised in Local Area	"Most"	86%
Identify as Appalachian (All Students)	Unknown	64%
Identify as Appalachian (Students Raised in Region)	Unknown	64%

Table 2: Sciotoville

	Campus	Class
Enrollment	3,500 students	18 students
Male-Female Enrollment	40% M, 60% F	60% M, 40% F (50-50 in regular attendance)
Average Age of Students	25	26.8
Race of Students	86% white, 10% unknown, 4% students of color	94% white, 6% African-American
Commuting Students	90%	75%
First Generation College	"Most"	32%
Born and Raised in Local Area	"Most"	62%
Identify as Appalachian (All Students)	Unknown	28%
Identify as Appalachian (Students Raised in Region)	Unknown	45%

This demographic information confirms what I found in interviews: Riverton students were less likely to self-identify as Appalachian, even when they had been raised in the region, and had negative perceptions of Appalachian-ness; almost all of the Sciotoville students self-identified as Appalachian and performed Appalachian-ness in positive, even romanticized ways. These performances of identities would echo in interesting ways throughout the students' discussions of their literacy.

Multiple Sources of Sponsorship

Spiritual Influences

Interviews with all of my participants indicated several literacy sponsors at work in their lives. Michelle and Mike told of the influence of sports team and fraternity membership, respectively. Katie May, a 19-year-old pre-med student from State University-Sciotoville, shared intertwining stories of literacy and spirituality. Many Appalachian Studies scholars focus their attentions on the role of religion and the church in Appalachians' everyday lives. Jones represents this approach to Appalachians' religious lives when he writes, "Mountain people are religious. This does not mean that we always go to church regularly, but we are religious in the sense that most of our values and the meanings we find in life spring from the Bible. To understand mountaineers, one must understand our religion" (39). Thus, I was not surprised when the church appeared prominent in Katie May's discussions of her literacy.

Some of Katie May's sponsors include the church as an institution, as well as individuals (such as a youth pastor who encouraged her to take notes during church services) who were directly connected to the church and representative of the church's role in her literacy beliefs and practices. Katie May's descriptions of her brother's sponsorship of her spiritually-based literacy practices led me to focus on the role not only of religion, but also of family, in the development of her literacy life. While work by literacy scholars such as Shirley Brice Heath and Denny Taylor points to parents as significant forces in the development of literacy, my research points to multiple family members, including parents, as sponsors of literacy. This family sponsorship seems particularly important in the cultural context of Appalachia, since, as previously discussed, the work of many Appalachian Studies scholars emphasizes the value Appalachians place on family and extended kinship networks.

Immediate Family Members

10 Katie May's brother played an important role in the intertwining of literacy and religion in her life, since he recommended that she begin daily devotionals when she was in eighth grade.[3] He also offered specific suggestions of religious texts for her to read. Katie May recalled, "My brother encouraged me a lot with books that he had read. He'd say, 'Hey, try this one; it's good.'" Her brother was four years older than Katie May and, at the time he began to take on this sponsorship role in her life, he was preparing to attend Bible college. Given their age difference, Katie May's brother was more mature and knowledgeable about both spirituality and literacy, making him an appropriate sponsor in her life.

Katie May's brother demonstrated his sponsorship in other ways as well. Her brother offered her a ride to church until Katie May was old enough to drive herself, and as Katie May stated, he "encouraged" her spiritual development through various uses of literacy. Describing his influence, Katie May said his communication came "through notes. I'd find a note in my school notebooks. I'd turn the pages and there would be something he'd written me a couple nights before. Also with the books [the devotionals]. He recommended a lot of things to me." The notes usually had a theme of encouragement, drawing on stories from the Bible to make a point. Katie May said, "I think he was trying to encourage me. He'd write things like, 'I've been praying for you.' He'd mention things from the Bible, about people who had gone through the same thing. He'd talk about characters from the Bible that I could relate with." After Katie May's brother moved across the country to become a youth pastor, they began exchanging e-mails once or twice a week as a way to stay in touch and to continue this spiritual sponsorship. The spiritual sponsorship Katie May's brother offered was inextricably tied to literacy, as almost all instances of sponsorship that Katie May shared with me involved print such as recommendations of specific readings, writing notes, making Biblical analogies, and e-mailing.

Extended Family Members

While for some students immediate family members exerted the most influence in their literacy lives, extended family members, such as Michelle's grandparents and cousins and Katie May's aunt, acted as significant sponsors as well. Michelle, a 19-year-old, chemistry/pre-pharmacy student who had just completed her first year at Riverton University, lived in rural Massie County, a 30-minute drive from the campus. This distance made it difficult for her to return home for lunch or studying during the day. Her grandparents lived in town, however, and they invited their grandchildren to come to their house during the school day. Several of Michelle's cousins also attended Riverton University, and all of those cousins would gather at their grandparents' house for lunch and study breaks. In an interview, Michelle described these visits to her grandparents' home:

> Grandma will cook lunch for whoever's there, but we're all in and out at different times due to our class schedules, so we'll bring our own food to eat, too. But the main thing is that it's a quiet place to study. Grandma and Grandpa will ask how things are going and that sort of thing, but then they'll leave you alone so you can get your work done. And if they're not going to be home, they'll leave the door open so we can come in and do our work.

Michelle's grandparents did not sponsor her literacy through teaching her particular literacy practices, modeling textual interaction, and the like. Instead, Michelle's grandparents' sponsorship arose from their offer of material goods—namely food and study space—that would assist in the development of her academic literacy and education. Michelle's grandparents did not have the necessary academic literacy themselves to assist Michelle and her cousins with their homework; however, they could, and did, offer their approval of academic literacy by offering a warm meal and a quiet place to study. These acts, which on the surface may seem unconnected to literacy, were a powerful show of support for the educations of their grandchildren.

Michelle also commented on the role the cousins played in each other's educations, noting that since the cousins were at varying stages in their college careers and had different academic strengths, they could support each other:

> There is always somebody around who can help you with your homework. Or you can help them. It's really nice to be able to talk with them, if I'm stuck on something or have a question. Or sometimes we just give each other advice about what classes to register for, which professors are good, that sort of thing.

Through this support, Michelle and her cousins became sponsors of each other's academic literacy practices and education, broadly speaking.

Other students also discussed the importance of family members who helped them learn how to "do school." For Katie May, one of her aunts was a pivotal sponsor of literacy. Katie May stated in an interview that her aunt "teaches me how to do school," and we later talked further of the specific suggestions her aunt gave her for "doing school." Though Katie May was taking summer classes at State University-Sciotoville, she was actually a rising sophomore at Big State University, her state's flagship university. Katie May had a difficult time during her first two quarters at Big State. Always an A student in high school, she found herself struggling to make Cs in the chemistry and calculus courses required for pre-med majors—grades that put her in danger of losing her scholarships, which required a B average. Her aunt, a dentist who earned her undergraduate and professional degrees at Big State, sat Katie May down over a break and gave her a "talking-to," which Katie May discussed in an interview.

> **Katie May:** "I brought my grades up a lot last spring quarter, and she definitely influenced me in that area. I felt like I had what it took [to do well in school], but I didn't know how to channel that. And so she really guided me and showed me, this is the way you do it. It really was. At first I didn't believe her, because I'd never done study groups. But it really helped."

> **Sara:** "How did she, how did she show you, 'this is how you do it?' Was is just the study groups, or did she give you other kinds of advice?"

> **Katie May:** "She would talk to me, she talked to me at the end of fall quarter [Katie May's first term of college], and said, 'This is what you need to do and went down the list. And then …"

> **Sara [interrupting]:** "What was the list?"

Katie May: "Do study groups. Talk to the professors. Do all the homework. She asked me how I studied, and I said I read the chapters but then I'm usually too tired to do the homework, so I just read the chapters. She was like, well maybe you should do the homework first and then go back and read the chapter. So she really helped me with that."

Katie May's responses indicate the pivotal acts of literacy sponsorship her aunt took on. Her aunt directed her as to which academic literacy practices were most important—doing the written homework as opposed to the reading homework—and directed her towards other, more local sponsors of literacy like her peers and professors. Here we see a sponsor whose importance came in part from her recommendations of other sponsors of literacy.

15   Katie May's aunt told her not only to seek out these other sponsors of literacy, but also how to approach them, and the aunt stayed in regular contact with Katie May so she could continue her sponsorship:

Sara: "Did she give you strategies about how to talk to professors?"

Katie May: "Yeah. She said, 'Go up to your Chemistry 122 professor and say, I got a C– in Chemistry 121, and I struggled for that, and I don't want to get another C– in this class. How can I improve?' [...] And then she'd talk to me once a week and ask me, so are you doing the things we talked about? Are you doing the study groups and talking to the professors? That sort of thing. [...] We have AIM instant messenger, so we talk at least once a week through that. At first it was probably two times a week, but then, as she saw I was doing what I needed to do, we went down to once a week."

Sara: "How did she come to sit you down and give you the talking-to? Did you kind of come home and cry on her shoulder, or did your parents tell her something was up? Or did she just ask you about how you were doing in school?"

Katie May: "My mom would call her and say, 'Katie May's crying! What should I do?!' That type of thing. And then I came home for break and we talked."

Here we see another sponsor of Katie May's literacy emerge: her mother, who first informed the aunt of Katie May's struggles in school. As I shall discuss in the next section, parents were important influences on the literacy practices and beliefs of many of the participants in my study.

Parents

In studies of family literacy, it is often parents who receive the most attention, and our culture's conventional wisdom places heavy emphasis on the role parents play in the development of their children's literacy practices. While part of my intent in this article has been to illustrate that many family members can become sponsors of literacy, I also recognize that for most individuals, their parents are among the earliest and most primary sponsors of literacy.

Parents' sponsorship can take different forms, however, as illustrated by the experiences of my case study participants. For some parents, such as Katie May's mother, sponsorship meant connecting their children with more knowledgeable sponsors. In the last transcribed section of the Katie May interview, Katie May stated that her mother had informed Katie May's aunt—her sister—of Katie May's problems with school and had asked for assistance: "Katie May's crying! What should I do?!." Katie May's mother did not attend college, whereas Katie May's aunt held undergraduate and professional degrees. Katie May's mother may not have had the knowledge of academic literacy practices to advise Katie May about difficulties in school, but she knew someone who did—her sister— and she asked her sister to work with Katie May. While this may have been an indirect form of sponsorship, it was incredibly important in helping Katie May acquire the literacy practices she needed during her first year of college.

Other parents engaged in indirect, as well as more direct, forms of sponsorship. Michelle's father earned two associate's degrees from Riverton University and worked at the local hospital as the supervisor of bio-medical engineering. He loomed large in Michelle's discussions of literacy. One of her earliest memories of books involved looking at her father's college textbooks when he was enrolled at Riverton while Michelle was a small child. After Michelle's father earned his last degree, he did not put away his books. Instead, he kept them displayed on the family bookshelf, and as she grew up, Michelle continued to read them:

> I loved looking at his books when I was little. Still do. I look at them now sometimes to see if they might explain something a little better, something I'm confused about. I know he's got a physics book up there that I should look at. [...] He never showed them to me. They were just always there. [...] As a kid I looked at them, not knowing what they were. But as I got older and thinking about college, it hit me, what they were, and I looked at them to see what college would be like.

In addition to the textbooks Michelle's father kept on hand, he also subscribed to and read several science magazines, partly to stay aware of new developments in his line of work, and partly for the pleasure of reading about science. Michelle frequently read these magazines and stated that she enjoyed doing so. While her father did not directly encourage her reading the magazines, his modeling of a certain type of behavior—an interest in continued learning and a love of science, combined with the easy availability of texts—led Michelle to develop an interest in science and read the books and magazines. Michelle directly credited her skill and interest in math and science to her father, an unsurprising development given the types of print materials her father brought into the house via his work and education. As Brandt notes:

> Though not always the focus of explicit instruction and not often school oriented, work-related reading and writing provided children real-world information about how literacy functions [… and] brought at least some children into contact with the material assets and social power of major literacy sponsors—corporations, industries, merchants, governments, and universities. (199)

While Michelle's mother worked at the hospital as well, she worked in the data entry department. She attended a business college for two years and did not earn a degree. Though Michelle did note in interviews that her mother always encouraged her to go to college, she made it clear that her father played a more active sponsorship role in her life through his sharing of texts and, as I will soon discuss, his specific guidance about her education. In Michelle's family, there was an unstated understanding that her father would be the one to develop Michelle's interest in science and to advise her about her education, since he had two associate's degrees and work experience in scientific fields.

Thus, it was Michelle's father who had the career path with more economic and cultural capital—one that a college-bound daughter would be more likely to emulate. Brandt writes that fathers are often overlooked in studies of family literacy, due to an emphasis on "the nurture of preschool children," a presumably "motherly" domain (200). But Michelle's case is representative of Brandt's notion that "[t]he historically privileged position that men have occupied in education and employment made fathers in many households the conduits of specialized skills and materials that could be of interest and use to other family members" (200). It was Michelle's repeated exposure to the world of scientific reading materials, via her father, that set her on the path of a chemistry/pre-pharmacy major.

20   Her father also played a direct role in her educational goals, advising her to take particular courses in high school:

> My sophomore year, I doubled up on math classes so I could go farther [take more advanced courses in high school]. I knew that I really wanted to go towards the medical field, and I knew, because my dad told me, that you had to have a lot of science, since obviously it's the big thing in the medical field. So you gotta get that in. So I doubled up in that.

The "doubling-up" in math and science courses paid off, as Michelle was quickly moving through her courses at Riverton and was looking into transferring to a joint B.S./PharmD program at a large state university a few hours from home. Given her father's educational background and work experience, he had the knowledge to tell Michelle what types of courses she needed to be taking and when—a critical factor in determining what careers would later be open to her and in enabling her success at Riverton. Michelle's father's ability to steer her towards particular courses—towards developing particular kinds of academic literacies, if you will—became a very important moment of sponsorship in her life.

Inhibitors of Literacy

While the students I interviewed told many positive and heart-warming stories of literacy sponsorship, as our interviews continued, other stories emerged as well. In these stories, a threatening side of literacy sponsorship emerged. Literacy, particularly academic literacy, became a dangerous force, one that could distance students from family members and loved ones. For a few students, their pursuit of academic literacy vis-à-vis a college degree put them at odds, in ways big and small, with some of the most important people in their lives. Some of these people sought to inhibit the students' development of this literacy through their sponsorship of competing meanings of literacy. These individuals did not inhibit the development of the students' literacy practices alone, however. Social forces, such as poor health care and stereotypical gender roles, played a significant part as well. Brandt writes, "Literacy spreads last and always less well to remote rural areas and newer, poorer industrial areas—a geographic and political legacy that, even today, in the United States, helps to exacerbate inequalities by race, region, and occupation" (88). The forces at work in these students' lives, sometimes presented in the form of individual inhibitors, reveal some of the inequalities still at work in parts of Appalachia.

Mike's Story

For Mike, attaining a college degree had been a long, drawn-out process. While he began college at the age of eighteen, at the time of our interview he was twenty-six and just entering his senior year. One reason why his college education had taken seven years to that point was repeated transfers between institutions, but his health was the factor that most slowed his progress to earning a degree. Mike developed a problem with his kidneys while he was enrolled in Riverton, a problem that required a minor surgery at the local hospital. The surgery involved inserting a stent into one of his kidneys to help improve its function and to reduce the pain he felt every day. While this was not a life-threatening operation, Mike had to withdraw from school for a quarter as he healed. As it turned out, however, Mike's surgery wasn't so simple: "I got an infection. It was pretty bad. They put me in the hospital for four or five days. I don't even remember being in the hospital, I was so sick. It was a staph infection. It was pretty bad."

After his hospital stay, Mike returned to his parents' home in a nearby town and continued to recover from the infection, which had left him weakened. During the course of his recovery, it was determined that the surgery had not corrected the problem with his kidneys. In fact, the condition had worsened. At this point, frustrated by the care their son was receiving and worried about his health, Mike's parents took him to the campus of Big State University so that he could be treated at the university's medical center:

> I was still in so much pain every day, which is what the first surgery was supposed to fix. And then I developed that staph infection, which you get from the [surgical] instruments not being sterile. So when that happened, we decided that I should change doctors, and I went up to Big State. They couldn't get me in for the surgery for a while, so I missed even more school. But at least they fixed my kidney.

All told, Mike lost a year of school as he went through the first surgery and recovery, the staph infection and recovery, and the second surgery and recovery. When I asked Mike if he ever wanted to give up during this time and quit school altogether, he responded, "Yes. But what kept me going was my parents. My parents were dead set on me getting through college."

Mike's story illustrates multiple forces at work in his literacy life. His first surgery, at a small country hospital, turned into a disaster, with the failure of the stent to treat the problem and the development of a staph infection. Mike attributed both of these problems to the health care he received, and, given the state of health care in Central Appalachia and Massie County, Riverton's home county, it is quite likely Mike received inadequate care. Massie County has been identified by the Appalachian Regional Commission as economically distressed, and, according to Richard P. Mulcahy, the "supply of doctors in the distressed counties is one primary-care physician for every 2,128 persons and one specialist for every 2,857 individuals" (1635). This is in comparison to one primary-care doctor for every 1,099 persons and specialist for every 588 in economically competitive Appalachian counties (1635). The lack of quality health care in the region caused serious hardship for Mike and very nearly derailed his college career.

25   But Mike's story also reveals the larger social forces that worked to help him return to college. His parents had the economic means to support him throughout his illness, to care for him in their home, to seek out second opinions, and to take him to Big State for further medical treatment. His parents also had the means to support him financially following the second surgery. Prior to these health problems, Mike had worked full time and gone to school. But Mike stated that after he recovered from his second surgery, "my parents told me they wanted me to focus on finishing school and staying healthy. They were afraid working would get me run-down and sick again. So they're paying for my school now and helping me with money to live on." The importance of this type of economic sponsorship, as well as his parents' insistence that he finish his degree, cannot be overrated. Simply put, without the sponsorship of his parents throughout this challenging time, it is highly debatable whether Mike would have returned to school or if his health would have permitted him to return.

Women's Stories

While Mike's story reveals some of the economic forces that sponsor or inhibit academic literacy, the stories of Pamela and Julie reveal how traditional gender roles can inhibit academic literacy—or, at the very least, sponsor competing notions of that literacy. I will first discuss Pamela, a thirty-three-year-old student at Riverton University.

Pamela

When I met Pamela during the first week of class, she was eager to participate in the case study, but she explained to me that she might have to drop the class due to problems at home. While she had just been accepted into the nursing program—a rigorous and competitive program at Riverton—she was considering withdrawing from it as well. Pamela was going through a divorce and was worried about its impact on her sons, who were nine and thirteen years old: "The kids, especially the little one, really need my support right now, and I'm worried he's not going to have that if I have my nose stuck in a book." There were also financial considerations. In order to accommodate the class schedule and homework the nursing major demanded, Pamela, who worked as a licensed practical nurse at the local hospital, would have to limit herself to sixteen hours of work a week. Given the pending divorce, she literally could not afford to make that change.

Pamela did in fact drop the course the following week; she also delayed her admission into the nursing program. Thus, what was to be our first interview became our only interview. During our short time together, Pamela explained why her plans for school were in a state of transition:

> I started here two years ago, full-time, but then last year I took a couple quarters off to deal with stuff at home. And now my status fluctuates. I can't predict what it will be. So much depends on my husband. Soon to be ex-husband. At first he was *very* supportive. And then his insecurities … [trailing off]. That's why we're getting a divorce. I'll just tell you: He's got a prescription drug abuse problem. He's buying them from the street.

Pamela's estranged husband suffered a back injury at work and, in the course of his treatment, was put on prescription painkillers, including OxyContin. During his disability leave from work and recovery, he eventually grew addicted to Oxy. His addiction is sadly representative of the problems facing many Central Appalachians. Oxy has become the drug of choice in the region, to such an extent that it is commonly referred to as "hillbilly heroin." And like heroin, Oxy can have a devastating effect. To give one example of the severity of the problem, the Appalachian Regional Commission states in "Substance Abuse in Appalachia" that "Appalachian Kentucky is experiencing drug related deaths at about four times the rate of the rest of the state"—deaths that, for the most part, are attributable to OxyContin. Though Pamela's estranged husband was alive, his addiction caused serious emotional and financial hardship for the family:

He had difficulty keeping a job, and he had emptied the joint bank accounts he had with Pamela in order to buy more Oxy. The consequences of his actions were mortgage and car payments so far behind that Pamela feared she might lose both her home and her car. Pamela continued to discuss her estranged husband and his addiction, directly relating his addiction to her pursuit of a college degree:

> And at first he was really supportive. In fact, before I went back to school, I actually wrote a paper about this for my first English class. It was something like, 'Why are you here?' And I had said, to my kids and my husband, I had said, 'Okay, here it is. I'm gonna go back to my school, you're going to have to help me pick up the slack with the house,' and everybody was in agreement. If one of them had said, 'No, I'm not willing to do that,' I probably wouldn't have come. But it was a family decision. And now his insecurities … [trailing off]. He thinks, he wants to blame me going to school for his problems, which it is not. It has nothing to do with me going back to school.

Indeed, even before we sat down for this interview after class, Pamela had related her estranged husband's attempts to attribute the cause of his addiction to her schooling. When she approached me after class, she told me that her husband had "problems" and stated, "He says it's my fault for going back to school. Because as the man, he should be the one to provide for the family, not me." Apparently, he was despondent over the loss of his income (due to his work injury) and threatened by Pamela's emergence as the breadwinner and most highly educated member of the family. In arguments with Pamela, her estranged husband connected these losses—both of money and of status—and perceived them as the cause of his subsequent addiction.

As this last anecdote suggests, gender roles can play a large part in circumscribing the opportunities available to men and women within the Central Appalachian region. More women go to college because they are deemed to "need" it, since it is hard for them to find a job that offers sustainable pay without a college degree. Men traditionally have not gone to college because jobs that could support a family were available to them without a degree. Yet given the exodus of jobs from this region, as well as changing life circumstances, gender roles are in flux. Whether it is due to a job being outsourced or being out of work due to workplace injury and subsequent addiction—as was the case in Pamela's marriage—many men are no longer the primary breadwinners for their families.

30   For couples steeped in the region's traditional gender roles (Bush and Lash 170), this break from tradition could have significant consequences. In her book *Whistlin' and Crowin' Women of Appalachia: Literacy Practices Since College,* Katherine Kelleher Sohn introduces us to Sarah, a former student of Sohn's and a woman whose marriage had been affected by her education, much like Pamela's. Sarah said of her husband, "He was a traditional man who wanted me to be more passive. He felt that he should be the breadwinner and felt that my being in college was a threat to his manhood in providing for his family" (131). Drawing on the old Appalachian maxim that "whistlin' and crowin' hens always come to no good ends," Sohn writes that in parts of Central Appalachia, "Women are not supposed to whistle or crow; those who objected [to women's changing roles] were threatened by these women's growth and change" (77). As we see from Sohn's study of Sarah and the example of Pamela in this study, some husbands may be intimidated by their wives' educations, given the confluence in the region of traditional gender roles, limited economic opportunities, and medical issues such as disability and addiction.

Julie

Like Pamela, Julie was also under a tremendous amount of pressure to live up to traditional gender roles and to abandon her pursuit of a college degree, though unlike Pamela, Julie's pressure came from multiple sources. Julie, a twenty-four-year-old mother of a kindergartner, first attended college as an eighteen-year-old fresh out of high school. Julie had been a good student throughout high school, and her mother and stepfather were generally supportive of her college plans. Thus, Julie enrolled at a community college in her hometown (while Julie is from Central Appalachia, she is not a native of Sciotoville or its home state). Soon after the fall semester started, however, Julie discovered she was pregnant, and her life quickly changed:

> I was under so much pressure. My mom and step-dad told me that I had to drop out of school, now that I was going to become a mother. I had to focus on my child and what was best for it. And he [the father of her child] and his mother said this, too. They all just wanted us to hurry up and get married. I really wanted to stay in school, but there was just no support for it at all. My ex-husband always went along with whatever his mother said, so there was no support there. And then I had terrible morning sickness and was constantly getting sick; I was so afraid of throwing up in class. Eventually, it seemed easier to stop fighting everybody and to quit, so I did.

For the first year of her son's life, Julie was a stay-at-home-mother, and while she enjoyed being home with her son, school was always in the back of her mind: "I knew I never should have dropped out." Then economic demands began taking a toll on the family. Julie described her ex-husband as young and irresponsible, and he lost several jobs. Julie found a job at a call center and went to work, eventually out-earning her husband—a fact that added stress to an already shaky marriage. When her son was four, Julie and her husband divorced. Shortly thereafter, Julie moved to Sciotoville and enrolled at the university. At the time of our interviews, she had just completed her first year.

Julie's family was aghast at these developments. Julie stated in interviews that numerous relatives told her she was "abandoning her child" by returning to school. Julie saw her return to school as a way to provide a better life for her son, but her relatives, especially her mother, did not agree:

> **Julie:** "Mom is always telling me that my place is in the home, that I should be taking care of him, that school is robbing him of me."
>
> **Sara:** "But you worked before you went back to school. So how is being away from him for work different from being away from him for school?"
>
> **Julie:** "That's just it. It's not. Well, I am working now, part-time, while I go to school, and they say it's too much, that I shouldn't be working and going to school. But I try to arrange my schedule so that I'm not away from him any more than I would be then if I worked full-time. Mom and my step-dad are always telling me that it's selfish for me to be in school, that I should just be working full-time and supporting my son. 'You made your bed, now you have to lie in it.' That's what they're always saying to me. It was one thing for me to go to school before I had him, but now it's something else."

Julie attributed her family's response to their strong religious beliefs, since "their church teaches a woman's place is in the home." But traditional gender roles were at work in complex and contradictory ways here. On one level, Julie's family recognized that her place was *not* in the home, since they felt she should be working full-time to support her son. Yet they also faulted her for not being home with him and told her she was "selfish"—an accusation typically hurled at working mothers. There was no way for Julie to win her family's approval, short of re-marrying and becoming a stay-at-home mother again.

Adding to her family's disapproval was the fact that Julie had come out as a lesbian. Shortly after moving to Sciotoville, Julie met Shelly, with whom she began a romantic relationship. They moved in together soon after they met. Her family's disapproval of homosexuality added to the already strained relationship and increased the tension in Julie's life. When I asked Julie in our first interview if Shelly had been a source of support for her during these trying times, she replied:

> **Julie:** "Oh, God, no. She's just as bad as they are about school. She tells me I have no business being in school. She says she was attracted to me because I was very femme, and she says school has changed that."
>
> **Sara:** "How?"
>
> **Julie:** "Well, she thinks it's my job to do all the stuff around the house, the cooking, the cleaning, and of course there's my son, who *is* my responsibility. She gets so mad when things aren't clean the way they should be and says that if I wasn't so busy with school I would take better care of the house."

Later in the same interview, Julie explained the other reasons why Shelly does not support her schooling:

> She says I don't have any time for her or our friends, that I'm always busy with homework. She says it can't be that hard, that it doesn't take that much time to do school work, that I just don't want to be with her. But how would she know? She came here a quarter when she was 18 and flunked out because all she did was party. So she never tried. (Sigh, then a short pause) She also says I think I'm better than everybody else now. She says I use big words and act all superior. And it's true, I do have a really good vocabulary, I've always been really verbal. But that's just the way I talk! It's not because I think I'm better than other people. I'm tired of fighting about it, though. So now I just don't talk about certain things, or say things in a certain way, just so I won't have to hear that.

Thus, Shelly emerged as an inhibitor of Julie's attempts to gain academic literacy, one who attributed academic literacy with other meanings. For Julie, her development of academic literacy was a way to gain a "better life" for her son. For Shelly, Julie's development of academic literacy was seen as an infringement on Julie's role in the home and their time together, as well as a force that distanced Julie from her, making her "uppity," to use another label Julie said had been applied to her by Shelly.

Shelly's disapproval of Julie's education had a noticeable impact on her schooling. As the summer term went on, Julie attended class less and less; she missed two classes to go on a camping trip that Shelly spontaneously announced, telling me, "I couldn't deal with telling her I couldn't go because of school." She also began a new job, one that required her to work more hours, because of pressure from Shelly that she wasn't contributing enough money to the relationship. The training for her new job overlapped with a couple of classes, and Julie missed class so she could attend those sessions. Before these absences, Julie was earning an A in the course. Between the penalty she earned due to the strict attendance policy and the self-admitted lack of time she put into doing assignments after she began her new job, Julie earned a B– for the course.

35   At the end of the summer, I met Julie for a follow-up visit, at which time she told me that she was taking fall quarter off: "I'm hoping it will make things better with Shelly," she said, sharing the details of their most recent argument about school. Throughout the summer, Julie had told me that she would not "give up" school for Shelly, noting, "If I have to choose between school or her, I'm choosing school." Yet, as fall approached, Julie's position had shifted: "I don't think it's worth it anymore. All the stress. All the fighting. I can't do it. Things are better now that I'm just working, and I want to keep it that way." I haven't been successful in contacting Julie since that day, and, as of the spring following that final conversation, her university e-mail account had been closed.

The Interplay of Literacy and Identity

The stories of literacy sponsorship presented here illustrate the complexities inherent in a discussion of literacy and identity. The sponsors profiled vary a great deal and at times exhibit contradictory or conflicting influences. The readily identifiable social problems discussed above affected my participants' literacy experiences in notable and dramatic ways. More pervasive, though harder to pinpoint, are the ways in which Appalachian identity—and the ways in which an individual performs that identity—affect his or her literacy beliefs and practices.

As noted in the introduction, familism is a value often constructed as part of a performance of Appalachian identity. Yet some of the most striking examples of those values in this article—Mike's relationship with his parents and Michelle's relationship with her grandparents—come from students who often sought to distance themselves from Appalachian identity in our interviews and in the classroom. What do the lives of these students suggest about Jones' construction of Appalachians?

Those students who most readily performed an Appalachian identity during my fieldwork evidenced ambivalence about their relationships with family members. While Katie May's mother was a sponsor of her literacy in important ways, Katie May also expressed a worry about being perceived by her mother as "rising above my raising"—similar to Julie's designation as "uppity" by her partner—when she talked about concepts she learned in school. Similarly, Julie appeared to embrace a romanticized performance of Appalachian identity more consciously and skillfully than any of the other students, yet in relation to her family and academic life, she stated, "All my life I've tried to do the absolute best I can do, and I never got the gratification from the people who love me. Most of the gratification I've got is from people who don't love me, my teachers and the students around me." This statement stands in stark contrast to Jones' description of Appalachians as "more truly themselves" when among family, a conceptualization that essentializes Appalachian-ness and assumes there is a stable, authentic Appalachian identity. Julie's comment undercuts this notion and reveals that the metaphor of the Appalachian family as a fortress is also a performance, much like the facets of Julie's romanticized Appalachian identity. But what might this "undercutting" reveal about overlapping and contesting performances of identity? How much of Julie's conflict, for example, is rooted in her performance of gender—a performance that clashes with the expectations for gender performance by Appalachian women? These are the questions that remain with me as I conclude.

Works Cited

Abramson, Rudy, and Jean Haskell, eds. *Encyclopedia of Appalachia*. Knoxville: The University of Tennessee P, 2006.

Borman, Kathryn, and Phillip J. Obermiller, eds. *From Mountain to Metropolis: Appalachian Migrants in the American City*. New York: Greenwood, 1993.

Brandt, Deborah. *Literacy in American Lives*. New York: Cambridge University P, 2001.

Bush, Kevin Ray, and Sheryl Beaty Lash. "Family Relationships and Gender Roles." *Encyclopedia of Appalachia*. 2006 ed.

Jones, Loyal. *Appalachian Values*. Ashland, KY: The Jesse Stuart Foundation, 1994.

Mulcahy, Richard P. "Health." *Encyclopedia of Appalachia*. 2006 ed.

Mullen, Patrick B. "Belief and the American Folk." *Journal of American Folklore* 113: 119–143.

Sohn, Katherine Kelleher. *Whistlin' and Crowin' Women of Appalachia: Literacy Practices since College*. Carbondale: Southern Illinois University P, 2006.

United States. Appalachian Regional Commission. *Substance Abuse in Appalachia*. 28 May 2006. Web.

Credit ———

Webb-Sunderhaus, Sara. "A Family Affair: Competing Sponsors of Literacy in Appalachian Students' Lives." *Community Literacy Journal 2.1* (2007): 5–24. Reprinted with the author's permission.

Mother Tongue

AMY TAN

I am not a scholar of English or literature. I cannot give you much more than personal opinions on the English language and its variations in this country or others.

I am a writer. And by that definition, I am someone who has always loved language. I am fascinated by language in daily life. I spend a great deal of my time thinking about the power of language—the way it can evoke an emotion, a visual image, a complex idea, or a simple truth. Language is the tool of my trade. And I use them all—all the Englishes I grew up with.

Recently, I was made keenly aware of the different Englishes I do use. I was giving a talk to a large group of people, the same talk I had already given to half a dozen other groups. The nature of the talk was about my writing, my life, and my book, *The Joy Luck Club.* The talk was going along well enough, until I remembered one major difference that made the whole talk sound wrong. My mother was in the room. And it was perhaps the first time she had heard me give a lengthy speech, using the kind of English I have never used with her. I was saying things like, "The intersection of memory upon imagination" and "There is an aspect of my fiction that relates to thus-and-thus'—a speech filled with carefully wrought grammatical phrases, burdened, it suddenly seemed to me, with nominalized forms, past perfect tenses, conditional phrases, all the forms of standard English that I had learned in school and through books, the forms of English I did not use at home with my mother.

Just last week, I was walking down the street with my mother, and I again found myself conscious of the English I was using, the English I do use with her. We were talking about the price of new and used furniture and I heard myself saying this: "Not waste money that way." My husband was with us as well, and he didn't notice any switch in my English. And then I realized why. It's because over the twenty years we've been together I've often used that same kind of English with him, and sometimes he even uses it with me. It has become our language of intimacy, a different sort of English that relates to family talk, the language I grew up with.

5   So you'll have some idea of what this family talk I heard sounds like, I'll quote what my mother said during a recent conversation which I videotaped and then transcribed. During this conversation, my mother was talking about a political gangster in Shanghai who had the same last name as her family's, Du, and how the gangster in his early years wanted to be adopted by her family, which was rich by comparison. Later, the gangster became more powerful, far richer than my mother's family, and one day showed up at my mother's wedding to pay his respects. Here's what she said in part:

> Du Yusong having business like fruit stand. Like off the street kind. He is Du like Du Zong—but not Tsung-ming Island people. The local people call putong, the river east side, he belong to that side local people. That man want to ask Du Zong father take him in like become own family. Du Zong father wasn't look down on him, but didn't take seriously, until that man big like become a mafia. Now important person, very hard to inviting him. Chinese way, came only to show respect, don't stay for dinner. Respect for making big celebration, he shows up. Mean gives lots of respect. Chinese custom. Chinese social life that way. If too important won't have to stay too long. He come to my wedding. I didn't see, I heard it. I gone to boy's side, they have YMCA dinner. Chinese age I was nineteen.

You should know that my mother's expressive command of English belies how much she actually understands. She reads the *Forbes* report, listens to *Wall Street Week,* converses daily with her stockbroker, reads all of Shirley MacLaine's books with ease—all kinds of things I can't begin to understand. Yet some of my friends tell me they understand 50 percent of what my mother says. Some say they understand 80 to 90 percent. Some say they understand none of it, as if she were speaking pure Chinese. But to me, my mother's English is perfectly clear, perfectly natural. It's my mother tongue. Her language, as I hear it, is vivid, direct, full of observation and imagery. That was the language that helped shape the way I saw things, expressed things, made sense of the world.

CRIENCRIENCRIEN

Lately, I've been giving more thought to the kind of English my mother speaks. Like others, I have described it to people as 'broken" or "fractured" English. But I wince when I say that. It has always bothered me that I can think of no way to describe it other than "broken," as if it were damaged and needed to be fixed, as if it lacked a certain wholeness and soundness. I've heard other terms used, "limited English," for example. But they seem just as bad, as if everything is limited, including people's perceptions of the limited English speaker.

I know this for a fact, because when I was growing up, my mother's "limited" English limited *my* perception of her. I was ashamed of her English. I believed that her English reflected the quality of what she had to say That is, because she expressed them imperfectly her thoughts were imperfect. And I had plenty of empirical evidence to support me: the fact that people in department stores, at banks, and at restaurants did not take her seriously, did not give her good service, pretended not to understand her, or even acted as if they did not hear her.

10   My mother has long realized the limitations of her English as well. When I was fifteen, she used to have me call people on the phone to pretend I was she. In this guise, I was forced to ask for information or even to complain and yell at people who had been rude to her. One time it was a call to her stockbroker in New York. She had cashed out her small portfolio and it just so happened we were going to go to New York the next week, our very first trip outside California. I had to get on the phone and say in an adolescent voice that was not very convincing, "This is Mrs. Tan."

And my mother was standing in the back whispering loudly, "Why he don't send me check, already two weeks late. So mad he lie to me, losing me money.

And then I said in perfect English, "Yes, I'm getting rather concerned. You had agreed to send the check two weeks ago, but it hasn't arrived."

Then she began to talk more loudly. "What he want, I come to New York tell him front of his boss, you cheating me?" And I was trying to calm her down, make her be quiet, while telling the stockbroker, "I can't tolerate any more excuses. If I don't receive the check immediately, I am going to have to speak to your manager when I'm in New York next week." And sure enough, the following week there we were in front of this astonished stockbroker, and I was sitting there red-faced and quiet, and my mother, the real Mrs. Tan, was shouting at his boss in her impeccable broken English.

We used a similar routine just five days ago, for a situation that was far less humorous. My mother had gone to the hospital for an appointment, to find out about a benign brain tumor a CAT scan had revealed a month ago. She said she had spoken very good English, her best English, no mistakes. Still, she said, the hospital did not apologize when they said they had lost the CAT scan and she had come for nothing. She said they did not seem to have any sympathy when she told them she was anxious to know the exact diagnosis, since her husband and son had both died of brain tumors. She said they would not give her any more information until the next time and she would have to make another appointment for that. So she said she would not leave until the doctor called her daughter. She wouldn't budge. And when the doctor finally called her daughter, me, who spoke in perfect English—lo and behold—we had assurances the CAT scan would be found, promises that a conference call on Monday would be held, and apologies for any suffering my mother had gone through for a most regrettable mistake.

15   I think my mother's English almost had an effect on limiting my possibilities in life as well. Sociologists and linguists probably will tell you that a person's developing language skills are more influenced by peers. But I do think that the language spoken in the family, especially in immigrant families which are more insular, plays a large role in shaping the language of the child. And I believe that it affected my results on achievement tests, I.Q. tests, and the SAT. While my English skills were never judged as poor, compared to math, English could not be considered my strong suit. In grade school I did moderately well, getting perhaps B's, sometimes B-pluses, in English and scoring perhaps in the sixtieth or seventieth percentile on achievement tests. But those scores were not good enough to override the opinion that my true abilities lay in math and science, because in those areas I achieved A's and scored in the ninetieth percentile or higher.

This was understandable. Math is precise; there is only one correct answer. Whereas, for me at least, the answers on English tests were always a judgment call, a matter of opinion and personal experience. Those tests were constructed around items like fill-in-the-blank sentence completion, such as, "Even though Tom was _____, Mary thought he was _____." And the correct answer always seemed to be the most bland combinations of thoughts, for example, "Even though Tom was shy, Mary thought he was charming:' with the grammatical structure "even though" limiting the correct answer to some sort of semantic opposites, so you wouldn't get answers like, "Even though Tom was foolish,

Mary thought he was ridiculous:' Well, according to my mother, there were very few limitations as to what Tom could have been and what Mary might have thought of him. So I never did well on tests like that.

The same was true with word analogies, pairs of words in which you were supposed to find some sort of logical, semantic relationship—for example, "*Sunset* is to *nightfall* as _____ is to _____." And here you would be presented with a list of four possible pairs, one of which showed the same kind of relationship: *red* is to *stoplight, bus* is to *arrival, chills* is to *fever, yawn* is to *boring.* Well, I could never think that way. I knew what the tests were asking, but I could not block out of my mind the images already created by the first pair, "*sunset* is to *nightfall*"—and I would see a burst of colors against a darkening sky, the moon rising, the lowering of a curtain of stars. And all the other pairs of words—red, bus, stoplight, boring—just threw up a mass of confusing images, making it impossible for me to sort out something as logical as saying: "A sunset precedes nightfall" is the same as "a chill precedes a fever." The only way I would have gotten that answer right would have been to imagine an associative situation, for example, my being disobedient and staying out past sunset, catching a chill at night, which turns into feverish pneumonia as punishment, which indeed did happen to me.

ᑫᔐᏬᏣᔐᏬᏣᔐ

I have been thinking about all this lately, about my mother's English, about achievement tests. Because lately I've been asked, as a writer, why there are not more Asian Americans represented in American literature. Why are there few Asian Americans enrolled in creative writing programs? Why do so many Chinese students go into engineering! Well, these are broad sociological questions I can't begin to answer. But I have noticed in surveys—in fact, just last week—that Asian students, as a whole, always do significantly better on math achievement tests than in English. And this makes me think that there are other Asian-American students whose English spoken in the home might also be described as "broken" or "limited." And perhaps they also have teachers who are steering them away from writing and into math and science, which is what happened to me.

Fortunately, I happen to be rebellious in nature and enjoy the challenge of disproving assumptions made about me. I became an English major my first year in college, after being enrolled as pre-med. I started writing nonfiction as a freelancer the week after I was told by my former boss that writing was my worst skill and I should hone my talents toward account management.

20   But it wasn't until 1985 that I finally began to write fiction. And at first I wrote using what I thought to be wittily crafted sentences, sentences that would finally prove I had mastery over the English language. Here's an example from the first draft of a story that later made its way into *The Joy Luck Club,* but without this line: "That was my mental quandary in its nascent state." A terrible line, which I can barely pronounce.

Fortunately, for reasons I won't get into today, I later decided I should envision a reader for the stories I would write. And the reader I decided upon was my mother, because these were stories about mothers. So with this reader in mind—and in fact she did read my early drafts—I began to write stories using all the Englishes I grew up with: the English I spoke to my mother, which for lack of a better term might be described as "simple"; the English she used with me, which for lack of a better term might be described as "broken"; my translation of her Chinese, which could certainly be described as "watered down"; and what I imagined to be her translation of her Chinese if she could speak in perfect English, her internal language, and for that I sought to preserve the essence, but neither an English nor a Chinese structure. I wanted to capture what language ability tests can never reveal: her intent, her passion, her imagery, the rhythms of her speech and the nature of her thoughts.

Apart from what any critic had to say about my writing, I knew I had succeeded where it counted when my mother finished reading my book and gave me her verdict: "So easy to read."

Memoria Is a Friend of Ours:
On the Discourses of Color

VICTOR VILLANUEVA

A memory. Seattle, 1979.

> *She is a contradiction in stereotypes, not to be pegged. He likes her right off. She wants to go to Belltown, the Denny Regrade, to take photos. He wants to go along. He does, feeling insecure and full of bravado, slipping into the walk of bravado he had perfected as a child in Brooklyn. Stops into a small café at the outskirts of downtown, at the entry to the Regrade. It's a French-style café, the Boulangerie, or some such. To impress her, he speaks French.*
>
> *"Une tasse de café, s'il vous plait. Et croissants pour les duex." Don't laugh. It's how he said it.*
>
> *He's an English major, a senior, quite proud of having gotten this far in college. But he's insecure about what this will lead to (since he had only gotten as far as deciding to stay in college till he's finally in over his head). He tells her of a novel he will write someday. His description goes something like:*
>
>> *I've been thinking about a novel about a white Puerto Rican kid who buys into the assimilation myth, hook, line, and sinker. He does all the right things—learns the language, learns how to pronounce "r's" in words like "motherrr" and "waterrr" and how not to trill the "r" when he says "three," and does well in school. He's even a war hero. Does it all, only to realize that assimilation just can't happen. Yet he can't really be Puerto Rican. So maybe he goes to Puerto Rico to find out who he might have been and what he is tied to. I don't have it all worked out.*

The plot line might not have been worked out, but this was the impulse nevertheless—to keep alive the memory of assimilation denied, a truism turned to myth, to try to hold on to, maybe even to regain, that which had been lost on the road to assimilation.

A reminiscence:

> *That morning I had spoken with Ceci, my friend the Cuban English professor. Her husband had said something to me over the phone that I had to unravel quickly, immediate translation from my first language to my only language, slipping the Spanish into English to understand. Their baby, I'm told, used to translate into Spanish for her mother when someone spoke in English at home, translated the English into Spanish so that the English professor would understand. Cute.*

During that phone conversation, I tried to come up with a familiar Spanish saying about how Cubans and Puerto Ricans are two wings of the same bird. It was there: at the tip of the mind. But I could never. I said it in English. Ceci said it for me in Spanish. Quickly. Then again more slowly. I heard it. I understood it. I recognized it. I still feel unsure that I could produce it. My Spanish is limited to single sentences, never extended stretches of discourse. I can't. At least I don't believe I can. And I listen to salsa and mambo and bomba and plena — the music of my childhood. But I can't dance to it in front of anyone. And phrases from the CDs slip by me, untranslated. I am assimilated. I am not.

So I was driving home from some chore or other on the afternoon of the morning I had spoken to Ceci. And in the midst of a left turn I thought: "I'm fifty now, maybe a third of my life left, I wonder if I'll die without ever being fluent in the language that first met my ears." English is the only language I know, really. Yet Spanish is the language of my ear, of my soul. And I try to pass it on to my children. But I'm inadequate.

In some sense, the impulse of the book I had described twenty-one years ago gets worked out in *Bootstraps*, the assimilation myth explicit in the title; the story told then elaborated upon with research and with theory. It's an attempt to play out a kind of Freirean pedagogy: the political explored through the experiential. And it does more. It's

an autobiography with political, theoretical, pedagogical considerations. The story includes ethnographic research. The story includes things tried in classrooms. The story includes speculations on the differences between immigrants and minorities, the class system and language, orality and literacy, cultural and critical literacy, Freire, ideology, hegemony, how racism continues and the ways in which racism is allowed to continue despite the profession's best efforts. And in [so doing] the story suggests how we are—all of us—subject to the systemic. This is the personal made public and the public made personalized, not for self-glory nor to point fingers, but to suggest how, maybe, to make the exception the rule. (xviii)

I wrote that in 1992. Now some part of that first impulse reasserts itself, fictionalizing, telling the story, reaching back to the heritage that is at risk of passing away quickly. To the kids before my father died last spring:

Remember to call your grandpa abuelo. He'll like the sound of that, since none of my sister's kids have called him that. If you let him, he'll watch baseball day and night and not say much. Push him for the stories of Puerto Rico during his childhood. Ask him about catching shrimp with his hands, and the stories of how the neighborhood boys got a Model A Ford, about the revolutionary who hid out in the El Yunque, about his time in the Army. Ask about my grandfather, Basilio, and gardening, and working as a groundskeeper and gardener for the university. And ask about Tio Benito, the tall farmer, inland, on the coffee bills. "Inland" is important about knowing about being Puerto Rican, about Puerto Rico. I remember when I met him. A tall PR. Man, that was very cool. And he gave me sugar cane from his farm, and a coffee bean, and a lemon that he had cut a hole on the top of. And he told me to chew on the bean, squeeze lemon juice on the tongue, and chew on the cane. I wish I could give you that memory, mi'jitas.

Now, Mom is easier. She loves to talk. But she'd rather forget the past. And I don't want the past forgotten, so press her too.

A poem: Victor Villanueva y Hernándes

Triste lucha la del árbol con espinas	Sad struggle of the tree of thorns
Fuerte ardor que solo a su alma	Fierce feeling covered solely by
se cobija.	your soul
Vano empeño para el ser que vive,	Vain striving for he who lives,
En tratar de comprender su propia vida.	In trying to understand his own life.
Muy dulce es percivir de la noche	So sweet to see your caresses in
sus caricios;	the night
Pero es terrible saber	But so terrible to know
Que más tarde en la madrugada	That later in the light of day
Agonizando todos ellos quedan. …	All the agonies remain. …
Triste lucha del irbol con espinas	Sad struggle of the tree of thorns
triste lucha la del que ya un	sad struggle of that which is
poquito tarde,	already a little late,
Ni siquiera el más leve	Without even the lightest
suspiro	sigh
su alma alienta.	your soul's breath
Triste e interminable lucha	Sad and interminable struggle
esta que jamás se aleja	that which will never leave
¡Oh, que triste lucha ésta	Oh, how sad this struggle
que a mi pecho	Weighing so on my chest!
Tanto apena!	
¡Triste lucha … triste lucha!	Sad struggle … sad struggle!
—"En el pasado	—"In the past
versa tu presente"	turns the present"
19 de enero 1951	19 January 1951

The fiction, the *Bootstraps* retold and fictionalized, would have to begin back then, not quite a generation after the change of hands, when the Spanish colony was handed over to the United States, the changes seen by three generations—*Boricua* to Nuyorican to the middle class of color far removed from the cultural soil of either of the generations, maybe even a wheat field in Eastern Washington. It's important. The memory.

5   So many have said this so well, that it's hard for me to reiterate without breaking into the academic discourse of cite-and-quote—Adell, JanMohamed and Lloyd, Omi and Winant, Saldívar, San Juan, Singh, Skerrett, and Hogan, Smorkaloff, and the "standards" like Anzaldúa or hooks—all have written about the connections between narratives by people of color and the need to reclaim a memory, memory of an identity in formation and constant reformation, the need to reclaim a memory of an identity as formed through the generations. And I'd say the need to reclaim and retain the memory of the imperial lords, those who have forcibly changed the identities of people of color through colonization.

> Nelly, the department's graduate secretary, hands me a flyer for a meeting of the Pacific Islanders' group, inviting me to join the students, staff, and faculty (which includes two department chairs I work with often). We smile at each other. Her cultural ways—Filipina—and mine are so different really—except that we have two out of three imperial lords in common: Spain and the United States. It binds us. Our first imperial lord was there before the world got large, more local: the Japanese and the Caribes. We laugh, while others look and listen on with looks of wondering. It's not their memory.

Memory simply cannot be adequately portrayed in the conventional discourse of the academy.

I am grateful for the acknowledgement of perceptions that academic discourse provides, for the resources the conventions of citation make available, for the ideocentric discourse that displays inductive or deductive lines of reasoning, a way to trace a writer's logical connections.

Academic discourse is cognitively powerful!

But the cognitive alone is insufficient. It can be strong for *logos*. It can be strong for *ethos*. But it is very weak in *pathos*. Academic discourse tries, after all, to reach the Aristotelian ideal of being completely logocentric, though it cannot be freed of the ethical appeal to authority. A demonstration: Agustín Lao, in "Islands at the Crossroads: Puerto Ricanness Traveling between the Translocal Nation and the Global City," writes that

> Puerto Ricans (like other racialized diasporas) function within multiple and ambiguous registers of race and racism. As colonized subjects, all Puerto Ricans are "colored" by colonial discourses. On the other hand, differential processes of racialization can either nominalize Puerto Ricans as "ethnic" and/or allow some light-skinned Puerto Ricans to "pass" as "white," [...] A single Puerto Rican "transmigrant" can be classified as *trigueña* on the island, black in Ohio, and Latina in New York. (178–79)

Now consider the rhetorical effect of Professor Lao's assertion (though with qualification) and a couple of stories from this light-skinned Puerto Rican. Both take place during the Summer of 2000:

> *He was picked up at the registration desk of the hotel in Iowa City. The limousine (really a van) driver walks up, a man in his late fifties or early sixties, buzz cut, thick build, surely one more accustomed to hard physical labor, a farmer, one would imagine, given the locale. Says at least the guest is on time, kind of to the person behind the registration desk, kind of to himself, maybe even to the guest. He goes on to say that the last guest he'd picked up had been fifteen minutes late, then didn't pay the fare.*

> *Once in the van, the story of the deadbeat develops. It was a family of four, including an infant. No car seat.*

> *"I could've had my license pulled, with no cat seat for the baby. Then he tries to pay me with a $100 travelers' check, like I carry that kind of money at five in the morning."*

> *"Were they foreigners?" assuming the passengers would have overestimated the fluidity of travelers' checks.*

> *"Who can know these days. The guy wore a turban. What are you?"*

> *Internal soliloquy: he didn't say "rag head," so maybe this is more the condition of the international seaports flowing into the middle of America, the in-migration of the newest immigrants and those new immigrants from*

*the 1930s, a land no longer completely owned by those of Scandinavian
and German ancestry. But 1898 and 1917 really should mean something
in a situation like this* [NB: 1898: the U.S. acquisition of Puerto Rico; 1917:
US citizenship conferred on all Puerto Ricans].

"Me? I'm American."

"Coulda fooled me!"

"Yeah, well. I'm from New York."

*The conversation ends. The next passenger turns out to be a black man
with a crutch coming out of an upper-middle-class home in the suburbs
of Iowa City. Kind of felt sorry for the driver and his uncomfortable
assumptions.*

Second story:

*It was another one of those receptions produced by the dean of the
graduate school. This one was to welcome doctoral fellows in residence.
Most were persons of color. I was there as a department chair and as one of
the mentors to a couple of the fellows.*

*The scene: Back porch of the house, clusters of folks with drinks in hand
or paper plates with guacamole and chips, talking, smiling, overlooking
cows grazing in the valley below and green soft rolling hills nearby, maybe
three hundred yards away, where there will soon be wheat blowing
beautifully in the wind.*

*A conversation ensues with one of the fellows, a woman who grew
up in the black area of Boston, Roxbury. Listening in is an associate
dean, originally from Central Asia, overly happy to be away from Russian
bureaucracy. The conversation turns to race in the wheatland.*

*VV: "Around here folks don't know if I'm Spanish, Jewish, Italian, from
the Middle East, or from South Asia."*

Associate Dean: "I would have thought you were Italian."

Roxbury: "I don' know. He looks pretty Portorican to me."

*Sure, she knows the hue, she sees the "niggerlips," one of those names I
endured as a child, just like Martín.*

Martín Espada:

Niggerlips was the high school name
for me.
So called by Douglas
the car mechanic, with green tattoos
on each forearm,
and the choir of round pink faces
that grinned deliciously
from the back row of classrooms,
droned over by teachers
checking attendance too slowly.

Douglas would brag
about cruising his car
near sidewalks of black children
to point an unloaded gun,
to scare niggers
like crows off a tree,
he'd say.

My great-grandfather Luis
was un negrito too,
a shoemaker in the coffee hills
of Puerto Rico, 1900.
The family called him a secret
and kept no photograph.
My father remembers
the childhood white powder
that failed to bleach
his stubborn copper skin,
and the family says
he is still a fly in milk.

So Niggerlips has the mouth
of his great-grandfather,
the song he must have sung
as he pounded the leather and nails,
the heat that courses through copper,
the stubbornness of a fly in milk,
and all you have, Douglas,
is that unloaded gun.

Professor Lao, I would contend, is not quite right. Those of us who are light-skinned don't pass for white; we're just not automatically sorted into the appropriate slot. But more to the point is that Lao's academic discourse (complete with scare quotes and nominalizations) is insufficient, lacks emotional appeal. And though Aristotle thought it not right to sway with emotional appeals, he knew that the greatest impact on listeners is in fact the emotional. The personal here does not negate the need for the academic, it complements, provides an essential element in the rhetorical triangle, an essential element in the intellect—cognition *and* affect. The personal done well is sensorial and intellectual, complete, knowledge known throughout mind and body, even if vicariously.

10   And for the person of color, it does more. The narrative of the person of color validates. It resonates. It awakens, particularly for those of us who are in institutions where our numbers are few. We know that though we really are Gramsci's exceptions—those who "through 'chance' [… have] had opportunities that the thousand others in reality could not or did not have"— our experiences are in no sense unique but are always analogous to other experiences from among those exceptions. So more that narrating the life of one so that "one creates this possibility, suggests the process, indicates the opening," in Gramsci's terms (*Selections from Cultural Writing* 132), we remember the results of our having realized the possibility, discovered the process, found the opening, while finding that there is in some sense very little change on the other side. This is what Ellis Cose describes as *The Rage of a Privileged Class*. This is Luis Rodriguez's call, that we'll read below.

Ellis Cose, I've written before ("On Colonies"), explains, mainly by way of anecdote, the reasons African Americans in particular continue to be angry even after having crossed over to the other side. He explains the ways in which little slights continue to display the racism inherent in our society. Those "Dozen Demons" are

1. Inability to fit in.
2. Exclusion from the club.
3. Low expectations.
4. Shattered hopes.
5. Faint praise.
6. Presumption of failure.
7. Coping fatigue.
8. Pigeonholing.
9. Identity troubles.
10. Self-censorship and silence.
11. Mendacity.
12. Guilt by association. (57–68)

I haven't been called a "spic" in many years (except by others of color, perhaps, in fun, I hope). Yet little things happen that betray the underlying racism that affects us all, no matter how appalled by racism we might be. I read Anzaldúa or hooks or the poetry of Espada or Cruz or Esteves or any other writings of color, and I know I haven't become clinically paranoid. I know that I've been poked by one of the demons. Some of the slights signified by Cose are self-imposed, instances of Frantz Fanon's internal colonialism. Some are externally imposed. All can be laid bare through the personal made public.

> *There's the story of the academics of color who wrote about the subtle ways in which they find themselves victims of some of Cose's demons—exclusion, expecting less, presuming failure, pigeonholing as "brown-on-brown" research rather than disinterested research (read: white and classical-empirical). Someone far away reads the essay once published and files suit for slander. The authors had never heard of the person. This is a very funny story to people of color who have heard it—the laughter of verification and white guilt gone awry.*

> *The converse:*

> *"Man, I loved your book [or article or essay], I could relate. The same things have happened to me," something I've heard time and time again wherever I travel. Identity minus troubles among Cose's demons, associating guiltless, a new club formed.*

Somehow, the spic does remain, despite all the good fortune and accolades, not only from within but from without. While a good academic piece would help me to remember, rich narrative does more for the memory.

And the precedent is old. *Memoria* was the mother of the muses, the most important of the rhetorical offices. Now rhetorics of writing seem to go no further than invention, arrangement, and style; when delivery is still there, it's the matter of "voice." But memory is tied in as well, surely for people of color. It's as if we have accepted Plato's prophecy that literacy would be the downfall of memory, leading only to remembrance. We have to remember Plato, because his writing is significant by virtue of its genre, an attempt at representation of dialogue, of storytelling, of the play. Plato's literacy took shape not as logocentric discourse but as a representation of discourse in action. Though folks like Volosinov have shown that all discourse, written as well as spoken, is dialogic. Plato is maybe the coolest of the philosophers because of the resonance of the dialogue, the possibility for humor, the clear presence of all three points in the rhetorical triangle and the often unspecified dimension which is context. I don't mean to be waxing Platonic, really, only to suggest that there's something to Plato's notion of memory as more than recollection and to his leaning on a written discourse that approximates orality as a means toward arriving at Memory. The narratives of people of color jog our memories as a collective in a scattered world and within an ideology that praises individualism. And this is all the more apparent for the Latino and Latina, whose language contains the assertion of the interconnectedness among identity, memory, and the personal. There is a common saying among Puerto Ricans and Cubans: *Te doy un cuento de mi historia*, literally rendered as "I'll give you a story about my history": me, history and memory, and a story.

> *A thousand years before the first Europeans arrived on Puerto Rico, the native people of the mainland and the lesser Antilles migrated to Puerto Rico, where they could live in relative peace, able to fish and live off the fresh vegetation—pineapple and varieties of tuber that have no name in English. We don't know the names of the first inhabitants of Puerto Rico. Our history is the history told by the Europeans, who, conferring their values on the land, took the language of the local imperial lords. We only know the names given the first Puerto Ricans by their first colonizers, the first to raid them, the first to enslave them, the ones the Europeans honored by naming a region after them. These first colonizers were the peoples of Carib. And they named the people of the island Arawak and the culture of the Arawak was called Taino. And their island was named Boriquén.*

> *Then came Columbus (or Columbo or Colón. I'm glad we've stopped translating people's names, or I'd have to walk around with the name Conqueror Newton). And then Ponce de León. Then the priests.*

> *And when the slaves of Puerto Rico rebelled, slaves from Africa were brought in, and the Boricuas ran inland, away from the fortressed walls of El Morro, acquiescing to the Spanish yet surreptitiously trading with Dutch and English, French and Italian pirates who would find other ways to enter the island. This subversion became jaibería. So I understand Angel Rama, when he says that it is in the Caribbean that "the plural manifestations of the entire universe insert themselves" (qtd. in Smorkaloff vii). My mother's name is Italian (the line is never lost in the Spanish tradition: my father's mother—Hernándes and my mother becoming Maria Socorro Cotto de Villanueva, my father was thus Victor Villanueva y Hernándes and me Victor Villanueva y Cotto until we both were Americanized and I became "Jr.") My mother's name: Italian. The memory of that first Italian, whether family or slavemaster (which is how so many of the Tainos got their names, just like the African Americans of the mainland)—lost.*

> *Centuries after the first Europeans later, I am Puerto Rican—a product of the first migrations of Puerto Ricans to New York in the late 1940s, though my mother arrived though what was euphemistically called "indenture servitude," what others called "white slavery," as if somehow more barbaric than the slavery of Africans. And I assimilate. And I don't. But I know how to seem to be—jaibería—and I have the memory—the memory provided by stories told. Memory does danger. And it's fed through the stories told.*

I'm trying to figure this out, somehow: who I am, from where, playing out the mixes within. It isn't a question for me, whether public or private discourses. I am contradictory consciousness. The discourse should reflect that. I am these uneasy mixes of races that make for no race at all yet find themselves victim to racism. The discourse should reflect that. I am an American (in every sense—a boy from Brooklyn, jazz and rock 'n' roll, and from the Americas, with an ancestry dating back before the Europeans), an academic, a person of color— an organically grown traditional intellectual, containing both of Gramsci's intellectual formations, yet not quite his new intellectual. The discourse should reflect that as well. And I am in a wheatfield, attempting to pass on a memory as I attempt to gather one. Personal discourse, the narrative, the auto/biography, helps in that effort, is a necessary adjunct to the academic.

Looking back, we look ahead, and giving ourselves up to the looking back and the looking ahead, knowing the self, and, critically, knowing the self in relation to others, maybe we can be and instrument whereby students can hear the call.

A Poem by Luis J. Rodriguez:

> The calling came to me
> while I languished
> in my room, while I
> whittled away my youth
> in jail cells
> and damp *barrio* fields.
>
> It brought me to life,
> out of captivity,
> in a street-scarred
> and tattooed place
> I called body.

Until then I waited silently,
a deafening clamor in my head,
but voiceless to all around;
hidden from America's eyes,
a brown boy without a name.

I would sing into a solitary
            tape recorder,
music never to be heard.
I would write my thoughts
in scrambled English;
I would take photos in my mind—
            plan out new parks,
            bushy green, concrete free,
            new places to play
            and to think.
Waiting.
Then it came.
The calling.
It brought me out of my room.
It forced me to escape
night captors
in street prisons.

It called me to war,
to be writer,
to be scientist
and march with the soldiers
            of change.

It called me from the shadows,
out of the wreckage
of my *barrio*—from among those
who did not exist.
I waited all of 16 years
for this time.

Somehow unexpected,
I was called.

Memoria calls and pushes us forward. *Memoria* is a friend of ours. We must
invite her into our classrooms and into our scholarship.

Works Cited

Adell, Sandra. *Double Consciousness/Double Bind: Theoreitcal Issues in Twentieth-Century Black Literature.* Urbana: U of Illinois P, 1994.

Cose, Ellis. *The Rage of a Privileged Class.* New York: Harper, 1003.

Espada, Martin. "Niggerlips." *Cool Salsa: Bilingual Poems on Growng Up Latino in the United States.* Ed. Lori M. Carlson. New York: Fawcett, 1994. 73–74.

Fanon, Frantz. *Black Skin, Wihte Masks,* Trans. Carles Lam Markmann. New York: Grove, 1967.

Gramsci, Antonio. *Selections from Cultural Writings.* Ed. Davide Forgacs and Geoffrey Nowell-Smith. Trans. William Boelhower. Cambridge: Harvard UP, 1985.

—————. *Selections from the Prism Notebooks.* Ed. and trans. Quintin Hoare and Geoffrey Nowell-Smith. New York: International, 1971.

Grosfoguel, Ramón, Frances Negrón-Muntaner, and Chloé s. Georas. "Beyond Nationalis and Colonialist Discourses: The Jaiba politics of the Puerto-Rican Ethno-Nation." *Puerto Rican Jam: Rethinking Colonialism and Nationalism.* Ed. Frances Negrón-Muntaner and Ramón Grosfoguel. Minneapolis: U of Minnesota P, 1997. 1–36.

JanMohamed, Abdul R., and David Lloyd, eds. *The Nature and Context of Minority Discourse.* New York: Oxford UP, 1990.

Lao, Agustin, "Islands at the Crossroads: Puerto Ricanness Traveling between the Translocatl Nation and the Global City." *Puerto Rican Jam: Rethinking Colonialism and Nationalism.* Ed. Frances Negrón-Muntaner and Ramón Grosfoguel. Minneapolis: U of Minnesota P, 1997. 169–188.

Omi, Michael, and Howard Winant. *Racial Formation in the United States*: From the 1960s to the 1990s. New York: Routledge, 1994.

Rodriguez, Luis J. "The Calling." *Cool Salsa: Bilingual Poems on Growng Up Latino in the United States.* Ed. Lori M. Carlson. New York: Fawcett, 1994. 123–124.

Saldivar, Ramón. *Chicano Narrative: The Dialectics of Difference.* Madison: U of Wisconsin P, 1990.

San Juan, F. *Racial Formations/Critical Transformations: Articularions of Power in Ethnic and Racial Studies in the United States.* Atlantic Highlands, NJ: Humanities, 1992.

Singh, Amritjit, Joseph Skerrett, Robert E. Hogan, eds. *Memory, Narrative, and Identity: New Essays in Ethnic American Literature.* Boston: Northeastern UP, 1994.

Smorkaloff, Pamela Maria. *Cuban Writers on and off the Ilsand: Contemporary Narrative Fiction.* New York: Twayne, 1999.

Villanueva, Victor. *Bootstraps: From an American Academic of Color.* Urbana, IL: NCTE, 1993.

——————. "On Colonies, Canons, and Ellis Cose's Rage of a Privileged Class." *JAC* 16(1996): 159–169.

Islamophobia in Classrooms, Media, and Politics

MAYIDA ZAAL

It was the second week of school in a sleepy town on the eastern coast of the U.S. Middle school students (mostly White, Christian, and middle class) were becoming familiar with one another, their routines, and their teachers.

Their history teacher had a special activity planned to commemorate the 10th anniversary of the attacks that occurred on September 11, 2001. First, students were to describe in writing how they felt about the building of a mosque near the World Trade Center site in New York City. Second, they were given the following vocabulary words and asked to construct a paragraph: *Al Qaeda, terrorist, Islam, Muslim, hijacker, and Islamist.*

The teacher did not provide any context (historical, political, or social) for the assignment, and several students were uncomfortable with it. A few students asked one another in disbelief, "Why is he saying that all Muslims are terrorists?" Becky (all names are pseudonyms) worried how her friend Aysha, a Muslim American, felt about the activity. Although they complied with the assignment, Becky and others did not agree with their teacher's implications.

Becky told Aysha after class, "I don't believe that all Muslims are terrorists and I'm sorry you had to hear that." After being alerted by Becky's parents about the U.S. History lesson, Aysha's parents knew they needed to address the issue.

5   At a meeting with the principal and the teacher, Aysha's parents described their concerns. They wished the teacher had taken a different approach, one that did not equate Islam with terrorism. The teacher was apologetic, but did not understand that pathologizing Islam could have a direct effect on his students. The principal exclaimed that he would have never taught a lesson on that topic, even though it was a significant event discussed in the news media.

Critical Pedagogy

Becky and Aysha's story was brought to my attention when Aysha's parents sought guidance regarding this incident. This classroom example and others like it point to the necessity for a critical pedagogical stance that addresses the manifestation of Islamophobia in the classroom.

The example raises many difficult questions and ethical considerations. What are the consequences (whether intended) of such a lesson taught in isolation? How could a lesson on the events of September 11th have been taught differently? How can educators use literacy as a way to engage with most pressing social contexts instead of oversimplifying or barring them? How do young Muslims across the U.S. experience growing anti-Muslim sentiment? What are our responsibilities as educators to create safer spaces for Muslim students and for all of our students?

Currents of Islamophobia

According to the Council on American Islamic Relations (2009), civil rights violations targeting Muslims in the workplace, at religious institutions, and in schools have escalated. For instance, in 2007 there were 118 reported cases of discrimination in schools, and in 2008 there were 153 reported cases.

Moreover, the Pew Research Center's (2010) survey in the wake of public debate on the proposed construction of an Islamic cultural center and mosque near the site of the former World Trade Center reveals that since 2005, Americans are tending towards less favorable views of Islam. In 2005, 41% of those surveyed held a favorable view of Islam, while 36% held an unfavorable view. In 2010, only 32% held a favorable view, while 38% looked at Islam unfavorably.

10   Remarkably, the Center for American Progress reports that over the last decade $43 million dollars in funding was contributed to support anti-Muslim thinkers in the U.S. (Hing, 2011). These are the same thinkers who are credited with influencing the Norwegian mass murderer, Anders Breivik, whose intent was to wage war against Muslims in Europe.

What fuels these acts of hatred? What influences the general public's perceptions of Muslims as a group? There are many inputs from mass media, both historical and current, that have served to facilitate people's perceptions of Muslims as a threat.

The effects of Islamophobia, defined as a generalized fear of Islam and Muslims (Shryock, 2010; Zine, 2004), are felt by Muslims and non-Muslims alike. For instance, Arabs, Sikhs, and South Asians are some of the groups that are often targets of anti-Muslim discrimination (American-Arab Anti-Discrimination Committee Research Institute [ADC], 2010).

Politics of Representation

Muslim Americans are not a monolithic group, nor can they be described in terms of one common experience. Nonetheless, it is a term that millions of Muslims living in the U.S. use to identify themselves (Bakalian & Bozorgmehr, 2009; Pew Research Center, 2011). Muslims in the U.S. originate from at least 77 countries and include native-born African Americans and other converts to Islam (Pew Research Center, 2011).

Therefore, it is imperative not to homogenize or essentialize the experiences of Muslims across the country. I employ the category of "Muslim Americans" to situate a growing Islamophobic trend within its historical, social, and political context and to generate discussion and interrupt the pedagogical practices that contribute to further oppression of Muslim students.

15   Muslims in the U.S., and Arabs specifically, have been vilified in images, cartoons, film, and television for many decades (and long before the attacks of September 11th took place). Social scientist Jack Shaheen (2001) has extensively documented the hundreds of images that portray Arabs as violent and barbaric. (Many Arabs, usually represented as Muslims, are Christians, Jews, and even Quakers [ADC, 2008]).

These demonized and dehumanizing images (often depicted in seemingly harmless ways, as in the Disney film *Aladdin*) have served to desensitize the U.S. populace and to legitimize fear and hatred against Muslims and Islam. Moreover, the persistent discourse in the media and in politics (e.g., Peter King's Congressional hearings on Muslim Americans and radicalization) that equates Muslims with terrorism and violence (Nisbet & Garrett, 2010) perpetuates Islamophobia.

How do these popular, discriminatory discourses manifest themselves in schools and in classrooms? They inform literacy practices like the ones illustrated in the opening vignette. These mainstream images, texts, and narratives form the basis of how students and teachers make sense of the world and reinforce the official curriculum in textbooks and state standards.

Common Concerns

In previously conducted research, the Muslim youth who shared their stories with me in the U.S. (Zaal, Salah, & Fine, 2007) and in the Netherlands (Zaal, 2009) had many concerns in common. They spoke of experiencing Islamophobia in blatant and insidious ways—being called names, being told they were oppressed by their backward religion, and told to return to where they came from. They reported feeling targeted at school, on the playground, and on the bus. They did not want to be burdened with educating others about their faith or to defend their religion or ethnicity. They described feeling alienated when adults and peers promoted stereotypes about Islam.

The young women who participated in my research based in New York City resisted having their identities defined in polarizing dichotomies—devout or progressive, Muslim or American, good citizen or feared neighbor. They wanted to claim all their identities—student, sister, national origin, friend, daughter, law-abiding citizen, Muslim—without compromise.

20   We have a responsibility as educators to expand our students' understanding of the world by engaging them critically in analyzing the social, political, and historical contexts in which they live. This responsibility can and should include difficult conversations about conflicts, war, discrimination, and oppression.

Unlike the principal in the vignette, I do not agree that the teacher should not have conducted a lesson about the events of September 11, 2001. But teachers must be prepared with pedagogical tools and age-appropriate curricula (see Table 1). When approaching socially sensitive issues, it is critical to deconstruct stereotypes and create anti-oppressive classrooms that allow for difficult dialogue in a responsible way.

Table 1: Resources for Educators

Organization	Websites
Colorlines	www.colorlines.com/911-anniv/
Rethinking Schools	www.rethinkingschools.org/war/readings/index.shtml www.rethinkingschools.org/static/special_reports/sept11/pdf/911insrt.pdf
Teaching Tolerance	www.tolerance.org/activity/debunking-muslim-myths
American-Arab Anti-Discrimination Committee	www.adc.org/education/educational-resources/

Classrooms are not simply spaces reserved for fiction, mock debates, and role-plays. They are microcosms where global–political, social, and historical tensions are enacted and reinforced in every action and interaction. Young people must negotiate torrents of information, and as educators we need to provide counternarratives and create learning environments in which students can engage as critical readers of their world.

Works Cited

American-Arab Anti-Discrimination Committee Research Institute. (2008). *2003–2007 Report on hate crimes and discrimination against Arab Americans.* Washington, DC: American-Arab Anti-Discrimination Committee. Retrieved August 15, 2011, from www.adc.org/PDF/hcr07.pdf

Bakalian, A., & Bozorgmehr, M. (2009). *Backlash 9/11: Middle Eastern and Muslim Americans respond.* Berkeley: University of California Press.

Council on American–Islamic Relations. (2009). *The status of Muslim civil rights in the United States 2009: Seeking full inclusion.* Washington, DC: Council on American-Islamic Relations.

Hing, J. (2011, September 11). The $43 million Islamophobia machine. *Colorlines.* Retrieved January 15, 2011, from colorlines .com/archives/2011/09/the_43_million_ islamophobia_machine.html

Nisbet, E., & Garrett, K. (2010). *FOX News contributes to spread of rumors about proposed NYC Mosque: CNN and NPR promote more accurate beliefs.* Retrieved November 11, 2010, from www.comm.ohio-state.edu/kgarrett/MediaMosqueRumors.pdf

Pew Research Center. (2010). *NYC mosque opposed, Muslims' right to build mosques favored: Public remains conflicted over Islam.* Retrieved June 11, 2011, from pewforum.org/Muslim/ Public-Remains-Conflicted-Over-Islam.aspx

Pew Research Center. (2011). *Muslim Americans: No signs of growth in alienation or support for extremism mainstream and moderate attitudes.* Retrieved November 5, 2010, from people-press.org/files/legacy-pdf/Muslim-American-Report.pdf

Shaheen, J.G. (2001). *Reel bad Arabs: How Hollywood vilifies a people.* New York: Olive Branch.

Shryock, A. (2010). *Islamophobia/Islamophilia: Beyond the politics of enemy and friend.* Bloomington: Indiana University Press.

Zaal, M. (2009). *Neglected in their transitions: Second generation Muslim youth search for support in a context of Islamophobia.* Unpublished dissertation. Graduate Center, New York.

Zaal, M., Salah, T., & Fine, M. (2007). The weight of the hyphen: Freedom, fusion and responsibility embodied by young Muslim-American women during a time of surveillance. *Applied Developmental Science, 11*(3), 164–177. doi:10.1080/10888690701454674

Zine, J. (2004). Anti-Islamophobia education as transformative pedagogy: reflections from the educational front lines. *The American Journal of Islamic Social Sciences, 21*(3), 110–119.

Credit

Zaal, Mayida. "Islamophobia in Classrooms, Media, and Politics." *Journal of Adolescent and Adult Literacy 55.*6 (2012): 555–558. Republished with permission of John Wiley and Sons Inc.

Collected Notes from Essays

The Inspired Writer vs. The Real Writer by Sarah Allen

1 See his "Autobiographical Digression" in the second chapter of *Writing without Teachers*.

2 Most universities have a Writing Center, too, and that can be a valuable resource, since the staff is trained to read papers and often allot as much as an hour to focus on your draft.

How to Tame a Wild Tongue by Gloria Anzaldúa

1 Ray Gwyn Smith, *Moorland is Cold Country,* unpublished book.

2 Irena Klepfisz, "*Di rayze aheym*/The Journev Home," in *The Tribe of Dina: A Jewish Women's Anthology,* Melanie Kaye/Kantrowitz and Irena Klepfisz, eds. (Montpelier, VT: Sinister Wisdom Books, 1986), 49.

3 R. C. Ortega, *Dialectologia Del Barrio,* trans. Hortencia S. Alwan (Los Angeles, CA: R. C. Ortega Publisher & Bookseller, 1977), 132.

4 Eduardo Hernandéz-Chávez, Andrew D. Cohen, and Anthony F. Beltramo, *El Lenguaje de los Chicanos: Regional and Social Characteristics of Language Used by Mexican Americans* (Arlington, VA: Center for Applied Linguistics, 1975), 39.

5 Hernandéz-Chávez., xvii.

6 Irena Klepfisz, "Secular Jewish Identity: Yidishkayt in America," in *The Tribe of Dina,* Kaye/Kantrowitz and Klepfisz, eds., 43.

7 Melanie Kaye/Kantrowitz, "Sign," in *We Speak in Code: Poems and Other Writings* (Pittsburgh, PA: Motheroot Publications, Inc., 1980), 85.

8 Rodolfo Gonzales, *I Am Joaquín/Yo Soy Joaquín* (New York, NY: Bantam Books, 1972). It was first published in 1967.

9 Gershen Kaufman, *Shame: The Power of Caring* (Cambridge, MA: Schenkman Books, Inc., 1980), 68.

10 John R. Chávez, *The Lost Land: The Chicago Images of the Southwest* (Albuquerque, NM: University of New Mexico Press, 1984), 88–90.

11 "Hispanic" is derived from *Hispanis* (*España,* a name given to the Iberian Peninsula in ancient times when it was a part or the Roman Empire) and is a term designated by the U.S. government to make it easier to handle us on paper.

12 The Treaty of Guadalupe Hidalgo created the Mexican-American in 1848.

13 Anglos, in order to alleviate their guilt for dispossessing the Chicano, stressed the Spanish part of us and perpetrated the myth of the Spanish Southwest. We have accepted the fiction that we are Hispanic, that is Spanish, in order to accommodate ourselves to the dominant culture and its abhorrence of Indians. Chávez, 88–91.

Between Acceptance and Rejection: Muslim Americans and the Legacies of September 11 by Moustafa Bayoumi

[1] "Dueling Demonstrations Held in NYC After 9/11 Memorial," *CBS New York,* September 11, 2010, <http://newyork.cbslocal.com/2010/09/11/dueling-demonstrations-begin-after-911-memorial/>.

[2] Sylviane Diouf, *Servants of Allah: African Muslims Enslaved in the Americas* (New York: NYU Press, 1998).

[3] For Internet links to many of these condemnations, see <http://www.muhajabah.com/otherscondemn.php>.

[4] "Washington Post-ABC News Poll," *The Washington Post,* <http://www.washingtonpost.com/wp-srv/politics/polls/postpoll_09072010.html?sid=ST2010090806236>.

[5] R.M., "Mosque Building and Its Discontents," *The Economist* August, 19, 2010, <http://www.economist.com/blogs/democracyinamerica/2010/08/islamic_cultural_centre_sorta_near_ground_zero>. The 55 percent figure comprises the 27.7 percent "somewhat unfavorable" and the 27.7 percent of "very unfavorable."

[6] David Cole, *Enemy Aliens* (New York: New Press, 2003), 25.

[7] Ibid., 31.

[8] Anushka Asthana, "Domestic Detainee Released," *The Washington Post,* July 21, 2006, A09.

[9] See U.S. Department of Justice Office of the Inspector General, *The September 11 Detainees: A Review of the Treatment of Aliens Held on Immigration Charges in Connection with the Investigation of the September 11 Attacks,* June 2003, <http://www.justice.gov/oig/special/0306/index.htm>, and a supplemental report on allegations of abuse while in detention published in December 2003.

[10] Eric Lichtblau, *Bush's Law* (New York: Anchor Books, 2009), 6.

[11] See, for example, "US: Misuse of the Material Witness Statute," *Human Rights Watch,* January 29, 2011. <http://www.hrw.org/en/news/2011/01/28/us-misuse-material-witness-statute>. This is an amicus brief for *Ashcroft v. Al-Kidd,* a case before the U.S. Supreme Court regarding the use of the Material Witness Statute.

[12] Nicole J. Henderson, et al., executive summary for *Law Enforcement & Arab American Community Relations after September 11, 2001: Engagement in a Time of Uncertainty* (New York: Vera Institute of Justice, 2006), <http://www.vera.org/policerelations>, 4–5.

[13] Gayle Fee, et al., "Bill Cosby down with plan for Muslim 'Cosby Show,'" *Boston Herald,* February 11, 2011, <http://www.bostonherald.com/track/inside_track/view/2011_0211bill_down_with_muslim_cosbys/>.

[14] *Muslim Americans: Middle Class and Mostly Mainstream,* (Washington, D.C.: Pew Research Center, May 22, 2007).

15 Associated Press, "Texas ed board adopts resolution limiting Islam in textbooks." *USA Today,* September 25, 2010, <http://www.usatoday.com/news/religion/2010-09-26-textbooks25_ST_N.htm>.

16 James McKinley, Jr., "Judge Blocks Oklahoma's Ban on Using Sharia Law in Court," *New York Times,* November 29, 2010.

17 "Controversies Over Mosques and Islamic Centers Across the U.S.," *Pew Forum on Religion,* September 24, 2010, <http://features.pewforum.org/muslim/assets/mosque-map-all-text-10-5.pdf>.

18 Phil Whillon, "Islamic Group Denounces planned Temecula mosque protest," *Los Angeles Times,* July 28, 2010.

19 Peter Catapano, "Freedom to Inflame," *New York Times,* April 8, 2011.

20 Justin Elliot, "Tea Party Leader: Defeat Ellison because he's Muslim," *Salon.com,* October 26, 2010, <http://www.salon.com/news/politics/war_room/2010/10/26/tea_party_nation_phillips_ellison_muslim>.

21 David Schanzer, Charles Kurzman, and Ebrahim Moosa, "Anti-Terror Lessons of Muslim Americans," *Triangle Center on Terrorism and Homeland Security,* January 6, 2010, 1.

22 Charles Kurzman, "Muslim-American Terrorism Since 9/11: An Accounting," *Triangle Center on Terrorism and Homeland Security,* February 2, 2011.

23 Laurie Goodstein, "Muslims to be Congressional Hearings Main Focus," *New York Times,* February 7, 2011.

24 Greg Sargent, "Pete King: No law enforcement officials will substantiate my claims about Muslims," *The Plum Line,* February 8, 2011, <http://voices.washingtonpost.com/plum-line/2011/02/what_if_pete_king_holds_a_hear.html>.

25 John Higham, *Strangers in the Land: Patterns in American Nativism 1860–1925,* 2nd ed. (New York: Antheum, 1977), ii.

26 Richard Hofstadter, *"The Paranoid Style in American Politics" and Other Essays* (New York: Vintage, 2008), 3.

27 *Ibid.,* 27.

28 *Ibid.,* 39.

29 Alex Altman, "TIME Poll: Majority Oppose Mosque, Many Distrust Muslims," *Time,* August 19, 2010; Josh Gerstein, "Poll: 46% of GOP thinks Obama's Muslim," *Politico.com,* August 19, 2010, <http://www.politico.com/blogs/joshgerstein/0810/Poll_46_of_GOP_thinks_Obamas_Muslim.html>.

30 Richard Hofstadter, *"The Paranoid Style in American Politics,"* 24–25.

Trans Media Moments: Tumblr, 2011–2013 by Marty Fink and Quinn Miller

1 Georgia Tech, Atlanta, GA, USA

2 University of Oregon, Eugene, USA

Is He Boyfriend Material?: Representation of Males in Teenage Girls' Magazines by Kirsten B. Firminger

1. Percentage of male-focused pages was taken out of total editorial pages, not including advertising pages. Confessional/embarrassing stories did not count toward the total number of pages because of inconsistencies in unit of analysis, with the confessional stories having a variable number of male-focused stories. I analyzed those separately. Feature articles (unique, nonregular) counted if the article focused on or if males significantly contributed to the narrative in the article (for instance, "Out of bounds: A cheerleader tells the story of how the coach she trusted attacked her"). If the feature was equally balanced with focused sections on both boys and girls (for example, if the article is sectioned into different topics or interviews), only pages that focused on males were counted.

   Because of the limited nature of the study, I chose to focus purely on the content that was decided upon by the editorial/writing (called "editorial content" within this article) staff of the magazines, since they establish the mission and tone of the content across all of the issues of the magazine. While I acknowledge the influential presence of advertising, I did no analysis of the content of the advertising pages or photographs. The analysis consists only of the written content of the magazines.

2. The magazines report that the question-and-answer columns and embarrassing/confessional tales are "submitted by readers." However, they do not report how they choose the questions and stories that are published, or whether the magazine staff edits this content.

3. *ELLEgirl* did not contain embarrassing or confessional stories.

4. The unit of analysis was the smallest number of sentences that contained a complete thought, experience, or response, ranging from one sentence to a paragraph. For example, "The fact is you can't change other people. He has to change himself—but perhaps your concern will convince him to make some changes." I took this approach so that the meaning and context of a statement was not lost in the coding. Whole paragraphs could not always be used because they sometimes contained contrasting or multiple themes.

5. The other articles that were not included in the coding focused predominantly on a specific boy or a celebrity male and his interests/activities, or on stories including a boy, or activities to do with a boy, rather than making broad statements about how all boys act (for example, "When he was in kindergarten, his mom enrolled Elijah [Wood] in a local modeling and talent school." or "One time, my boyfriend dared me to sneak out of the house in the middle of the night while my parents were sleeping and meet him at a park.").

A Herstory of the #BlackLivesMatter Movement by Alicia Garza

1 http://dignidadrebelde.com

2 http://work.robdontstop.com

3 http://designaction.org

4 http://www.colorlines.com/articles/get-bus-inside-black-life-matters-freedom-ride-ferguson

5 http://www.nbc.com/law-and-order-special-victims-.../.../n41296/

6 http://apen4ej.org/justice4trayvon/

7 http://www.notonemoredeportation.com/2014/08/18/marisa-franco-if-michael-brown-was-the-last-not-the-latest/

8 http://www.liberationink.org/content/assata-unisex

Learning to Read by Malcolm X

1 Charles H. Parkhurst (1842–1933); American clergyman, reformer, and president of the Society for the Prevention of Crime.

2 A native Egyptian Christian church that retains elements of its African origins.

3 Evil plots or schemes. Faust was a fictional character who sold his soul to the devil for knowledge and power.

4 The "Opium War" of 1839–1842 was between Britain and China and ended when Hong Kong was handed over to Britain.

5 The Boxer Rebellion of 1898–1900. An uprising by members of a secret Chinese society who opposed foreign influence in Chinese affairs.

Reading Games: Strategies for Reading Scholarly Sources by Karen Rosenberg

1 In this discussion I draw on Norgaard's excellent discussion of reading as joining a conversation (1–28). By letting you, the reader, know this in a footnote, I am not only citing my source (I'd be plagiarizing if I didn't mention this somewhere), but I'm also showing how I enter this conversation and give you a trail to follow if you want to learn more about the metaphor of the conversation. Following standard academic convention, I put the full reference to Norgaard's text at the end of this article, in the references.

2 I draw on—and recommend—Rounsaville et al.'s discussion of rhetorical sensitivity, critical reading and rhetorical reading (1–35).

Queer Characters in Comic Strips by Edward H. Sewell, Jr.

1   Terminology is always something of a problem. Throughout this chapter, the term "queer" is used rather than cumbersome combinations of gay, gay men, lesbian, bisexual, and transgender. It is used in two different ways. First, it is used to identify a sexual orientation different from heterosexual or straight. Second, it is used as a collective term for all the combinations of gay, gay men, gays, lesbians, bisexuals, homosexuals, and transgendered. In instances of direct quotations or paraphrases, the term used by the quoted or paraphrased source is retained. For a recent discussion of this debate, see Rotello (2000).

2   The role of the Internet in the queer community cannot be overemphasized. It provides a type of "community forum" where people can meet, talk, and have no fear of being "outed" or harassed.

3   The Doonesbury website (http://www.doonesbury.com) has an excellent search engine that locates all dates when a specific topic or character appeared in the strip.

4   Robert Triptow (1989) provides an excellent collection of early queer comics art that is not readily available from any other source. A brief overview of the beginnings of queer comic books and strips is also found in Sabin (1996, p. 124), but without any visual examples.

5   *Kyle's Bed & Breakfast* can be found on-line at URL members.aol.com/KylesB&B

"God Don't Never Change": Black English from a Black Perspective by Geneva Smitherman

1   For examples of such programs, see *Non-Standard Dialect*, Board of Education of the City of New York (National Council of Teachers of English, 1968); San-Su C. Lin, *Pattern Practices in the Teaching of Standard English to Students with a Non-Standard English Dialect* (USOE Project 1339, 1965); Arno Jewett, Joseph Mersand, Doris Gunderson, *Improving English Skills of Culturally Different Youth in Large Cities* (U.S. Department of Health, Education and Welfare, 1964); *Language Programs for the Disadvantaged* (NCTE, 1965).

2   Don L. Lee. "Malcolm Spoke/Who Listened?" *Don't Cry, Scream*. Detroit: Broadside Press, 1969. 33.

3   Don L. Lee, "But He was Cool or: he even stopped for green lights,: ibid., pp. 24–25.

4   Etheridge Knight, "Hard Rock Return to Prison from the Hospital for the Criminal Insane," *Poems from* Prison (Detroit: Broadside Press, 1968), p. 12.

5   Maya Angelou, *Just Give me a Cool Drink of Water 'fore I Diiie* (New York: Random House, 1971), pp. 46–47.

6 John Oliver Killens, *The Cotillion or One Good Bull is Half the Herd* New York: Trident Press, 1971), pp. 29–42.

7 Richard Wright, "Fire and Cloud," *Uncle Tom's Children* New York: Harper and Row, 1936), pp. 137–39.

8 Imamu Amiri Baraka (LeRoi Jones), "Expressive Language," *Home* (New York: William Morrow & Co., 1996), pp. 171–72.

A Family Affair: Competing Sponsors of Literacy in Appalachian Students' Lives by Sara Webb-Sunderhaus

1 Urban Appalachian is a term that refers to a subgroup of Appalachians who migrated out of the Appalachian region and relocated to urban centers; the term also includes the children of these migrants. See Borman and Obermiller's *From Mountain to Metropolis: Appalachian Migrants in the American City* for further discussion.

2 Pseudonyms have been substituted for the names of all locations and individuals in order to protect participant anonymity.

3 Devotionals are short books designed to reinforce daily prayer and reading of the Bible. They direct readers to read a particular Bible passage and to use the devotional as supplementary material that encourages further reflection. Finally, the readers are to conclude the reading with prayer. Some devotionals even include suggested prayers for the day, though not all do, thus blending silent reading of the devotional with the reading aloud of prayers.